FACING the
SHADOW

FACING *the* SHADOW
SECOND EDITION

STARTING SEXUAL AND RELATIONSHIP RECOVERY

A Gentle Path to Beginning Recovery from Sex Addiction

Patrick J. Carnes, Ph.D.

Gentle Path
P R E S S
CAREFREE, ARIZONA

GENTLE PATH PRESS
P.O. BOX 3172
Carefree, AZ 85377
www.gentlepath.com
800-708-1796

Library of Congress Cataloging-in-Publication Data

Carnes, Patrick
Facing the Shadow: Starting Sexual and Relationship Recovery, Second Edition/Patrick Carnes

p. cm.
Includes bibliographical references
ISBN 0-9774400-0-1
1. Sex Addiction   2. Recovery

Author's note:
The stories in this book are true; however, each has been edited for clarity. Names, locations, and other identifying information have been changed to protect confidentiality.

Editor: Marianne Harkin
Cover: Martin Wilkes, Summation Design
Interior Design: George Sarratt

Contents

Introduction to the Gentle Path Series

Years ago I learned something of great value as I followed the recoveries of a thousand people. It became clear that if people did certain activities, they got well. If they did not, relapse was likely. Success in recovery was linked in an essential way to what the recovering person actually did.

My research staff and I broke these activities down into tasks, such as getting a sponsor and completing a consequences inventory. As our understanding deepened, we designed experiences that we assigned to recovering patients. When they completed the assignment, it signaled they had completed the task, grasped its concepts, and made progress toward recovery.

We were teaching specific competencies, or skills, that people could use to manage their lives and their illnesses. To simply identify the tasks was not enough. We had to make explicit the skills we were helping to develop. This series is based on these skills. We summarized these skills into thirty tasks. At the conclusion of this book is a guide which maps out the thirty tasks. *Facing the Shadow* mentors you through the critical first seven tasks that addicts need in order to create the foundation of their recoveries. *The Recovery Zone* series will lead you through tasks eight through thirty. A brief summary is provided at the conclusion of this introduction.

One of the biggest problems in avoiding relapse is follow-through. In the real world of recovery, people are told by their therapists and their sponsors what to do, yet addicts focus on the sobriety part – ignoring the hard-won lessons of long term sobriety. Getting sober is not hard. Staying sober is. Attaining sobriety is just the beginning of recovery. After leaving residential treatment, patients feel as though they have completed their work when, in fact, the window to recovery has just opened. Sadly, this is when they often lose their momentum. There is not a structure to support the long-term work on an outpatient basis. Once sobriety from the addiction has been established, people need a guide for future steps. That's what this book aims to do.

Another problem is multiple addictions. It is now clear that for success, the recovering person will probably have to work on multiple issues. If they do not, untreated addictions may escalate and the treated addictions will be replaced by others. Treatment approaches have to be specific enough in each addiction so that recovering people have all the skills and information they need to deal with it. Yet the process must get at the core issues for which addictions have become the "solution."

In my experience, recovery is no "walk in the park." As members of Alcoholics Anonymous say, "it's a *simple* program, not an *easy* program." Recovering sex addicts face pain and damage that goes to the core of their being. They have countless questions, and even more doubts and fears. This book addresses those questions and deep feelings, too. Therefore, this series is designed to:

- Be Comprehensive
- Be Specific
- Be Long term
- Be Focused on cause
- Be Inclusive of all addictions

- Be helpful with internal issues such as shame, grief, and trauma
- Gain new understandings around work, finances, and health

Facing the Shadow assists in creating a revitalized, interpersonal network of family, friends, and recovery support. You will learn to:

- Break free from denial
- Make sense of your own sexual history
- Understand your behaviors (chaos)
- Face the unmanageability
- Access resources and support
- Take the mystery out of arousal and your behavior
- Learn fundamentals of recovery
- Avoid relapse

When I wrote *A Gentle Path through the Twelve Steps* in 1989, I learned that the book's users always add to the recovery process with suggestions. The authors in this series invite you to contact us with your ideas and feedback at info@gentlepath.com. With your help, we can fill in the gaps that have troubled recovering people for years.

Best wishes,

Patrick J. Carnes
Cave Creek, Arizona

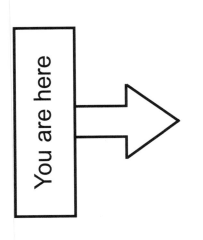

You are here →

Tasks 1–7

Break through denial
Understand addiction
Surrender
Limit damage
Establish sobriety
Physical integrity
Culture of support

Facing the Shadow **(2005)**

Tasks 8–19

Multiple addictions
Cycles of abuse
Reduce shame
Grieve losses
Closure to shame
Relationship with self
Financial viability
Meaningful work
Lifestyle balance
Building support
Exercise and nutrition
Spiritual life

Recovery Zone: Creating Personal Recovery **(2008)**

Tasks 19–30

Spiritual life
Resolve conflicts
Restore healthy sexuality
Family therapy
Family relationships
Recovery commitment
Issues with children
Extended family
Differentiation
Primary relationship
Coupleship
Primary intimacy

Recovery Zone II: Creating Family Recovery **(2009)**

Preface

For all addicts, a moment comes when they realize they have a problem.

I wrote that statement twenty years ago in the beginning of my book *Out of the Shadows*, and I am still convinced it is true. In this moment of lucidity, it suddenly hits home how out of control life is. Then the old rationales and cravings rush back in to blur reality.

Think of an addiction as being caught in a wild and dangerous whitewater stream. Those flashes of understanding are footholds when addicts regain stability. If they act quickly, there is a chance of escaping danger before they are pulled back into the roiling and thrilling current.

Others recognize their peril and know they must get out in order to survive, but the stream is too strong and those lucid moments too rare. There are some who have reached a point where they refuse to be pushed around any longer. They seize the opportunity and with courage and work manage to find tranquil pools or beaches. They pull themselves out and discover they had forgotten, or maybe never knew, a calmer, more ordered world. With perspective they realize the last choice they would make would be to spend their lives in the raging river. If you are looking at this book, you may be wrestling with the problem of sex addiction. If you are, this doesn't mean you are bad or perverted or hopeless. It means you may have a disease, an obsession from which many have healed. It also doesn't mean you're one of the lonely few - experts estimate there are 18 million sex addicts in this country, or up to six percent of the population. If you are a "normal" addict, you have probably made the following statements to yourself:

- Nothing will help

- I am overreacting to "normal things

- Others (my family, my boss, my neighbors) are overreacting to "normal" things

- I am "perverted" and too abnormal to change

- The problems will blow over

- I can stop if I just try harder (as opposed to trying therapy or recovery)

- I will be OK if I just do less of my behavior

- I will be OK if I can be more skillful or clever about my behavior so I will not be caught

- The reason I do this is because of my spouse or parents or work or religion or culture or drinking or _____fill in the blank)

- My situation is different

- No one will understand what I do (or did)

If any of those thoughts occur to you, you are exactly where you should be. This is what most addicts think when first beginning to confront their addiction. If you are starting to acknowledge your problem, this is significant progress. You may be open at last to the possibility that hope and healing can enter your life.

If you have reached the moment where you know that your sexual behavior is out of control, this book is for you. Fortunately, there are now many books on sexual addiction (see the Resources listing at the back of the book). But this is the first one that takes techniques used with thousands of recovering sex addicts and uses these to teach you step by step how to break free from the raging current of addiction and make your life better.

Decades of research and clinical experience have taught me that breaking recovery down into defined tasks makes it easier to leave the addictive life. As recovering people perform these tasks, they learn speficic competencies with which to manage their problems. Taken together, these skills form a map for success. If they follow the map, they will reach the goal of recovery. If not, they will end up back in the whitewater.

This book is the tool many of us now in recovery wish we had when we started. It is intended to be used as part of therapy, either in an outpatient or inpatient treatment program. It is also designed to support a Twelve Step recovery program such as Sex Addicts Anonymous (SAA), Sex and Love Addicts Anonymous (SLAA), or Sexaholics Anonymous (SA). (Look for a listing of such support groups in the Resources listing in the back of this book.) We have found that both therapy and Twelve Step support are keys to success.

Doubtless your internal "addict voice" will supply rationales for not doing therapy or Twelve Step work.

- Therapy does not work

- Therapists are crazy or they would not be in the business

- Twelve Step groups will not work for me

- I can do this on my own

- I do not like the therapist, the group, the program, the Twelve Steps, the people there, talking about myself, or _____(fill in the blank)

- My situation is different

- No one will understand what I do (or did)

It is at this point that addicts must try to see what is really going on because they soon will be caught up in the rapids again. That is why we start with the first chapter about "What is Real?"

Since *Out of the Shadows* appeared, I have personally known close to fifty people who have died because of their sex addiction and have heard the stories of countless others who have met the same fate. The last was a man who left my office after trying to convince me that his therapist and his family were wrong. Outraged with me for pointing out the obvious, he declared he was capable of handling things his own way. Five days later he was dead, killed while being arrested for his behavior.

In that same week, another of my patients faced a similar turning point -- but she chose differently. She found a break in the raging current where she could listen to her grown children and husband. I watched her 26-year-old son figure out how much trouble his mother faced. "Mom, you can't keep living like this!" he cried. His plea moved her and, though it was excruciating, she finally saw herself and what was happening to her. She committed to getting help. I have great hope for her.

Delusion is the deadliest part of this illness. Those rushing rapids kill. If you are in a moment where you can see them, I invite you to come out of the river.

CHAPTER ONE: What Is Real
Recognizing Self-Delusion

Mental health is commitment to reality at all costs.
—M. SCOTT PECK

ADDICTION IS AN ILLNESS OF ESCAPE. Its goal is to obliterate, medicate, or ignore reality. It is an alternative to letting oneself feel hurt, betrayal, worry, and—most painful of all—loneliness.

The hardest challenge for some addicts is acknowledging that they have a problem. Addiction cripples the core ability to know what is real—our most essential skill—because addicts weave a string of rationalizations and delusions that make it impossible to cope with details like jobs or families.

In this chapter, we will look at why denial holds such strong sway over addicts and what to do to counter it. We will define addiction and who is likely to become an addict.

Addiction often begins simply: reality becomes too much to bear, so we try to escape through drugs, alcohol, or sex. Escaping reality for even the briefest time brings some relief. But when escaping becomes habitual, we have a mental health illness known as addiction. If mental health can be defined, as M. Scott Peck says, as a commitment to reality no matter what the cost, addiction can be defined as its most direct opposite: evading reality no matter the cost—though it may even bring death.

Reality distortion starts within the family. Sex addicts typically come from families in which addiction is already present. Often, parents, grandparents, siblings, or extended family members struggle with alcoholism, compulsive gambling, nicotine addiction, eating problems, illicit drug use, or compulsive sex. Even more likely, those family members battle a combination of addictions.

As children, sex addicts grow up in environments where there is the classic "elephant in the living room" syndrome: everyone pretends there is no problem although there's a huge issue interfering with everyone's lives. In such a situation, children learn very early with everyone pretending there is no problem and everyone pretends to avoid the painful and the obvious: to look at addiction and not see it.

Sex addicts also tend to come from rigid, authoritarian families. These are families in which all issues and problems are black and white. Little is negotiable and there is only one way to do things. Success in the family means doing what the parents want to such an extent that children give up being who they are. Normal child development does not happen. By the time children enter adolescence, they have few options. One is to become rebellious. The other is to develop a secret life about which the family knows nothing. Both positions distort reality. Both result in a distrust of authority and a poor sense of self.

If the family's rigidity is also sex negative (that is, children are taught that sex is dirty, sinful, bad, or nasty), sex becomes exaggerated or hidden. Worse yet, the forbidden can become the object of obsession. Or all of the above may happen. The worst-case scenario happens when the child finds out that parents are not living up to their sexual standards. For example, if the parents preach against sexual promiscuity but one or both chronically have affairs, this teaches the acceptability of sexual duplicity. The norm is to deceive others and to pretend that what is true is not true.

One essential way to check reality is to share with others and find out their perception of a situation. This requires a capacity for intimacy. Most sex addicts, however, come from families in which members are "disengaged" from one another—there is little sharing or intimacy. Children develop few skills about sharing, being vulnerable, or risking anything about themselves. As a result, they learn to trust no one but themselves in such families. The further result is that self-delusion is then hard to break, and secrets become more potent than reality. The worst effect is that the children are unable to ask for help.

Abuse and neglect deepen this distrust of others and further distort reality. Children who are neglected conclude they are not valuable. In addition, they live with a high level of anxiety because no one teaches them common life skills or provides for their basic needs. Children find ways to deaden the anxiety they inevitably feel, and they do so compulsively. For sex addicts, compulsive masturbation is a good example of an anxiety-reduction strategy. Food and alcohol can be controlled by parents, but it is difficult to stop a young person from masturbating. Other forms of physical and sexual abuse intensify poor self-esteem and the need for relief from fear.

Abuse victims tend to distort reality. They can overreact or under-respond to life problems. Being so terrified makes them reactive. Further, they "compartmentalize," meaning they learn to split reality, acknowledging parts of their life but disallowing or denying problem areas. That may mean acting a certain way in one context and totally different in another. They may pretend part of their life, such as a dead sibling or a family member who is in prison, does not exist. Robert Louis Stevenson wrote about this compartmentalization when he described Dr. Jekyll and Mr. Hyde. Hyde personified the monster underneath the normal exterior of Dr. Jekyll. He was essentially describing the phenomenon of alcoholism, but it is an apt metaphor for all forms of addiction.

A final characteristic of abuse victims is that they tend to distort or minimize the impact of abuse. "It was not so bad" or "it did not hurt me much." This adds yet another layer of reality distortion.

Sex addicts have so much experience in distorting reality that they become comfortable with it. Here are examples of the extremes some have gone to:

- A 35-year-old man is president of a company owned by his wife's family. He has been sexually involved with his wife's sister on and off for over three years. He thinks his wife will not find out and even if she did, he would not lose the company he has built with her family money.
- A priest in his 40s has a compulsive prostitution problem. He has gone through his family

inheritance and now finances his habit from parish funds. He believes no one will ever find out and that he has not violated his vow of celibacy because he has maintained "emotional" virginity.

- A police officer has sex with his neighbors, many of whom are friends of his wife and have children who are friends of his children. He also has had sex with friends of his wife who do not live in the neighborhood. Though he has been confronted by his wife, he has managed to convince her he has been faithful. He counts on the fact that he only picks married women who have to keep the secret, too.
- A woman has sex in high-risk situations including adult bookstores. One man secretly films her having sex with him and then threatens to send it to her husband if she does not continue to have sex with him.
- A lawyer cost his partners millions of dollars because of having sex with employees. He started having sex with prostitutes who were also medical students. He believed he found an adequate solution to his sexual needs. After all, he was doing it with "doctors."
- An executive charged hundreds of thousands of dollars to his company for cybersex. He counted on the company's immense size and cumbersome accounting practices to bury his problem.
- A physician would initiate relationships with women after he examined them. He knew none of the women he had sex with would ever report him because of the "meaning" they still had for one another.

In each of these cases, the truth came out with horrible results. Every one of these people was stunned by their capacity for self-delusion.

This is why we start by looking at denial. As you progress in recovery, you will start to understand how this process will work for you. Our purpose now is simply to say it is normal at this point to be confused about all this. It is also normal to punish yourself because you feel bad about sexual activities you have done. And it is true you have not been honest with yourself or others. It will, however, be easy to see how you got to this point.

There are two challenges:

First you must be honest with yourself. Then you need to be honest with those who can help you, such as your therapist or your support group.

This may surprise you, but I suggest that spouses, family, friends, and bosses can wait until 1) you understand what is wrong, and 2) you have support from people who understand your problem.

There are three activities that can help you focus on reality.

First you must list what you think your problems are. This list will be an important resource as you go through your recovery process.

Second, as you review these problems, notice what secrets you have. In other words, how many instances can you find in which people are unaware of the truth. These are cases in which you have told lies, failed to tell the whole story, or decided to tell nothing at all.

Finally, what excuses or rationales have or do you use for your sexual behavior? Make every effort to be as honest as possible.

We will start to work here on breaking through these barriers to reality. It may be hard at first, but take heart. This process has worked for countless others before you.

Journal as a Tool

As you go through this workbook, I encourage you to keep a journal or notebook. You can record the "overflow" in your assignments there. Any reflections or notes you write as you go through the exercises will become invaluable to you as time goes on.

I would also suggest finding a secure place to keep your journal. If you have confidence no one but you or a trusted confidant such as a sponsor or therapist will see what you have written, you can feel free to write openly. This kind of unrestricted honesty is crucial to your recovery.

Problems, Secrets, and Excuses

The Problem List:

The goal of this exercise is to reveal your current perception of what is happening in your life. It will give you a "big picture" of what has brought you to this point. Making the list will assist you in talking to your therapist and others in your recovery about what is wrong.

It is important to be as complete as possible because doing so will make your recovery much stronger. If you run out of room feel free to use another sheet of paper or write in your journal.

It may feel uncomfortable or frightening at first to make this list. If necessary, take a break and come back to it later. Some addicts find that as they write, more layers of their problems are revealed. Again, this can be unnerving, so if you need to discuss the emotions that are welling up for you with a sponsor or therapist, do so and then return to this exercise.

List all of your problems here. Include both sexual (ran up credit card for porn videos, lied to my boss about lunch-time liaisons, have to get AIDS test, and so on) and nonsexual (teenager having trouble in school, car transmission making funny noise) issues.

_____

_____

_____

_____

_____

_____

_____

_____

Problem One: _____

_____

_____

_____

_____

Problem Two: _____

_____

_____

_____

Problem Three: _____

_____

_____

_____

Problem Four: _____

_____

_____

_____

Problem Five:

_____

_____

_____

_____

Problem Six:

_____

_____

_____

_____

Problem Seven:

_____

_____

_____

_____

Problem Eight:

_____

_____

_____

_____

Problem Nine: _____

_____

_____

_____

Problem Ten: _____

_____

_____

_____

Problem Eleven: _____

_____

_____

_____

Problem Twelve: _____

_____

_____

_____

Problem Thirteen: _____
_____
_____
_____

Problem Fourteen: _____
_____
_____
_____

Problem Fifteen: _____
_____
_____

The Secret List:

Usually sex addicts have a significant number of secrets: out-of-wedlock children, credit cards their wives don't know about, cyber lovers their husbands have no clue exist. In fact many of the problems on your Problem List are probably problems because of the secrets they involve. You might ask yourself how many of the problems listed would be worse if everybody knew the truth about your behavior.

Secrets themselves are a problem.

First, you may carry the emotional stress of knowing you are being dishonest.

Then you have the anxiety of trying to remember who you told what so that you do not trip yourself up.

And then there is the fear of discovery of the truth.

Each of these problems takes a toll on you. What's worse, you end up believing some of your distortions. By telling a story often enough, an addict starts to live as if the story is the reality. You must start with reality.

Remember to include the omissions, not just the lies you have told, but what you have left out.

As you list each secret, note who does not have an accurate picture about you by indicating those from whom you have kept the secret. If you need more room, use your journal or notebook.

Secrets

First Secret:

_____

_____

From whom have you kept this?

_____

Second Secret:

_____

_____

From whom have you kept this?

_____

Third Secret:

_____

_____

From whom have you kept this?

_____

Fourth Secret:

_____

_____

From whom have you kept this?

_____

Fifth Secret:

_____

_____

From whom have you kept this?

_____

Sixth Secret:

_____

_____

From whom have you kept this?

_____

Seventh Secret:

_____

_____

From whom have you kept this?

_____

Eighth Secret:

_____

_____

From whom have you kept this?

_____

Ninth Secret:

_____

_____

From whom have you kept this?

_____

Tenth Secret:

_____

_____

From whom have you kept this?

_____

The List of Excuses:

Addicts create rationales for their behavior. Usually they state the rationales in terms of deprivation (my spouse is not sexually responsive) or blame (my partner does not understand me). Or they argue for their uniqueness; some special circumstance or situation causes them to do what they do (I have extra pressures because I'm a surgeon, priest, teacher, lawyer). Whatever the rationale, the list's purpose is to help addicts come to terms with unhealthy behavior.

It is important at the outset to label these rationales as excuses. Only when we start realizing we're making excuses can we begin stripping away the layer of lies covering our behavior.

List in the space below the excuses for your behavior you have used over time. Frequently, people will add to this list as they progress through the workbook. Note the date at which you realized you were distorting reality so that you can see your progress.

RATIONALE:	DATE RECOGNIZED:
1.	
2.	
3.	
4.	
5.	
6.	
7.	
8.	
9.	
10.	
11.	
12.	
13.	
14.	

RATIONALE:	DATE RECOGNIZED:
13. _____	_____
14. _____	_____
15. _____	_____
16. _____	_____
17. _____	_____
18. _____	_____
19. _____	_____
20. _____	_____
21. _____	_____
22. _____	_____
23. _____	_____
24. _____	_____
25. _____	_____
26. _____	_____
27. _____	_____
28. _____	_____
29. _____	_____
30. _____	_____

Consequences Inventory

Most addicts have some expectation that everyone will overlook the damage caused by what they do. Some become indignant when they do experience consequences—getting docked or fired, bouncing checks, jail.

Consequences, however, are signposts to reality. Addicts receive them because the world does not share their thought distortion. Lies, broken promises, and exploitive behavior will eventually cost, and cost dearly.

In these ways, addicts discover that their denial is the beginning of a grief process. In other words, the losses begin mounting and the addict tries to stave off the moment of truth by clinging to denial. But ultimately that moment arrives and disaster is at hand.

Addicts find it extremely useful to do a complete inventory of their consequences. All addicts who have experienced out-of-control sexual behavior, used sex to cope with stress, or acted out sexually have had consequences due to their behavior. You have had consequences, too.

Sadly, people sometimes don't call what has happened to them consequences, or they use their sexual behavior as a way to avoid having to feel or to admit what has happened. Though it is difficult to face the "wreckage of our past," as Alcoholics Anonymous puts it, an honest assessment of your consequences will dramatically improve your recovery.

Look realistically at the consequences of your behavior in each of the categories below. Put a check in the box by each of the ones that you have experienced.

Emotional Consequences

☐	1.	Thoughts or feelings about committing suicide
☐	2.	Attempted suicide
☐	3.	Homicidal thoughts or feelings
☐	4.	Feelings of hopelessness and despair
☐	5.	Failed efforts to control your sexual behavior
☐	6.	Feeling like you had two different lives—one public and one secret
☐	7.	Depression, paranoia, or fear of going insane
☐	8.	Loss of touch with reality
☐	9.	Loss of self-esteem
☐	10.	Loss of life goals
☐	11.	Acting against your own values and beliefs
☐	12.	Strong feelings of guilt and shame
☐	13.	Strong feelings of isolation and loneliness
☐	14.	Strong fears about the future
☐	15.	Emotional exhaustion
☐	16.	Other emotional consequences:

_____

_____

Physical Consequences

- [ ] 1. Continuation of addictive behavior despite the risk to health
- [ ] 2. Extreme weight loss or gain
- [ ] 3. Physical problems (ulcers, high blood pressure, etc.)
- [ ] 4. Physical injury or abuse by others
- [ ] 5. Involvement in potentially abusive or dangerous situations
- [ ] 6. Vehicle accidents (automobile, motorcycle, bicycle)
- [ ] 7. Injury to yourself from your sexual behavior
- [ ] 8. Sleep disturbances (not enough sleep, too much sleep)
- [ ] 9. Physical exhaustion
- [ ] 10. Other physical consequences related to your sexual behavior such as venereal disease, HIV/AIDS, bleeding, etc.

Spiritual Consequences

- [ ] 1. Feelings of spiritual emptiness
- [ ] 2. Feeling disconnected from yourself and the world
- [ ] 3. Feeling abandoned by God or your Higher Power
- [ ] 4. Anger at your Higher Power or God
- [ ] 5. Loss of faith in anything spiritual
- [ ] 6. Other spiritual consequences

Consequences Related to Family

- [ ] 1. Risking the loss of partner or spouse
- [ ] 2. Loss of partner or spouse
- [ ] 3. Increase in marital or relationship problems
- [ ] 4. Jeopardizing the well-being of your family
- [ ] 5. Loss of family's or partner's respect
- [ ] 6. Increase in problems with your children
- [ ] 7. Estrangement from your family of origin
- [ ] 8. Other family or partnership consequences

Career and Educational Consequences

☐ 1.   Decrease in work productivity
☐ 2.   Demotion at work
☐ 3.   Loss of co-workers' respect
☐ 4.   Loss of the opportunity to work in the career of your choice
☐ 5.   Failing grades in school
☐ 6.   Loss of educational opportunities
☐ 7.   Loss of business
☐ 8.   Forced to change careers
☐ 9.   Not working to your level of capability
☐ 10.   Termination of job
☐ 11.   Other career or educational consequences

_____

_____

Other Consequences

☐ 1.   Loss of important friendships
☐ 2.   Loss of interest in hobbies or activities
☐ 3.   Few or no friends who don't participate in or condone your sexual behavior
☐ 4.   Financial problems
☐ 5.   Illegal activities (arrests or near-arrests)
☐ 6.   Court or legal involvement
☐ 7.   Lawsuits
☐ 8.   Prison or workhouse
☐ 9.   Stealing or embezzling to support behavior
☐ 10.   Other consequences

_____

_____

You will need to refer to this inventory later in this book. In addition, it would be of great benefit to you to talk about it with your therapist or sponsor for later work.

This is the tough part. Often addicts will feel that consequences are unfair. Remember that no one promised you justice and fairness. You have to deal with what is real. You may have lived with the illusion that others will respond to perceived inequities or will be sympathetic because of all the good you have done or how hard you have tried. None of that will help you now.

The people who gave you the consequences are not your enemies. By seeing those who give the consequences as the enemy, you keep yourself stuck in justifying your behavior. The real problem is your denial and your capacity for self-delusion. You are responsible for making yourself vulnerable to them. When you chose your behavior, you opened the door to consequences. You have to ask whether the risk was worth it. And if you can do this, you've already made significant progress toward recovery.

What helps at this point is to see your consequences as your teachers. You have been sent a lesson to learn. If you don't learn the lesson this time, it will manifest itself again, and probably in a more painful form next time.

Denial

To deny something is to say it is not true, to say "no" to it, or to prevent it from happening. Denial, of course, can be an honest, straightforward disagreement or refusal. When coupled with out-of-control sexual behavior, however, denial becomes a potent and powerful, though often destructive, way of protecting oneself from discovery—and from help.

For addicts, denial is a confused kind of thinking and reasoning used to avoid the reality of behavior or the consequences of behavior. It is a way to try to manage and explain the chaos caused by addictive behavior. It is an effort to protect sexual behavior that addicts believe they can't live without. It is a way to deflect attention and responsibility. Here are some examples:

- It was only once in awhile
- No one was hurt because no one knows
- I had to get my needs met somewhere
- She started it, so why is she upset
- We are all adults
- I am just being a man (woman)
- If you think I'm bad, you should see so-and-so
- My situation is different

Denial Worksheet

This exercise will help you look at the role denial is playing in your life. List all of the reasons you believed—or still believe—you don't belong in therapy or a group for your sexual behavior and acting out

1. _____

2. _____

3. _____

4. _____

5. _____

6. _____

7. _____

8. _____

9. _____

10. _____

11. _____

12. _____

13. _____

14. _____

15. _____

There are many kinds of denial. A few of the primary categories are listed below. Beneath each of them is room for you to write your own examples of each type.

Global Thinking. Attempting to justify why something is not a problem using terms like "always," "never," "no problem whatsoever."

_____

_____

Rationalization. Justifying unacceptable behavior. "I don't have a problem—I'm just sexually liberated." "You people are such prudes!" "You're crazy."

_____

_____

Minimizing. Trying to make behavior or consequences seem smaller and less important than they are. "Only a little." "Only once in awhile." "It is no big deal."

_____

_____

Comparison. Shifting the focus to someone else to justify behaviors. "I'm not as bad as
."

_____

_____

Uniqueness. Thinking you are different or special. "My situation is different." "I was hurt more." "That's fine for you, but I'm too busy to go to group right now."

_____

_____

Avoiding by creating an uproar or distraction. Being a clown and getting everyone laughing; angry outbursts meant to frighten; threats and posturing; shocking behavior that may be sexual.

_____

_____

Avoiding by omission. Avoiding by omission—trying to change the subject, ignore the subject, or manipulate the conversation to avoid talking about something. It is also leaving out important bits of information like the fact that a lover is sixteen years old, or that the person is your friend's partner.

_____

_____

Blaming. "Well, you would cruise all night, too, if you had my job." "If my wife/husband/partner weren't so cold, I wouldn't have to have an affair." "I can't help it—the baby cries day and night and makes me nervous."

_____

_____

Intellectualizing. Avoiding feelings and responsibility by thinking or by asking why. Explaining everything. Getting lost in detail and storytelling. Pretending superior intellect and using intelligence as a weapon.

_____

_____

Hopelessness/helplessness. "I'm a victim, I can't help it." "There is nothing I can do to get better." "I'm the worst."

_____

_____

Manipulative behavior. Usually involves some distortion of reality including the use of power, lies, secrets, or guilt to exploit others.

_____

_____

Compartmentalizing. Separating your life into compartments in which you do things that you keep separate from other parts of your life.

_____

_____

Crazymaking. When confronted by others who do have a correct perception, telling them they are totally wrong. Acting indignantly toward them is an attempt to make them feel crazy by telling them, in a sense, that they cannot trust their own perceptions.

_____

_____

Seduction. The use of charm, humor, good looks, or helpfulness to gain sexual access and cover up insincerity.

_____

_____

There Really is No Excuse

Most addicts discover there really is no excuse for their behavior. It is not easy to be honest with oneself, much less to be honest with the rest of the world. But staying in denial and staying dishonest guarantees staying in old, destructive patterns of behavior.

Accountability

When you begin to accept responsibility for your behaviors and their consequences, you will get a glimmer of what life in recovery can be. You know all too well that denial creates constant anxiety. Trying to remember the lies you have told, and to whom you have told them, is an ongoing source of stress. The good news is that honesty and accountability bring peace and freedom, a feeling of serenity that comes from integrity.

In denial, you say that you did not hurt anyone; accountability is facing the fact that you hurt others. For example, if we act out with compulsive masturbation, we might not recognize any damage to others. Yet if we are sexually unavailable to our partner, so preoccupied that the kids are neglected, and sneak off during work time, the impact and the damage are very real.

Powerless or Pointless

In addiction recovery, we talk about powerlessness. Because of your addiction, you have been unable to stop your behavior on your own. That is why you have asked for help. Despite the fact that you are powerless, you are still responsible and accountable for what you have done.

The concept of accountability is central to the Twelve Step process. Accepting your accountability helps you to break through denial and admit the extent of the problem.

In the space that follows, list as many examples as possible of people who were hurt by your behavior and in what ways they were hurt. Make your examples as concrete as possible.

You need to know that this task is one of the hardest in recovery. Though it will be painful, it is not about punishing yourself; it is about facing reality and leaving denial behind. So be gentle with yourself, but also be thorough.

1. _____

_____

2. _____

_____

3. _____

_____

4. _____

_____

5. _____

_____

6. _____

_____

7. _____

_____

8. _____

_____

9. _____

_____

10. _____

_____

If you are like most addicts, you are starting to realize how far from reality you have been living. To reassure yourself that you are not alone, we have included comments from other addicts describing what this phase was like for them. As you read, note how reality inserted itself in their lives.

Ending up in a massage parlour when I promised myself I wouldn't.
Not being able to refuse sex with women—felt no right to say no.
Unable to honor marriage commitment.
In high school I had sex with older women for money.
Sleeping with serial partners in one night.
Out six nights a week to pick up or be picked up in bars.
Took sexual risks with employees.
Would masturbate in library and never study.
Attempted to start an affair with sister-in-law.
Lost two close friends because I tried to seduce their wives.
Involvement with total strangers.
Exchanged sex for drugs.
Being sexual in public places like bars.
Masturbating in car despite accidents and near accidents.
Stole money to keep sexual relationship.
Accumulated heavy debt "to buy" person.
Whenever I was alone, I felt compelled to be sexual.
Arrested for lewd behavior.
Every time I went shopping I felt compelled to go to restroom for sex.
Involved in more than one intense relationship at once.
Many anonymous partners.

Could not form friendships/only find sex partners.

Hitchhiking at night hoping to have sex.

Went to a pornographic bookstore after getting negative HIV test.

Exhibiting self while driving (woman).

Could not practice safe sex even when trying hard to do so.

Sex with married men.

Calling a guy who tortured me—went over and had sex with him.

Dangerous situation with strangers.

At age 14, already had multiple lovers in daytime.

Stole woman's clothes for cross-dressing.

Masturbating on porch in the middle of the night, nude.

Sex on a passenger train with a stranger.

Took risks with pimps and prostitutes.

Sexualizing clients on the job.

Brought men home in the middle of the day when children were there.

Slept with circle of one man's friends to stay close to him.

Waking up with strangers.

Could not say no to husband's suggestion of wife swapping.

Physician masturbated me during examination and I could not say no.

So you see, you are not alone. These are people who managed to change their lives dramatically. They started by admitting they needed help.

Getting the Help You Need

After realizing that you have a problem—even though you may not want to call it an addiction—there are two steps you must take:

You must start therapy.
You must join a Twelve Step program for sex addiction.

It is quite common at this stage to wonder if you are really an addict and need to go through all this. The next two chapters will help you decide whether you are.

It's also important to understand that if addiction is a problem in your life, these materials will not help you recover if you use them in isolation. Because of the shame and guilt addiction involves, it's tempting to think, "I'll just pick up the materials, do them at home, and talk to you when I'm all better." You *must* talk with people who have more experience in recovery than you. It is the nature of denial to reassert itself when a person becomes isolated from others. Your ability to recognize your addiction and its consequences in your life and in the lives of others increases dramatically when you are with people who have struggled as you have. "Stick with the winners," urges Alcoholics Anonymous, meaning find people who have walked in the same shadows now clouding your life and who are now standing in the light.

Therapists are trained to help people understand what is happening to them—you can get an important perspective from them. What's more, therapists are trained to guide you over time and can help you through what can be a painful and bewildering process. If you already have a therapist, he or she may have handed you this book. Your therapist will become one of your guides for this process.

My experience in working with sex addicts has taught me what an addict has to do to heal and find sustained recovery—and that is what this book offers you. I know, too, that it doesn't happen overnight—the process takes three to five years.

Be aware that our research has shown that Twelve Step work and therapy are linked in an essential way. While therapy accelerates the process and dramatically reduces the risk of relapse, therapy alone is not enough. The Twelve Step process is simply indispensable for recovery. Being in a community of supportive people who are also recovering addicts seems to be absolutely key to recovery.

There are several ways you can find recovery groups. Start by looking in the Resources list at the back of this book. Your therapist may also be able to connect you with a person who can serve as a temporary sponsor. Your local medical or psychological information and referral services may be of help. Also, look in the phone book. For a guide to fellowships at a national level that can put you in touch with someone in your community check our website at *www.sexhelp.com.* Once you find a group, it takes a lot of courage to walk through those doors. But this is a path to the kind of healing and wholeness you've looked for all your life.

Finding a Sponsor

One of the great traditions that has grown out of the Twelve Step movement is sponsorship. A sponsor is another individual with more recovery experience whom we ask to help us work through our own recovery and healing. We seek out someone who has what we want—serenity, wisdom, humor—or who has walked a similar path. It's perfectly all right to find a temporary sponsor, someone who can help you understand the Twelve Step process and language when you're beginning recovery.

You may feel awkward asking someone to be your sponsor, especially when you are new in the program. You may assume you are imposing on them and this may hold you back from reaching out for help. Overcoming these negative assumptions becomes a way of nurturing yourself, and it is a crucial first step in the road to recovery.

Start by sharing all that you know with your therapist and sponsor. Use the exercises in this chapter to help you talk with them.

Finally, this workbook is based in part on two of my previous books, *Out of the Shadows* and *Don't Call It Love*. I encourage you to read the first chapters in each of them. They will give you more understanding of the challenges of recovery—and the gifts yet to be revealed.

By reading this chapter, you've taken a significant step. Breaking free from denial is one of the hardest steps we addicts take. If you need to take a break or nurture yourself in some way (eating in a nice restaurant, enjoying a hot bath, going for a walk on a beautiful evening), give that to yourself. And know that the strength you need to continue will be given to you.

CHAPTER TWO: What Is an Addiction?
Understanding Addictive Behavior

"Masturbation is the one great habit that is a primary addiction. The other addictions, for
alcohol, morphine, tobacco, etc., only enter in to life as a
substitute and replacement for it."
SIGMUND FREUD

WE HAVE COME A LONG WAY since Freud first speculated about sex addiction. But progress
has not been easy. There was a period in the 1930s and the 1940s when alcoholics and drug
addicts were seen as untreatable. Compulsive gamblers were, at best, objects of curiosity and
more often deemed people without character. Perverts and gluttons were perceived to have a
moral problem, if they were talked about at all.

Today we understand that addiction is an illness a very serious disease. Furthermore, problems such as drug, food, gambling, and sex addiction are actually related and rely on similar physical processes. Most important, we know that people can get help and that a good prognosis
exists. Sex addiction is the last addiction to be understood.

When I wrote *Out of the Shadows* in 1983, the definition used at the time described addiction
as pathological relationship with a mood-altering experience. People who grew up in difficult family situations learned not to trust. As adults, they searched for something to trust and rely on to
relieve the pervasive unease they felt. Since alcohol, sex, food, and risk always do what they promise at least temporarily they often became the answer, and thus the pathological relationship
begins.

For sex addicts, sex becomes the priority for which they sacrifice everything. They put sex
before their children, spouses, and friends, despite great cost to themselves. Just as an alcoholic
has an affair with the bottle, the sex addict s relationship is with sex and romance. Distorted fantasies and satiating behaviors that are obsessive to the point of physical harm are used in an
attempt to resolve the addict s desolate loneliness. Addiction can be viewed then, as an intimacy
disorder. As you go through this workbook, you will see how distorted relationships lie at the center of the addiction process.

Addiction also has a physiological component. In the mid-70s, scientists started to understand that addiction reflected a problem in the brain. When they were lonely, stressed, or depressed, addicts would access key neural pathways in the brain through mood-altering chemicals or behaviors. They would feel better temporarily. The addiction solution works through continuous stimulation. Pleasure could obliterate pain, numb loneliness, and help diminish shame. When behaviors become repetitive, we call them compulsive. Compulsion is the core of the addictive process and it relies on these neural pathways in the brain.

It s important that you understand how these neural pathways work and affect your addiction. You will learn more about this intricate chemical process in chapter seven.

The stimulation for the neural pathways comes from what I call the addictive system, and understanding addiction as a repetitive system will help you identify what in your life needs to change.

The Addiction Cycle

It was always the same for Jim. He would get this feeling in his stomach, scary but exhilarating and sexually arousing. He had a lot to do at work, but for a little time no one would know where he was. He would drive past massage parlors and strip joints, trying to decide if he would do it or not. He would stare at attractive women and become more aroused. He decided to stop at a nude bar that served sandwiches. He watched the women strip.

When he left, a decision had been made. No cruising or looking now. Definite in his purpose, he drove to a neighborhood massage parlor. Afterward he felt like he always did sad, defective, and ashamed. He asked himself why he did this when he knew that it always ended like this. Worse, he had taken much more time than he thought, so now he faced problems at work, forced to invent lies to cover up where he had been.

Kathy had a similar problem. She was a romance junkie who discovered the Internet. She was married but had an affair going even on the day of her wedding. During 13 years of marriage she had never been without one, or more often two, lovers, with numerous flirtations on the side.

She went to a therapist who told her she was a sex addict. She was furious because it was so clear to her that she had married the wrong man and was now trapped. Then she discovered the Internet and was captivated by chat rooms and their intrigue.

Pretending to work at her computer, she would wait until her husband was asleep, and then go online. Even the sound of the modem connecting was arousing. She would set a goal of being in bed by 11:00, but that seldom happened. Some nights it was 5:00 in the morning before she dragged herself away. She told herself it would be only computer sex, but eventually it became phone sex, and then hotel sex. Every new relationship added more complications. She suffered extreme fatigue. Her ability to perform at work diminished. Professionally, she felt like she was barely treading water. It just kept getting worse. If she could only stay within the limits she set for herself. But she couldn t.

Kathy and Jim are caught in a repetitive cycle. We call this the addiction cycle. It starts off with preoccupation, which involves obsessing about being sexual or romantic. All humans have fantasies and sexual thoughts, and that is a wonderful part of being human. For Kathy and Jim, however, fantasy became an obsession that serves in some way to avoid life. Used consistently, obsession sets the stage for loss of control.

These obsessions are intensified through the use of ritual. Jim first cruises and then goes to a strip show to heighten his arousal until he is beyond the point of saying no. Similarly, Kathy has a predictable set of actions she takes to warm up, including starting her computer and engaging people in chats. Ritualization helps to put further distance between reality and sexual obsession. Rituals are a way to induce trance and further separate oneself from reality. The goal is to reduce the ability to say stop.

The next phase of the cycle is sexual compulsivity, the acting out phase of the cycle. When therapists use the words acting out, they mean that the tensions addicts feel are reduced by acting on their sexual feelings. They feel better for the moment, thanks to the release that occurs. Compulsivity simply means that addicts regularly get to the point where sex becomes inevitable, no matter what the circumstances or the consequences. Thus, very smart, grown-up people end up doing things others would see as immoral or foolish.

Almost immediately reality sets in. Addicts for a moment will see the significance of their behavior and feel ashamed. This point of the cycle is a painful place where they have been many times. The last time they were at this low point, they probably promised themselves they would never do it again. Yet once again, they act out, and that leads to despair. For many addicts, this dark emotion brings on depression or a chronic feeling of hopelessness. For others, it results in an aversion to sex (sexual anorexia). In other words, sex becomes the enemy until the next time. One easy way to cure feelings of despair is to start obsessing again. The cycle then perpetuates itself.

The Addictive System

The addiction cycle is embedded in a larger addictive system which starts with a belief system. The belief system is a collection of convictions, myths, and values that affect the decisions we make. Beliefs about men, women, spouses and marriage, and sex are usually part of this internal paradigm. If you believe that "women always leave" or "men always lie" it will skew how you look at relationships. You will not trust in your primary relationship. For example, Kathy did not believe she could leave her husband, but she also could not share how unhappy she was or the dangerous risks she was taking.

At the core of this belief system are ideas you hold to be true about yourself. For the sex addict they are:

I am basically a bad, unworthy person.
No one would love me as I am.
My needs are never going to be met if I have to depend on others.
Sex is my most important need.

Basically, there is an internal logic that flows like this: Because I am unworthy, no one would love me if they really knew what I was like on the inside. Consequently, my needs are never going to be met if I have to tell the truth about who I am. Given that sex is my most important need, I will never be able to depend on another person who really knows me to get it. This logic is a recipe for desperation and disaster. Sex becomes an end in itself.

Figure 2.1

THE ADDICTIVE SYSTEM

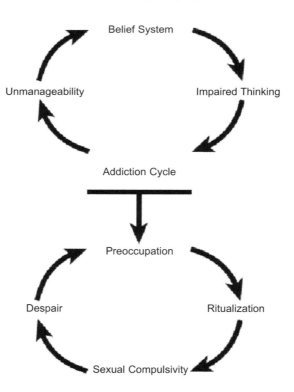

Out of this situation flows the kind of delusional thinking we explored in the first chapter. This impaired thinking allows the addictive cycle to flourish. It essentially distorts reality or even blocks your awareness of what is going on around you. Just think of times when you ignored a key reality such as a deadline at work or financial limits. For example, Jim s pressing obligations at work were pushed out of his consciousness by his obsession.

The addictive cycle becomes the driving force in the addict's life. Bad things start to happen. What we call unmanageability. Consequences start to occur. Because the addict is out of control and also out of touch with reality the problems compound. Lies, covering up, and inventing ways to keep the losses at bay do not stop the accumulation. Sooner or later, their life becomes a mess. Addicts find themselves despairing about how complex, stressful, or awful their lives have become. The feelings of despair confirm their dysfunctional beliefs about being an unlovable person. Thus, the system perpetuates itself. Figure 2.1 is a graphic map of how the system looks.

Unfortunately, most addicts do not understand until they accept that their lives have gotten so bad that they simply cannot go on. In the statements below, addicts tell how they knew they could not go on living as they d been. Review the list on pages 23 and 24 and then make one of your own, listing times when you started to understand that you could not continue your behaviors.

People were lying for me at work to cover for my absences.
Lost a job for taking sexual liberties with a customer.
Had a crisis with the promiscuity of my daughter who, at age fifteen, was doing exactly
   what I did.
Lost our family business.
Had two pregnancies in two years, giving up both children for adoption.
Rejected by roommates several times because of sexual behavior.
Realized that my exhaustion from sexual cruising was seriously affecting my work.
Realized I lost three marriages all because of affairs.
Became suicidal because of multiple intense involvement.
Was being sexual with my therapist and two of my graduate professors at the same time.
Was kicked out of bars for being publicly sexual.
Had to drop out of school because I couldn t concentrate due to obsessive
   fantasies.
Spent money on sex when I needed it for my children s clothes.
Didn t know which man was the father of my child.
Stayed in my marriage despite destructive sex.
Went to porn movies during work time.
Crossed professional boundaries with my patients.
Got herpes and gave it to my spouse.
Had no girlfriends due to stealing their boyfriends.
Lost promotion opportunities and a scholarship because coworkers discovered my sex life.
Constantly late for work or too tired to work.
Stayed out all night and slept all day despite kids to care for.
Lost whole weekends in bed with multiple partners.

List of Unmanageable Moments and When I Realized I Could Not Continue

1. _____
2. _____
3. _____
4. _____
5. _____
6. _____
7. _____
8. _____
9. _____
10. _____
11. _____
12. _____
13. _____
14. _____
15. _____
16. _____
17. _____
18. _____
19. _____
20. _____

Your Addictive Cycle

Below is a graphic representation of the addictive cycle. Each phase of the cycle has a place for you to record examples of your cycle. Provide as many examples as you can:

PREOCCUPATION

Example: _____

_____

_____

_____

DESPAIR

Example: _____

_____

_____

RITUALIZATION

Example: _____

_____

_____

SEXUAL
COMPULSIVITY

Example: _____

_____

_____

Diagram Your Own Addictive System

Some people have found it helpful to take a large piece of newsprint and diagram their own addictive system. Take each component—beliefs, thinking, addiction cycle, and unmanageability—and map out what happens in your addiction. Talk to your therapist, sponsor, and support groups. Sometimes it simply helps to have the big picture.

Sexual Anorexia—The Mirror of Sex Addiction

Systems often work just as well in reverse. I collect old outboard motors built in the days before clutches and transmissions. These engines shifted into reverse simply by spinning the motor in the opposite direction.

This image of a boat motor as a system capable of spinning in both directions can be used to help understand another sexual disorder called sexual anorexia. Sexual anorexics have an aversion to being sexual. As a beginner in recovery from sex addiction, you may well wonder what on earth this has to do with you. The answer is that many sex addicts have an aversion problem too, and they will not become healthy until they understand this. Many addicts also switch to sexual anorexia, mistaking sexual inactivity for recovery. But by trying to avoid sex completely, they only make themselves vulnerable to relapse. Recovering addicts must understand the dynamics of aversion from the start.

The sexually anorexic simply avoid sex. They hate all things connected with sex. In its most pure form, it means that the anorexic will go to extreme lengths to avoid being sexual.

Consider the story of Stan who, at the age of 38, was suicidal due to his loneliness and isolation. He had never touched a woman, held hands, kissed, or dated. Further, he never wanted to. He came from a family with an alcoholic mother who was sexually out of control. His father had killed himself at the discovery of yet another affair by his mother. After his dad's death when Stan was 12, most of Stan's teenage years were filled with embarrassment at his mother's sexual escapades. He also had to fend off her sexual initiatives with him to the point where he actually had to forcibly take her hands off of him on different occasions. She argued that she had friends who were sexual with their sons and it was good for them. As an adult, he perceived sex as the source of all his pain and refused to allow himself to have sexual feelings. As a result, he found himself isolated and fearful.

Anorexics like Stan have common characteristics:

- dread of sexual pleasure
- fear of sexual contact
- despair after sexual contact
- obsessive vigilance about sexual matters
- avoidance of anything connected with sex
- preoccupation with other people being sexual
- distortions about personal body appearance
- extreme loathing of body functions
- obsessional self-doubt about sexual adequacy
- excessive fear of sexually transmitted diseases
- rigid judgmental attitudes
- self-destructive behavior to limit, stop, or avoid sex

The sexually anorexic system works the same way the addictive system works. It starts with unhealthy beliefs about sex and relationships. The same core beliefs exist about feeling defective, unworthy, and unlovable as a person. Anorexics also believe that sex is dangerous and are terrified of their own sexual needs. Out of these dysfunctional beliefs stems impaired thinking. To think,

for example, that "everyone will take sexual advantage of me if I let them" is a major distortion of reality. Yet anorexics use many such distortions to keep sex at a distance. Similar compulsive cycles also exist, only the anorexic is preoccupied and obsessed with avoiding sex. Likewise, anorexics go through elaborate rituals, or distancing strategies, to avoid bringing sexual attention to themselves. Some, for example, go to extreme lengths to look unattractive and are then compulsively nonsexual or aversive. Then, they despair about this. The unmanageability is often harder to see than in sex addiction. Yet to lose a marriage because of being sexually unavailable to your partner is still to lose a marriage. To sexual anorexics, such events merely confirm their original premise of being unlovable. Figure 2.3 compares the addictive system and the anorexic system.

Figure 2.3

SEXUAL ANOREXIA AND SEXUAL ADDICTION COMPARED

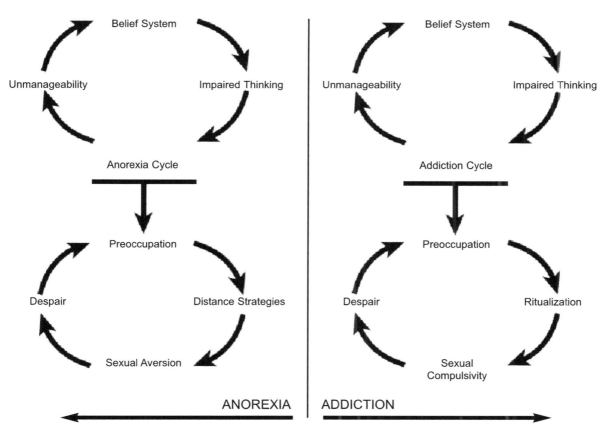

Many sex addicts are also sexually aversive. The following are examples of ways aversion fits with sex addiction:

- When sex addicts act outside of their relationship easily but find themselves avoiding sex with their partner. (Many anorexics find it difficult to be sexual with people they really care for or are vulnerable to.)
- When addicts binge and then go through a period in which they avoid all sex. (Addicts feel so bad about the binge, they "diet.")
- When addicts compartmentalize their lives so that one part is out of control while the other is under "super" control. (Think of a clergyman who preaches against promiscuity and pornography, yet in private, his life is out of control sexually.)
- When long periods of acting out are followed by long periods of sexual deprivation, the addiction has simply switched to the anorexic mode.
- When sex addiction and anorexia switch with other addictions. (An example would be a sex addict, who is also a food anorexic, who gets married and then begins to overeat compulsively and becomes sexually anorexic.)
- When the use of one addiction switches sexual behavior from addictive to anorexic. (For example, the sexual abuse survivor and alcoholic who is compulsively sexual when she drinks but compulsively nonsexual when sober.)

There are many patterns in sex addiction and sexual anorexia. Seventy-two percent of addicts can identify some degree of binge-purge behavior in their sexuality. Fifteen percent do addiction and anorexia simultaneously. Some people are so driven by both patterns that they will mutilate, harm or destroy their own genitals as a way to stop living in these extremes. Many addicts say they have considered some form of permanent self-harm as a solution. It is crucial to understand the aversive as well as the addictive part of yourself.

The contradictory combination of addiction and aversion is a potent, often overwhelming affliction, especially because it causes extreme shame and guilt on both ends of the spectrum. I would reassure you that there is hope. Many people, once having faced the conflicting demons in their life, use the tools outlined in this book to find hope and healing.

Sexual Anorexia List

You may still think this situation does not apply to you. Do the following exercises and see if it starts to make more sense to you.

List five examples of times you have become aversive to sex. Think of times when you have avoided sexual contact, felt sexual self-hatred, or have entered into a period of extreme deprivation.

1. _____
_____
_____

2. _____
_____
_____

3. _____
_____
_____

4. _____
_____
_____

5. _____
_____
_____

Describe three examples of ways your sex addiction and sexual anorexia go together.

1. _____
_____
_____

2. _____
_____
_____

3. _____
_____

How Do Professionals Know When Addiction Is Present?

Illnesses have a pattern of symptoms professionals can recognize. With all addictions, a screening test or assessment instrument can usually indicate that more in depth searching for a pattern is necessary.

Your counselor may have given you a SAST (Sexual Addiction Screening Test). There are different versions of the SAST, including one for men, one for women, and one for gay men. These instruments have been used tens of thousands of times and are proven to separate sex addicts from non sex addicts. If you have scored high in one of these tests, your therapist then probably did a series of interviews using specific criteria to discern addictive patterns. When addiction is present, the following criteria are easily identified:

1. Recurrent failure (pattern) to resist impulses to engage in specific sexual behavior.
2. Frequent engaging in those behaviors to a greater extent or over a longer period of time than intended.
3. Persistent desire or unsuccessful efforts to stop, reduce, or control those behaviors.
4. Inordinate amount of time spent in obtaining sex, being sexual, or recovering from sexual experience.
5. Preoccupation with the behavior or preparatory activities.
6. Frequent engaging in the behavior when expected to fulfill occupational, academic, domestic, or social obligations.
7. Continuation of the behavior despite knowledge of having a persistent or recurrent social, financial, psychological, or physical problem that is caused or exacerbated by the behavior.
8. Need to increase the intensity, frequency, number, or risk of behaviors to achieve the desired effect, or diminished effect with continued behaviors at the same level of intensity, frequency, number, or risk.
9. Giving up or limiting social, occupational, or recreational activities because of the behavior.
10. Distress, anxiety, restlessness, or irritability if unable to engage in the behavior.

Research shows that if at least three of these criteria are met, addiction is present. Follow-up studies indicate that after a period of recovery (as their awareness grows), addicts themselves can identify five of the criteria in their behaviors, with many acknowledging up to seven of them.

Similar criteria exist for sexual anorexia:

1. Recurrent pattern of resistance or aversion to any sexual activity, initiative, or behavior.

2. Persistent aversion to sexual contact even though it is self-destructive or harmful to relationships.

3. Extreme efforts to avoid sexual contact or attention, including self-mutilation, distortions of body appearance or apparel, and aversive behavior.

4. Rigid, judgmental attitudes towards personal sexuality and sexuality of others.

5. Extreme shame and self-loathing about sexual experiences, body perceptions, and sexual attributes.

6. Sexual aversion affects work, hobbies, friends, family, and primary relationship.

7. Preoccupation and obsession with avoiding sexual contact and with sexual intentions of others.

8. Despair about sexual adequacy and functioning.

9. Avoiding intimacy and relationships because of fear of sexual contact.

10. Distress, anxiety, restlessness, or irritability because of sexual contact or potential sexual contact.

Again, our research shows that early in recovery, meeting as few as three of the criteria can mean that compulsive behavior exists. For our purposes we also can look at signs that binge-purge conditions exist. Here are criteria that professionals use.

1. Pleasure or relief at time of sexual acting out, but experience despair after.

2. Periods of time where all sexual interest and behavior ceases.

3. A pattern of bingeing followed by periods of being compulsively non-sexual.

4. Sexually excessive in some areas and simultaneously compulsively non-sexual in others.

5. Take extreme measures such as self-mutilation as an attempt to disrupt acting out cycle.

6. Other family members who are sexually addicted.

7. Other family members who are sexually anorexic.

8. My significant other is a sex addict.

9. My significant other is sexually anorexic.

10. My significant other and I have sexual binge-purge patterns.

The following pages contain worksheets that will help you explore these criteria in greater depth so you can see for yourself how you fit them. It s important that you review them in a supportive atmosphere with a therapist or professional team, your support group, and your sponsor. It will help you to understand the strength of your addictive system and whether sexual anorexia has any part in your acting out. Remember that all addicts struggle with impaired thinking. If in doubt, ask others in your group or your therapist for help about whether certain criteria fit or not.

Sexual Addiction Criteria

Each of the addiction criteria is listed below, along with suggestions and examples to help you. Record whether you think your sexual patterns fit the criteria by circling yes or no. For those that you mark yes, use the space underneath to provide examples showing why you think the criterium fits. Mark your total at the bottom. We will discuss what your total may mean after you finish the exercise.

Yes   No   1.   Recurrent failure (pattern) to resist impulses to engage in specific sexual behavior.

_____

_____

Yes   No   2.   Frequent engaging in those behaviors to a greater extent or over a longer period of time than intended.

_____

_____

Yes   No   3.   Persistent desire or unsuccessful efforts to stop, reduce, or control those behaviors.

_____

_____

Yes   No   4.   Inordinate amount of time spent in obtaining sex, being sexual, or recovering from sexual experience.

_____

_____

Yes   No   5.   Preoccupation with the behavior or preparatory activities.

_____

_____

Yes   No   6.   Frequent engaging in the behavior when expected to fulfill occupational, academic, domestic, or social obligations.

_____

_____

Yes   No   7.   Continuation of the behavior despite knowledge of having a persistent or recurrent social, financial, psychological or physical problem that is caused or exacerbated by the behavior.

_____

_____

Yes   No   8.   Need to increase the intensity, frequency, number or risk of behaviors to achieve the desired effect, or diminished effect with continued behaviors at the same level of intensity, frequency, number or risk.

Yes   No   9.   Giving up or limiting social, occupational, or recreational activities because of the behavior.

Yes   No   10. Distress, anxiety, restlessness or irritability if unable to engage in the behavior.

Total: _____

Each of the sexual anorexia criteria is listed below along with suggestions and examples to help you. Record whether you think your sexual patterns fit the criteria by circling yes or no. For those that you mark yes, use the space underneath to provide examples showing why you think the criterion fits. Mark your total on the bottom. I will discuss what your total can signify after the exercises.

Yes   No   1.   Recurrent pattern of resistance or aversion to any sexual activity, initiative, or behavior.

Yes   No   2.   Persistent aversion to sexual contact even though it is self-destructive or harmful to relationships.

Yes   No   3.   Extreme efforts to avoid sexual contact or attention including self-mutilation, distortions of body appearance or apparel, and aversion behavior.

Yes   No   4.   Rigid, judgmental attitudes towards personal sexuality and sexuality of others.

Yes   No   5.   Extreme shame and self-loathing about sexual experiences, body perceptions, and sexual attributes.

Yes   No   6.   Sexual aversion affects work, hobbies, friends, family, and primary relationship.

_____

_____

Yes   No   7.   Preoccupation and obsession with avoiding sexual contact and with sexual intentions of others.

_____

_____

Yes   No   8.   Despair about sexual adequacy and functioning.

_____

_____

Yes   No   9.   Avoiding intimacy and relationships out of fear of sexual contact.

_____

_____

Yes   No   10.   Distress, anxiety, restlessness, or irritability because of sexual contact or potential sexual contact.

_____

_____

Total: _____

Binge-Purge Critera

The following binge-purge criteria include both family characteristics as well as personal patterns. Record whether you think your sexual patterns fit the criterion by circling yes or no next to each. For those that you mark yes, use the space underneath to provide examples showing why you think the criterium fits. Mark your total on the bottom.

Yes   No   1.   I feel pleasure or relief at the time of sexual acting out, but experience despair after.

_____

_____

Yes   No   2.   I have periods of time where all sexual interest and behavior ceases.

_____

_____

Yes   No   3.   I have a pattern of bingeing followed by periods of being compulsively nonsexual.

_____

_____

Yes   No   4.   I am sexually excessive in some areas and simultaneously compulsively nonsexual in others.

_____

_____

Yes   No   5.   I take extreme measures such as self-mutilation as an attempt to disrupt acting out cycle.

_____

_____

Yes   No   6.   I have other family members who are sexually addicted.

_____

_____

Yes   No   7.   I have other family members who are sexually anorexic.

_____

_____

Yes   No   8.   My significant other is a sex addict.

_____

_____

Yes   No   9.   My significant other is sexually anorexic.

_____

_____

Yes   No   10. My significant other and I have sexual binge-purge patterns.

_____

_____

Total: _____

If you answered yes to three or more of the criteria for any category in the above exercises, this suggests you probably are struggling with that issue.

Take a deep breath. Though it can be frightening to realize you have a serious problem, many addicts find it very helpful and relieving to finally have a name for what s been bothering them for so long. Remember, this is the beginning of a healing process that will work for you.

How Did I Get This Way?

By this time it must be clear to you whether or not you have a problem. Typical questions emerge with the realization that you do have a problem. First, you wonder how this happened to you. Following is a brief explanation (see the Resources list in the appendix for other sources of information on the origins of addiction).

¥ Addicts typically inherit a genetic structure which predisposes them to addictions in general. Scientists believe there is a problem with the way an addict's brain processes neurochemicals such as dopamine or seratonin (often associated with pleasure, pain and relief in the brain). There may actually be a problem with the way the synapses fire in the brain or how connections are made. Regardless of the reason, we do know part of the problem is genetic.

¥ Often addicts come from families in which other members suffer from addictions. Parents, siblings, and extended family members will have types of addictive and compulsive behaviors. This increases the probability of actually acquiring addictive behaviors through modeling, family dysfunction, and child abuse all of which can also activate a predisposed nature.

¥ One of the primary failures that plays a role in making an addict is the inability to sustain intimacy. There is fundamental failure to trust others enough to bond with them. Addiction in many ways is about the failure to bond, which is why we consider it as an intimacy disorder.

¥ Sex addicts families tend to be rigid and authoritarian or at least some members are. This results in a resistance to being accountable. Further, the presence of extreme sexual negativity will likely intensify sexual obsession. For example, living in a religious tradition that does not support healthy sexual attitudes can create obsessive thinking.

¥ Childhood abuse is a factor for many, leading to extreme reactivity or hypersensitivity to pain and emotional upset. Some sex addicts actually repeat abusive themes in their sexual acting out.

¥ Depression frequently accompanies both sex addiction and sexual anorexia. Feelings of despair intensify both addiction and anorexic obsessions.

¥ High stress situations such as medical school, business, or danger such as warfare can create addicts when there were no other predisposing factors.

¥ Other addictions can also precipitate an addictive sexual pattern. Addictions can actually migrate from one form to another.

It will take you some time to understand how you acquired your addiction. In order to start making change, you simply have to start with the fact that you do have the problem. The upcoming chapters will help to further your understanding.

Professionals look for twenty collateral indicators or accompanying signs that are usually present for sex addicts as another way to confirm a diagnosis. Usually six or more are present in most sex addicts. By reviewing them it also helps to better understand the factors that led to your illness. This next section is designed to help you gain that perspective.

Collateral Indicators

Below are twenty collateral indicators that are often used to confirm the presence of sex addiction. They are usually part of the profile of a sex addict. The purpose of this section is to list how many fit your experience. Circle yes or no to indicate if the statements are true about you. For those that you mark yes, use the space underneath to provide examples showing why you think the criterion fits. Mark your total on the bottom. Remember that sex addicts typically have six of the following:

Yes No 1. I have had severe consequences because of sexual behavior.

Yes No 2. I have struggled with depression and it appears related to sexual acting out.

Yes No 3. I have struggled with depression and it appears related to sexual aversion.

Yes No 4. I have a history of sexual abuse.

Yes No 5. I have a history of physical abuse.

Yes No 6. I have a history of emotional abuse.

Yes No 7. I see my sexual life in self-medicating terms (intoxicating, tension-relief, pain-relief, sleeping pills).

Yes   No   8.   I have persistently pursued high risk or self-destructive behavior.

Yes   No   9.   I find high risk or self-destructive behavior is more arrousing to me than safe sexual behavior.

Yes   No   10.   I have other addictions.

Yes   No   11.   I simultaneously use sexual behavior in concert with other addictions (gambling, eating disorders, substance abuse, alcoholism, compulsive spending) to the extent that desired effect is not achieved without sexual activity and other addiction present.

Yes   No   12.   I have a history of deception around sexual behavior.

Yes   No   13.   Other members of my family are addicts.

Yes   No   14.   I often feel extreme self-loathing because of sexual behavior.

Yes   No   15.   I have few intimate relationships that are not sexual.

Yes   No   16.   I am in crisis now because of sexual matters.

Yes   No   17.   I have a history of crisis around sexual matters.

Yes   No   18. I experience diminished pleasure now from the same sexual experiences.

Yes   No   19. I come from a rigid family.

Yes   No   20. I come from a disengaged family.

Is There Hope for Sex Addicts?

Do sex addicts ever really recover? That is the question I most frequently hear. The answer is a definite yes. A way to understand this is to think of other chronic illnesses. Diabetes is a very debilitating illness. However, if you learn how to eat appropriately, manage your weight, and watch for signs of blood sugar problems, you can live and thrive.

Similarly, addicts can learn to live a happy, joyous, and free life as long as they maintain the processes essential to recovery. They must learn to live in a recovery zone in which their sexual behavior is healthy. This workbook is built on that proven premise. The last chapter of this workbook provides more information about how this program works by creating an overview of the steps successful recovering people have taken to live in the recovery zone.

Some people in early recovery find their problems are too overwhelming and see no hope. They keep relapsing, or they become so hopeless and despairing that they consider suicide. Here again, the problem is not hopeless. What these people often need is more support, such as an inpatient (residential), outpatient (nonresidential) program or, if they are already in therapy, a more structured outpatient program with more frequent appointments and group therapy.

What's Best for You: Outpatient or Inpatient Therapy?

Basically, you deal with the same issues in each setting, but either may be appropriate. A residential program creates a more focused and supportive environment for developing skills for success. You may benefit more if you can build that momentum in the community in which you live through an outpatient program. But if the illness is too strong, residential treatment may be appropriate.

Outpatient programs work best if the recovering person can stay relapse free, has very strong family support, and is committed to the process.

The bottom line is that hope is connected to your courage. In order to change, you must confront the denial and delusion of your addictive system. This can be very painful. Usually this means that what you believed to be true does not turn out to be so.

Most addicts early in recovery felt resentful when they were confronted by others about their behavior. They vigorously defended themselves, only to later find that they had seriously misunderstood what was happening and how serious their situation was. They would protest to therapists, rebel against sponsors, and distance themselves from other recovering people. It is hard to face being out of control.

At a later point, we will talk in depth about what has to happen. For now it is important to learn to have compassion for yourself. This is why we talk about the gentle path rather than being hard on yourself. When someone is presenting reality to you, listen rather than spooling up to defend yourself. Admit to the possibility that the other person might be right. People are not out to get you, but rather love you and want to help you.

Remember that you are not alone. We live in a culture that supports addiction in many forms. Notice how long it has taken to understand tobacco and nicotine as a problem. Or gambling. There are still mental health professionals who do not believe in alcoholism. We are constantly invited to exceed our limits with food, sex, work, money, and chemicals. Historically, we have come a long way in our understanding of the nature of addiction. Living in this culture, it is no wonder that you are confused about addictive sex. To further clarify this, we will look at specific sexual behavior in the next chapter.

Reading Assignment

To prepare for the work of the next section, read *Out of the Shadows*, pp. 23—61, and *Don't Call It Love*, pp. 39—72. If you found significant aversion problems, please read *Sexual Anorexia*, pp. 37—79.

CHAPTER THREE: What Are Your Behaviors?
Understanding Compulsive Sex

A man "who imputes his indisposition to his excessive devotedness to Venus requested me to render him impotent, if I could not give him command
of himself any other way."
—BENJAMIN RUSH, 1812

WHEN THE FAMOUS RESEARCHER Alfred Kinsey was asked, "What is abnormal?" he responded, "Anything you cannot do." I have thought of that many times over the years because I constantly encounter people who do things sexually that you might never imagine or expect. I say to myself, "I did not know you could do that." And then I meet five other people who have done the unthinkable. One of my biggest revelations about sex is that people are extraordinarily diverse in their sexual behavior.

The problem is that sex is not talked about much so most people are unaware of the diversity and intensity of human sexual behavior. This is our culture's big secret and it has several effects:

- People feel great shame about what they do because they do not know how common their behavior is; they think they are abnormal.
- There has been a societal delay in understanding what constitutes healthy or unhealthy sexual behavior.
- Most important, it has been difficult to understand those whose sexual compulsion is the core of an addictive process.

In this chapter, we will focus on helping you understand the range of sexual behavior and see that you are not alone in your behavior.

The quote that starts this chapter comes from Benjamin Rush, commonly regarded as one of the grandfathers of modern psychiatry. Even in the early nineteenth century, he noticed that some people experienced problematic sexual behavior. The quote was taken from a case in which a man was so distraught over his sexual situation that castration would have been a relief. Most of us who work with sex addicts have heard that sentiment often. A few of us have had patients who actually castrated themselves out of desperation. Recently a colleague of mine treated a patient who used a shotgun to destroy his genitals. Such anguish goes beyond tragic.

By the twentieth century, professionals had developed a list of paraphilias—extreme or unusual behaviors regarded as "perverted" in the sense that they are either illegal or very dysfunctional. Pedophilia, exhibitionism, and voyeurism are commonly recognized paraphilias. Basically paraphilia happens when a person focuses on a specific aspect or practice of sex such as coprophilia (aroused by feces); a body part such as axillism (aroused by arm pits); or age such as ephebephilia (aroused only by adolescents). This is a changing list that reflects society's acceptance of behavior. For example, homosexuality was at one time listed as a problematic behavior but is now no longer identified as a mental health problem.

Understanding social conventions is part of the issue. For example, a man who exhibits himself and is aroused by that exposure runs the risk of arrest. A woman who exposes herself on the highway to passing motorists and finds it pleasurable is also an exhibitionist but has a low risk of arrest—or of being designated with a paraphilia.

Further, to define people by their unconventional sexual preferences or acts totally misses the mark. Many sex addicts do things that are problematic for them that are quite conventional. Consider a man whose sexual compulsion within his marriage is so great that his wife locks herself in the family car at night in her desperation to avoid his advances. Intercourse with your spouse is normal and expected in a loving relationship. To demand sex so many times a day your partner has to elude you is a problem.

By far the biggest issue we must address is that sex addicts will blend unconventional and normal behaviors in a pattern. The exhibitionist who goes to a massage parlor so that a woman looks at him in the nude may change the context so there is less likelihood of being arrested. But the scenario of exposing himself may continue. The shoe salesman who has a foot fetish may also have a problem with compulsive affairs in which he may or may not be interested in the women's feet. Some sex addicts have distinct compartments of their lives in which their behaviors are very different. A man may arrange elaborate threesomes when he's drunk. When he uses cocaine, however, he will cross dress and masturbate for 15 to 20 hours if undisturbed.

Addicts need to understand their patterns. First, they need to look at which sexual behaviors for them have a pattern of causing problems. Second, they must notice when there has been a loss of control, such as failed efforts to stop or continuation despite consequences, or knowing something will be bad and doing it anyway.

Usually, most addicts notice that they have more than one pattern. Think of types of sex as modules. If one activity cannot be done, you substitute another. We call this modularity. To switch from exhibitionism to prostitution is just switching the venue.

Most addicts also have a hierarchy of preference. A man goes to a hotel while traveling. He gets into his room and checks out the Yellow Pages to find an escort or massage service. The pages have already been torn out so he goes down to the hotel lounge to see if there are any prostitutes working the hotel. There is no one there. He then may scan to see if there are lonely women who could be picked up. He can find no one so he returns to his room and attempts to view adult movies, but this hotel offers none. He opens up his laptop to view pornography on the web but for some reason he cannot get online. So he returns to the lobby and buys a *Penthouse* or *Playboy*. He returns to his room and masturbates. He spends the evening working the alternatives until he can find some sexual outlet. Knowing what your modules are and what their hierarchy is becomes incredibly important to successful recovery.

The Ten Types

From 1985 to 1991, I followed the recoveries of over 1000 sex addicts. During that time, they were asked to complete an extensive inventory of their sexual behavior. Initially, 114 behaviors were identified; currently the figure is close to 200.

Through a statistical technique called a factor analysis, we discovered that these behaviors clustered into distinct types and each category had a set of issues that were important to understand. The following is an overview of the ten types we found.

1. *Fantasy Sex*—Sexually charged fantasies, relationships, and situations. Arousal depends on sexual possibility.
2. *Seductive Role Sex*—Seduction of partners. Arousal is based on conquest and diminishes rapidly after initial contact.
3. *Voyeuristic Sex*—Visual arousal. The use of visual stimulation to escape into obsessive trance.
4. *Exhibitionistic Sex*—Attracting attention to body or sexual parts of the body. Sexual arousal stems from reaction of viewer whether shock or interest.
5. *Paying for Sex*—purchase of sexual services. Arousal is connected to payment for sex and with time the arousal actually becomes connected to money itself.
6. *Trading Sex*—Selling or bartering sex for power. Arousal is based on gaining control of others by using sex as leverage.
7. *Intrusive Sex*—Boundary violation without discovery. Sexual arousal occurs by violating boundaries with no repercussions.
8. *Anonymous Sex*—High-risk sex with unknown persons. Arousal involves no seduction or cost and is immediate.
9. *Pain Exchange Sex*—Being humiliated or hurt as part of sexual arousal; or sadistic hurting or degrading another sexually, or both.
10. *Exploitive Sex*—Exploitation of the vulnerable. Arousal patterns are based on target "types" of vulnerability.

In the following pages we will help you review your sexual behaviors to see what patterns emerge. Be aware that your behaviors may appear in more than one type; in fact many addicts fit into multiple types. Becoming aware of potential multiple addictions becomes very important in working a relapse-free recovery. It will also bring you a step closer to understanding the issues at the core of sexual acting out.

In each page, you will be asked to check the following indicators. In the "history column," check those behaviors that are part of your sexual history. In the "problem column," check behaviors that have caused you distress, regret, or negative consequences. In the "loss of control" column, check an item if you have made efforts to control that behavior or if you knew it was bad for you but you did it anyway. Some items will have checks in each column. Some users of this workbook may have therapists who have access to a software program that will compare your answers to those of other sex addicts and will arrange it in a format for you and your therapist to review. If so, use the program for this section of the workbook.

It is entirely possible that you'll find only a few items that are problematic, but which are nevertheless destructive. Also it is possible to have no distinct type or pattern emerge. For example, if compulsive masturbation is what you do, you can still be incapacitated by it even though you do not use other behaviors compulsively. Many addicts find that they actually have a profile in a number of different types.

Fantasy Sex—Sexually Charged Fantasies, Relationships, and Situations

- Arousal depends on sexual possibility.
- Obsession and preoccupation is a way to prolong the feeling.
- Obsession can be heightened by masturbation, supercharged relationships, and sexualized environments.
- Observing or "spying" adds to obsessive life as does "acting out" the fantasy.
- Orgasm or even sexual contact may destroy the obsession; it is best when on the verge of being sexual.
- While direct sexual contact with others is avoided, sexual contact with self may be very compulsive, e.g., visiting fantasy websites and masturbating.

Although a wide variety of behaviors characterize the fantasy sex addict, the most common include chronic and compulsive masturbation that may or may not involve pornography. For the fantasy sex addict, the mental imagery is the pornography that fuels acting out. Feelings that accompany these obsessive fantasies often include such myths as "in order to be loved I must be sexual;" or "sex and love are one in the same." These individuals often feel anxious and depressed, and use sex as a way to medicate those feelings. Neglecting responsibilities in order to engage in fantasy and/or prepare for the next sexual episode is common among fantasy sex addicts.

History	Problem	Loss of Control	
_____	_____	_____	Thinking or obsessing about sex
_____	_____	_____	Fantasizing about past or future sexual experiences
_____	_____	_____	Spending a large amount of time preparing for a sexual episode
_____	_____	_____	Neglecting responsibilities and commitments in order to prepare for your next sexual episode
_____	_____	_____	Thinking that sex is love
_____	_____	_____	Thinking that your "special" sexual needs make you different from others
_____	_____	_____	Thinking that the next time things will be different
_____	_____	_____	Feeling a need to be sexual in order to feel good about yourself
_____	_____	_____	Denying or suppressing your sexuality and sexual feelings for periods of time
_____	_____	_____	Rationalizing or denying consequences of your sexual addiction
_____	_____	_____	Thinking deluded thoughts
_____	_____	_____	Having sex even though you didn't really want to or feel like it
_____	_____	_____	Feeling depressed, hopeless, or unworthy following a sexual encounter
_____	_____	_____	Feeling desperate or anxious between periods of sexual acting out
_____	_____	_____	Maintaining an open calendar and failing to make commitments because you fear missing an opportunity to be sexual

_____	_____	_____	Seeking sexual fantasy stories in books
_____	_____	_____	Using online fantasy websites
_____	_____	_____	Acting on a fantasy which turned out not to be true

Seductive Role Sex—Seduction of Partners

- Arousal is based on conquest and diminishes rapidly after initial contact.
- Arousal can also be a function of power and the maintenance of power as in sexual harassment or multiple families.
- Arousal can be heightened by increasing risk and/or number of partners.
- Use sexuality to gain control over others.
- Often have many relationships at the same time or a series of successive relationships.
- Often have extramarital affairs and hustles in singles clubs, health clubs, or bars.
- Often flirtatious with others and believe that seducing victims gives power over them.
- Using instant messging, emails, and chat rooms to discover and cultivate potential partners

History	Problem	Loss of Control	
_____	_____	_____	Thinking that if you are sexual with someone, you will have them in your power
_____	_____	_____	Feeling that you have to follow through with sex because you successfully hooked someone through your ritual
_____	_____	_____	Using sex as a means to find love
_____	_____	_____	Having many relationships at the same time
_____	_____	_____	Having rapid, successive relationships

_____	_____	_____	Having affairs outside your primary relationship
_____	_____	_____	Using sexual seduction to gain power over another person
_____	_____	_____	Hustling in singles clubs, bars, or health clubs
_____	_____	_____	Using flirtatious or seductive behavior to gain attention of others
_____	_____	_____	Finding sex partners over whom you have control or more power (as in money, age, or vulnerability)
_____	_____	_____	Using chat rooms, instant messaging, or websites to find partners
_____	_____	_____	Using online services that help find sex partners
_____	_____	_____	Cruising date services on or offline
_____	_____	_____	Seducing people who work for you
_____	_____	_____	Being sexual with professional clients (attorneys, physicians, therapists, etc.)

Voyeurism—Visual Arousal

The use of visual stimulation to escape into obsessive trance.
- Arousal may be heightened by masturbation, risk (e.g., peeping), or violation of boundaries (e.g., voyeuristic rape), but in order for arousal to be maintained it is illicit somehow and must be visual.
- Orgasm may or may not be part of the pattern.
- Behaviors for the voyeur include viewing sexually explicit videos and photographs, strip/peep shows, patronizing adult bookstores, and watching people through their house windows (both with or without binoculars).
- Often maintain a collection of pornography in various places (work, car, home) to always have a "stash" available.
- Using computers, disks, or jump drives to hide downloaded material.

It is also important to note that voyeurs often sexualize material that is not necessarily sexual. For example, magazines, advertisements, and catalogs that are not sexual in nature become pornography to the voyeur.

History	Problem	Loss of Control	
_____	_____	_____	Masturbating yourself
_____	_____	_____	Masturbating to the point of physical injury or infection
_____	_____	_____	Looking at sexually explicit magazines
_____	_____	_____	Keeping sexually explicit material or magazines at home or at work
_____	_____	_____	Watching sexually explicit video tapes
_____	_____	_____	Patronizing adult book stores
_____	_____	_____	Watching strip or peep shows
_____	_____	_____	Sexualizing people or materials that are not sexually explicit
_____	_____	_____	Watching people through windows of their houses or apartments
_____	_____	_____	Using binoculars or telescopes to watch people
_____	_____	_____	Hiding in secret places in order to watch or listen to people
_____	_____	_____	Sexualizing others that you observe in public places
_____	_____	_____	Maintaining a collection of pornographic materials
_____	_____	_____	Using online voyeur sites
_____	_____	_____	Observing others online such as webcam, nudist, or strip websites
_____	_____	_____	Accessing sites with cameras watching others

Exhibitionism—Attracting Attention to Body or Sexual Parts of the Body

Sexual arousal stems from reaction of the viewer whether with shock or interest. Often this attention-seeking pushes cultural norms or violates social conventions and laws.

- Orgasm may or may not be important.
- Often expose themselves from a car or within a public area such as a park, street, or school yard.
- May pretend that they did not intend for others to notice them (exposing self by choice of clothing, dressing/undressing in public areas, or from within their own home). However, others masturbate in their cars or in public places such as movie theaters, tanning salons, or dressing rooms with the hopes of another noticing their sexual behavior.
- Use of internet to expose self in real time such as on web cams or posting pictures on specialty websites.

History	Problem	Loss of Control	
_____	_____	_____	Exposing yourself from a car
_____	_____	_____	Exposing yourself in public places such as parks, streets, or school yards
_____	_____	_____	Exposing yourself from home
_____	_____	_____	Exposing yourself by being sexual or dressing/undressing in public or semipublic places
_____	_____	_____	Masturbating in cars
_____	_____	_____	Masturbating in public places such as movie theaters, tanning salons, or store dressing rooms
_____	_____	_____	Masturbating or exposing yourself on live web cams or on sites that post explicit pictures
_____	_____	_____	Sending photos of self to people who did not ask for them such as in an email or website link

Paying for Sex—Purchase of Sexual Services

Arousal is connected to payment for sex and, with time, the arousal actually becomes connected to money itself. Payment creates an entitlement and a sense of power over meeting needs, but the arousal starts with "having money" and the search for someone in the "business."

- Actual sexual activities can be very diverse, but this common scenario exists in most cases: (1) having means; (2) search; (3) payment; (4) preferred acting out (often a replication of childhood scenario); (5) extreme shame
- Often profoundly unable to protect or take care of themselves.
- May involve seeking out a prostitute. It can also include patronizing massage parlors, escort services, and lounges in order to find sexual favors.
- May call pornography lines, use personal ads to find sex partners, and spend money on someone in order to receive sexual favors.

History	Problem	Loss of Control	
_____	_____	_____	Patronizing saunas, massage parlors, or rap lounges
_____	_____	_____	Paying someone for sexual activity
_____	_____	_____	Using an escort or phone service
_____	_____	_____	Using the personal columns to find sex partners
_____	_____	_____	Paying for sexually explicit phone calls
_____	_____	_____	Spending money on someone in order to have sex
_____	_____	_____	Using online services to find escorts or prostitutes
_____	_____	_____	Paying to take pictures of nudity or sexual acts
_____	_____	_____	Arranging to financially support someone in exchange for sex
_____	_____	_____	Giving extraordinary gifts to gain sexual access

Trading Sex—Selling or Bartering Sex for Power

Arousal is based on gaining control of others by using sex as leverage.

- Prostitution, in this sense, is not about the financially desperate, but rather about the addicts' hook on the rush of high risk and power.
- Mutual sex can be unrewarding.
- Use currencies seldom acknowledged by the culture.
- Often make sexually explicit photographs and videotapes in which they may or may not be the subject.
- Receive money, services, or other goods in exchange for their sexual activity.
- Often swap partners, encourage a partner to have sex outside their relationship, or join sex clubs and nudist camps to find sexual partners.
- Often preoccupied with body image and will often "accessorize" their bodies with tattoo, and piercing.
- The swinger ads in magazines, newspapers often serve the trading addicts' addiction.

History	Problem	Loss of Control	
_____	_____	_____	Making sexually explicit video tapes
_____	_____	_____	Taking sexually explicit photographs
_____	_____	_____	Receiving money in exchange for sexual activity
_____	_____	_____	Receiving drugs in exchange for sexual activity
_____	_____	_____	Pimping others for sexual activity
_____	_____	_____	Swapping partners
_____	_____	_____	Urging your partner to have sex with persons outside your relationship
_____	_____	_____	Belonging to a nudist club to find sex partners
_____	_____	_____	Exposing yourself from stage or for hire
_____	_____	_____	Exposing yourself for home videos or photographs
_____	_____	_____	Being sexual because someone spent money on you
_____	_____	_____	Placing and answering ads in swinger magazines

_____	_____	_____	Participating in sexually explicit websites
_____	_____	_____	Producing or owning pornographic or sex-related site
_____	_____	_____	Performing, modeling, or being a subject of a sex-related site

Intrusive Sex—Boundary Violation without Discovery

- Sexual arousal occurs by violating boundaries with no repercussions.
- The high is about violation with orgasm being the secondary goal.
- Arousal related to having sexual contact often without permission or knowledge of victim and no accountability for behavior.
- Intrusive addicts are "sex thieves."
- Often sexualize conversations with inappropriate people (acquaintances or children) and at inappropriate times (work, social settings).
- Sexual acting out includes making inappropriate sexual advances or gestures towards another and would encompass issues such as sexual harassment.
- Often use explicit sexual phone lines and may place sexually harassing phone calls.
- Will often sexually touch others and pretend it was accidental.

History	Problem	Loss of Control	
_____	_____	_____	Participating in phone sexual activity
_____	_____	_____	Asking strangers or acquaintances inappropriate personal details about their sex lives
_____	_____	_____	Touching or fondling people inappropriately
_____	_____	_____	Telling sexually explicit stories or using sexually explicit language at inappropriate times or places
_____	_____	_____	Bringing sex or sexualized humor into conversations
_____	_____	_____	Making inappropriate sexual phone calls
_____	_____	_____	Making inappropriate sexual advances or gestures towards others
_____	_____	_____	Touching people but acting as if it were an accident

_____	_____	_____

Using chat rooms to make inappropriate or out of context sexual remarks

_____ _____ _____

Intruding in others' computers without their knowledge for sexual arousal

_____ _____ _____

Watching others' online activities for sexual arousal

Anonymous Sex—High-Risk Sex with Unknown Persons

- Arousal involves no seduction or cost and is immediate.
- Arousal has no entanglements or obligations associated with it, and is often accelerated by unsafe or high-risk
- Seek ultimate objectification by engaging with unknown partners, which may include regular partners or one-night stands
- Spend a great deal of time cruising beaches, parks, parking lots or bath houses to find anonymous sexual partner
- Often sexualizes others in showers, locker rooms, or public restrooms and may expose themselves in these places
- Using the internet for risky or anonymous encounters

History	Problem	Loss of Control	
_____	_____	_____	Having one night stands
_____	_____	_____	Engaging in sex with anonymous partners
_____	_____	_____	Cruising beaches, parks, parking lots, or baths
_____	_____	_____	Exposing yourself in showers, locker rooms, or public restrooms
_____	_____	_____	Sexualizing others in health clubs, locker rooms, restrooms, or showers
_____	_____	_____	Meeting people online for anonymous sex
_____	_____	_____	Having sex with people whose only identity is a screen name
_____	_____	_____	Traveling to meet someone met online who is unknown with sexual intent

Pain Exchange Sex

- Being humiliated or hurt as part of sexual arousal; or sadistic hurting or degrading another sexually, or both.
- Arousal is fused with pain, degradation, or both.
- Often arousal is built around specific scenarios or narratives of humiliation and shame.
- Orgasm and pleasure is elusive or may not even occur without pain or violence.
- The trigger for arousal is fear or reenactment of fearful situations. This arousal can be achieved by watching others hurt or be hurt as part of sex. This category also includes masochistic activities whereby the addict is self-inflicting pain or extreme fear in order to heighten sexual arousal (e.g., autoeroticism).
- Addicts in this category vary the ways they may cause or receive pain, fear, or humiliation. They may use sexual aids (vibrators, other objects) that are painful during masturbation or intercourse. Taking the passive role is also categorized in this area because the role involves giving up power and being willfully victimized in some way.
- Using chemicals to enhance sexual arousal is common with the pain exchange addict, particularly those who use inhalants to heighten erotic feeling.

History	Problem	Loss of Control	
_____	_____	_____	Dramatizing a particular role as part of your ritualizing behavior
_____	_____	_____	Masturbating with objects
_____	_____	_____	Willingly giving up power or acting out the victim role in your sexual activity
_____	_____	_____	Cross-dressing
_____	_____	_____	Using sexual aids to enhance your sexual experience
_____	_____	_____	Engaging in sex with animals
_____	_____	_____	Using drugs to enhance your sexual experience
_____	_____	_____	Receiving physical harm or pain during your sexual activity to intensify your sexual pleasure
_____	_____	_____	Causing physical harm or pain to your sex partner during sexual activity to intensify your sexual experience

_____	_____	_____	Masturbating with mechanical or electrical devices
_____	_____	_____	Seeking humiliating or degrading experiences as part of sex
_____	_____	_____	Using websites that specialize in bondage and pain
_____	_____	_____	Seeking websites that involve humiliation or degradation
_____	_____	_____	Focusing on internet sites that focus on the abnormal, bizarre, and painful

Exploitive Sex—Exploitation of the Vulnerable

- Arousal patterns are based on target "types" of vulnerability: Clients/patients of professionals, children, adolescents, or distressed persons become the focus of arousal.
- In cases of professional misconduct, perpetrators will become very aroused when the patient shares emotional pain.
- For street sex offenders, arousal may occur when they see a potential victim in a distressed situation.
- Arousal may occur in the "grooming" process of building trust in a potential victim.
- The boundary violations are explicit if not always illegal.
- Often seek other high-risk situations. Exploitive sex addicts cross the boundaries of their victims by forcing sexual activity, administering drugs or alcohol to their victims, or using their position of power. They may also share inappropriate sexual information with children or view child pornography.

History	Problem	Loss of Control	
_____	_____	_____	Watching or looking at child pornography
_____	_____	_____	Forcing sexual activity on a child outside your family
_____	_____	_____	Forcing sexual activity on a spouse or partner
_____	_____	_____	Forcing sexual activity on a person whom you know
_____	_____	_____	Forcing sexual activity on a person you do not know
_____	_____	_____	Engaging in sexual activity with a consenting minor
_____	_____	_____	Exposing children to your sexual activity
_____	_____	_____	Sharing inappropriate sexual information with children
_____	_____	_____	Using a power position to exploit or be sexual with another person
_____	_____	_____	Administering drugs to another person in order to force sexual activity
_____	_____	_____	Using alcohol to take sexual advantage
_____	_____	_____	Using the internet as a way to "find" vulnerable people or children
_____	_____	_____	Cruising chat rooms for someone to cultivate for exploitive purposes

Sexual History

This section will help you to identify key events or factors in your sexual history. Please answer the following questions by giving the approximate age and the specific event that was part of your sexual development.

Your Age _____ Key childhood sexual experiences up to age 10 (strong memories; traumatic events; events that evoke strong feelings; child abuse by parents or other adults).

_____
_____
_____
_____
_____

Your Age _____ Key adolescent sexual experiences up to age 18 (sexual experimentation; masturbation; onset of menstruation; sexual abuse by family member or other adults; fantasy life; other).

_____
_____
_____
_____
_____

Your Age _____ Key young adult experiences up to age 25 (dating; same-sex relationships; marriage; divorce; other).

_____
_____
_____
_____

Your Age _____ Key adult experiences up to present (include current sexual patterns).

_____
_____
_____
_____
_____

What has been the impact of any or all of the following on your sexual development?

How have family attitudes about sex affected your sexual development?

_____
_____
_____
_____
_____

How has the influence of religion affected your sexual development?

_____
_____
_____
_____
_____

How has your ethnic or cultural heritage impacted your sexual development?

_____
_____
_____
_____
_____

How has your work or career impacted your sexual development?

_____
_____
_____
_____
_____

Courtship Gone Awry

Implicit in most compulsive sexual patterns is a distortion of normal courtship. For example, it is very normal even for children to play "I'll show you mine if you show me yours." It is normal to be curious about your partner's body and pleasurable to have your body examined. As you grow up you learn how to handle that part of getting to know someone appropriately. Exhibitionists and voyeurs, however, have become stuck in this one part of courtship. They have become so focused on this phase that it becomes more pleasurable than the rest of the courtship. In other words, courtship has gone awry.

Consider the case of Carrie. Emotionally and physically abused, she was sexually abused by her father, who fondled her regularly until she was 14. At one point she got pregnant and her parents forced her into an abortion. Her mother had the doctor place the fetus next to Carrie's head after the surgery so she would "learn a lesson." As an adult, Carrie found it very difficult to allow herself to be sexual with a man that she cared for. She was always very anxious and fearful if the relationship mattered at all. However, when she was with men who were "slime" and for whom she did not care, she could be sexual with abandon. She also was intensively sexual with herself. She would masturbate whenever she got anxious.

It was a tremendous relief to her when she finally understood that being abused created a disordered sense of courtship, and prevented her from being sexual with a man who really mattered. Her father mattered and yet he had betrayed her. A further legacy of the betrayal was that men who did not matter and were unreliable were attractive.

One problem is that there is no systematic and reliable way in our culture to learn the basics of courtship. You probably never attended a course that taught you how to appropriately and successfully flirt. Courtship failure can mean that you start repetitive patterns because what you do does not work. So it is important to learn the basic elements of courtship. There are twelve components to courtship. They are as follows:

Noticing—This is the ability to notice attractive traits in others. With an existing partner this means the ability to stay conscious of the desirable traits in that partner. This dimension requires the capacity to filter out traits that, while desirable, are not a good match for you. In other words, noticing also means to be discriminating.

Attraction—This is the ability to feel attraction towards others and imagine acting on those feelings. This dimension assumes a functional arousal "map" in which you select behavior and persons appropriate for you. Attraction involves curiosity as well as desire about the physical, emotional, and intellectual traits of others. In an existing relationship it means the ability to maintain an openness to change and the unknown. In reality relationships, partners keep "discovering" the other. Attraction is where passion starts and how relationships endure.

Flirtation—Everyone needs to know how to flirt. Successful flirting uses playfulness, seductiveness, and social cues to send signals of interest and attraction to the desirable person. This ability extends to noticing and accurately reading flirtation from others. The critical factor in flirtation is knowing when it is appropriate to send and receive. Success in long-term relationships requires an ongoing flirtation with your partner.

Demonstration—Sometimes inaccurately described as "showing off," this is where one demonstrates "prowess"—either a physical trait, skill, or capability. Sexually, this is the classic "I will show you mine and you show me yours." There is in fact a pleasure or eroticism in having a potential partner show interest in your sexuality. Behaviors here include demonstrating a skill such as in an athletic ability, dressing to attract the other person, or doing specific sex-related actions to further the partner's interest. It is important to be aware of what you're doing and that you are being appropriate to the context and to the person.

Romance—The ability to experience, express, and receive passion. Romance assumes the ability to be aware of all the feelings of attraction, vulnerability, and risk. More important, a lover must be able to express them and have sufficient self-worth to accept the expressions of care from a lover as true. Included in romance is the ability to test the reality of the feelings. Is what is perceived in the other person accurate, or merely a projection of what you want to exist? Are the people selected consistently positive or bad choices for you?

Individuation—In the midst of the romance, healthy persons are able to be true to themselves. They feel absolutely free to be who they are. They feel no fear of disapproval or control by the other. They tell the truth and do not feel intimidated. Nor do they have to give in on important matters. They can ask needs to be met and they do not have to defer to the other. They trust that people care for them as they are.

Intimacy—As the exhilaration of early passion subsides, partners enter the "attachment" phase where the relationship deepens in its meaning and integrity. This requires profound vulnerability that is ongoing and more difficult than the exhilaration of discovery during early romance. This is the "being known fully and staying anyway" part of relationships.

Touching—Physical touch requires trust, care, and judgment. Touching affirms the other but is respectful of timing, situation, and boundaries. Touching without permission or sexualizing touch betrays trust. While touch can be seductive and misleading, it can also be extraordinarily healing. In adults who were not touched or who were otherwise neglected as children, touch deprivation can be very extreme. People deprived of touch will go against their judgment and their needs simply to be touched.

Foreplay—Sometimes referred to as the most important part of sexual contact, it is the expression of sexual passion without genital intercourse. Holding, fondling, kissing, and sexual play build sexual tension and are erotic and pleasurable. As a stage it includes the verbal expression of passion and meaning. In repeated surveys, most people say it is the best part of sex. It is often skipped over in our culture because of time pressure and stress.

Intercourse—More than the exchange of body fluids, this is the ability to surrender oneself to passion, to let go and trust yourself and your partner to be vulnerable. While extremely pleasurable, intercourse is also an indicator of how you are able to give up control. To give oneself over to passion requires a true abandonment of how things are supposed to turn out. Many people limit themselves or fail in orgasm simply because of problems with trust and control.

Commitment—Commitment is the ability to bond or attach to another. Some describe addiction as the failure to bond or to lack the capacity to form a deep, meaningful relationship. If someone matters enough, you honor the relationship by your fidelity to it. Many addicts refer to the "black hole" they are searching to fill. This is it—being bonded in meaningful relationships, including nonsexual ones. If you grew up in a family in which you learned not to count on others, you look for what you can count on. Alcohol, sex, drugs, and high risk always do what they promise, but this "pathological" relationship with a mood-altering behavior does not fill that void.

Renewal—The capacity must exist to sustain all the above dimensions in an existing relationship. To be married does not mean you stop flirting or expressing passion. There is a difference between being attached to someone out of habit and being devoted because of the meaning that has evolved in your journey together. Successful couples continue courtship, continue to show the other they are a worthy partner, continue to make efforts to attract their mate, and continue to express the value they have for each other. If a relationship is not working, partners take responsibility to change it. If the relationship is not tenable, they leave.

Courtship and the Ten Types

Think again about the Ten types you just examined. Each type in some way reveals a problem in courtship. We will review each type of sex addict and each component of courtship so you can see where courtship has failed for you—and where you can work to repair it. It is important to do this task now to understand that your problem is not just "sexual" but also an intimacy disorder. You struggle with addiction because you have not formed the kind of relationships that meet your needs, and your behavior provides an important clue about where your intimacy problems lie. We will start with the courtship problems in each type:

Fantasy Sex—These people notice attractive traits in others and feel attracted, but they do not move beyond it. There is safety in staying in the fantasy world as opposed to acting on the fantasy. Romance and sex can flourish when there is no reality testing. They also can become obsessional. Masturbation to fantasies is how we learn about our own desire. When masturbation becomes compulsive, we make it a way to escape our loneliness. It is about fear of rejection, fear of reality, and reduction of anxiety. It can also be self-indulgent in the sense of seeking comfort as opposed to risking relationship. Many sex addicts find refuge in fantasy sex because other forms of acting out are simply too complicated, too risky, or too much effort. Fantasy sex is a way to disassociate from reality including relationships.

Voyeurism—Voyeurs are also nonparticipants in the sex game. They move beyond fantasy to search out sexual objects in the real world. It is normal to enjoy looking at others sexually. When that means looking at people who do not know they are being viewed it becomes a problem. When it involves compulsive pornography use it becomes isolating. Voyeurs also venture into flirtation. Sitting in a strip bar and having someone do a table dance is to focus on another's sexual demonstration behavior without doing anything yourself. To put it in childhood terms, "you show me yours and I'll watch." Usually voyeurism means objectifying the other person—this is not a personal relationship.

Exhibitionism—Exhibitionism is the "I will show you mine" part. It is pleasurable and normal to have others notice you sexually. With a partner, it is a significant part of sex play. Some addicts focus only on being noticed and have difficulty moving beyond this point. Eroticism for them is being looked at. For some it is the power of realizing they have captured the other's attention. For some, it is forcing their sexuality on the other, which is angry and aggressive. From a relationship perspective it is introducing yourself in an inappropriate way. It is seeking attention from others with no intent of going further, which is merely to tease. Sometimes it is about the pleasure of breaking the rules. In either case, when exhibitionism is obsessional and compulsive, it is a significant distortion of normal courtship.

Seductive Role Sex—Here relationships are about power and conquest. Flirtation, performance, and romance are the erotic keys for sex addicts in this category. They are hooked on falling in love and winning the attention of the other. Often once they have done so, sexual interest subsides. While they can quickly gain the confidence of others and can be intimate in the early-discovery romantic stage, establishing a deeper relationship eludes them. They are on the hunt for another. People in this type feel trapped, as though they cannot be themselves, so they have multiple relationships in which they can present and act differently with different people. They have a hard time being themselves. Often they fear abandonment, so having more than one relationship is a way to prevent the hurt of a break-up that they are sure they will receive. They are crippled in their ability to form lasting bonds and enduring relationships.

Trading Sex—Some sex workers actually do form some attachment for their clients, but typically bartering sex for money is devoid of relationship. The goal is to simulate flirtation, demonstration, and romance. What actually happens in most cases is a replication of childhood sexual abuse in which the child gained power in a risky game of being sexual with the caregiver. If a prostitute is a sex addict, he or she has found sex more pleasurable with clients than in personal relationships and is "hooked on the life." This represents a significant distortion of normal courtship. Often the money is a sign of having been successful at the sexual "game" and then the client can be disregarded except as a repeat customer. Forging significant, enduring bonds or being true to yourself is not part of the bargain.

Intrusive Sex—People who do intrusive sex, such as touching others in crowds or making obscene calls, are really perverting the touching and foreplay dimensions of courtship. In most cases, they are using others for sexual arousal with little chance of being caught. Their behavior represents both intimacy failure and individuation difficulties. In their behavior, they do not see themselves as predatory although they are. An implicit anger exists because they do this "stealing" of sex. They believe no one would respond as they would really like to. Their goal is to take sex without the other's knowledge. They become quite expert in their subterfuge. For example, professionals such as physicians, clergy, or attorneys will look quite compassionate when in fact they use their clients' vulnerability for their own arousal. Stolen intrusion becomes the obsession. Ongoing relationship life suffers because of their secret shame.

Paying for Sex—Here sex addicts are willing participants in simulated intimacy. They are focused, however, on the touching, foreplay, and intercourse dimensions without the hassle of relationship. Frequently they tell themselves that they resort to prostitution because of their partner's inadequacies. Compulsive prostitution is a larger problem, but it does in fact reflect relationship failure. Often times, the failure is connected to sex addicts' inability to communicate feelings to their partners or to be willing to work on their own attractiveness behaviors. For some, sex *is* intimacy—or as close as they will allow themselves to be. Frequently, sexual anorexia is present in that it is difficult to be aroused in the presence of someone whom you care about. Commitment to and renewal of relationships are profoundly undermined by the secret life of this behavior.

Anonymous Sex—By definition, this sexual behavior is not about relationship. You do not have to attract, seduce, trick, or even pay for sex. It simply is sex. Ironically the sexual anorexia counterpart is often present, too, along with its associated loneliness and isolation. Frequently for sex addicts, part of the high is the risk of unknown persons and situations. In part that stems from early sexual relationships that were fearful. Having to experience fear in order for arousal or sexual initiation to work fundamentally distorts the courtship process. The safety of an enduring bond is never there to allow the deeper, profound risks of being known by another.

Pain Exchange Sex—People who compulsively take part in painful, degrading, or dangerous sexual practices such as "blood sports" (creating wounds which bleed as part of sex) or asphyxiation often have significant distortions of courtship. Touching, foreplay and intercourse become subordinated to some dramatic story line that usually is a reenactment of a childhood abuse experience. For a woman to be aroused only if a man is hurting her is a distortion of sexual and relationship health. Enduring relationships are difficult to build given arousal scenarios that are embedded in high-risk sex.

Exploitive Sex—To exploit the vulnerable clearly is distorted courtship. Sex offenders who rape have deep problems with intimacy and anger. Less obvious are nonviolent predators who seduce children or exhibit professional sexual misconduct with clients. In the workplace where a differential of power exists, employees can be exploited. When arousal is dependent on the vulnerability of another in order to be attractive, there is a significant courtship problem all along the courtship continuum. Addicts in this category will use "grooming" behavior, carefully building the trust of the unsuspecting victim. So attraction, flirtation, demonstration, romance, and intimacy are all used to gain the confidence of the person for sexual exploitation. Addicts will go so far as to profess an enduring bond, though they have only a much more malevolent intent.

Figure 3.1 summarizes the stages of courtship and the ten types. The chart shows how each type of behavior is affected by problems in specific courtship dimensions. To further clarify these issues we have included a courtship inventory. By using it, you will be able to connect what you have learned about the patterns of your sexual behavior to the ways you learned about courtship.

Figure 3.1
Courtship Disorder and the Ten Types

COMPULSIVE TYPE	Notice	Attraction	Flirtation	Demonstration	Romance	Intimacy	Individuation	Touching	Foreplay	Intercourse	Commitment	Renewal
Fantasy	•	•										
Voyeurism	•	•	•									
Exhibitionism			•	•								
Seductive Role			•	•	•	•	•				•	•
Trading			•	•	•	•	•				•	•
Intrusive					•	•	•	•			•	•
Paying					•	•	•	•	•		•	•
Anonymous					•	•	•	•	•		•	•
Pain Exchange								•	•	•	•	•
Exploitive	•	•	•	•	•	•	•	•	•	•	•	•

Courtship Inventory

The following are ten dimensions of courtship. Rate yourself on each dimension and record any comments you have about your rating. Remember you do not have to do this perfectly. Your goal is to identify places where you are stuck in understanding courtship. Use your work on the ten types to see how your behavior and intimacy issues are aligned. Record specific examples of problems you have had with relationships that relate to your sexual behaviors.

Noticing—The ability to recognize attractive traits in others. With an existing partner, to be conscious of the desirable traits in that partner. This dimension requires the capacity to filter out traits that, while desirable, are not a good match for you. Do you notice attractive traits in others? Are you able to keep noticing them with a current partner even after years of being together? Are you able to recognize attractive traits and decide they are not a good match for you or are inappropriate for you to pursue? This dimension requires both noticing and discriminating about what you notice.

LOW									HIGH
1	2	3	4	5	6	7	8	9	10

_____

_____

Attraction—The ability to feel attraction towards others and imagine acting on those feelings. This dimension assumes a functional arousal pattern or template in which you select someone appropriate for you. Attraction involves curiosity as well as desire about physical, emotional, and intellectual traits. In an existing relationship, it means having the ability to maintain openness to change and the unknown. Are you attracted to healthy, appropriate people? Can you maintain your attraction for a person over time? Are you able to have fantasies and recognize which are appropriate? Are you able to move beyond fantasies and feelings, to initiate a relationship with someone to whom you are attracted?

LOW									HIGH
1	2	3	4	5	6	7	8	9	10

_____

_____

Flirtation—The ability to use playfulness, seduction, and social cues to send signals of interest and attraction to the desirable person. This ability extends to noticing flirtation from others. A critical factor in successful flirtation is knowing when it is appropriate to send and receive. Are you capable of flirting? Do you flirt with appropriate persons and in appropriate contexts? Do you notice when others flirt with you? Do you accurately read what the other person means by flirting? In an existing relationship, are you flirtatious?

LOW									HIGH
1	2	3	4	5	6	7	8	9	10

_____

_____

_____

Demonstration—Sometimes inaccurately described as showing off, this is where "process" (skill and capability) is used to further attract a suitable partner. Demonstration behavior must be appropriate to the context and the person. Are you able to attract attention to yourself and show your good qualities and traits? Are you able to do that sexually? Sexually, are you appropriate with context and age? Are your sexual behaviors specific to a relationship or intended to be noticed by just anyone? Are you a tease, which means wanting attention with no intent to connect?

LOW									HIGH
1	2	3	4	5	6	7	8	9	10

_____

_____

_____

Romance—The ability to experience, express, and receive passion. This requires a difficult balancing act of extreme vulnerability and testing feelings against reality: Does this person match the feelings and the image you have of that person? Do you feel passion when attracted to another person? Can you clearly express how important the other person is by using those feelings? Are the people you select consistently inappropriate for you? Do you romanticize your partners so they are not who you thought they were?

LOW									HIGH
1	2	3	4	5	6	7	8	9	10

_____

_____

_____

Individuation—The ability to like and be true to yourself in a relationship. Are you able to be yourself in a relationship? Do you worry about the other's approval? Do you defer to them? Are you able to express your needs effectively? Do you feel that you are giving in or that you let the other take over?

LOW									HIGH
1	2	3	4	5	6	7	8	9	10

_____

_____

_____

Intimacy—The ability to sustain connection and vulnerability while being accountable and worthy of trust. Can you sustain a long-term relationship that matters? Can you be totally truthful about the worst aspects of yourself to your partner? Do you get bored with your primary relationship? Are you able to talk about how meaningful it is to be with your partner?

LOW									HIGH
1	2	3	4	5	6	7	8	9	10

_____

_____

_____

Touching—Conscious touching and contact with the other. Touching affirms the other and the relationship while still being respectful of timing, situation, and boundaries. Are you able to use touch to connect with a partner? Have you been conscious of your touching? Do you use touch seductively? Are you touch-deprived? Do you observe appropriate boundaries with touch? Do you touch without permission? Do you touch people sexually without their knowledge?

LOW									HIGH
1	2	3	4	5	6	7	8	9	10

_____

_____

_____

Foreplay—Sometimes referred to as the most important part of sexual contact, it is the expression of sexual passion without the use of the genitals. It includes verbal and emotional as well as physical initiatives. Is your foreplay very ritualized? Does it degrade or humiliate either you or your partner? Does your foreplay put anyone at risk physically? Do you take sufficient time?

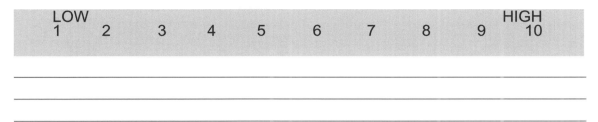

_____

_____

_____

Intercourse—More than the exchange of body fluids, this is the ability to surrender oneself to passion, letting go and trusting that both self and other can be totally vulnerable. Does orgasm occur easily for you with someone you care for? Do you find intercourse easier with people whom you do not know or in whom you have no investment? Do you have to have control in some way over the person you are with to have orgasm? Does intercourse work best with new or unknown persons?

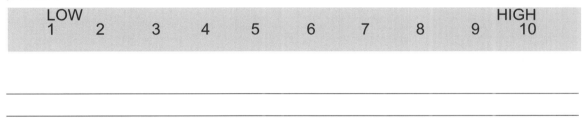

_____

_____

_____

Renewal—The capacity to sustain intimacy and all other courtship dimensions in an existing relationship. This requires the ability to see when a relationship is not working and actively work to change it or leave it. Do you take sufficient responsibility to make your relationship work? Do you continue to court and attract your partner? Are you able to consistently express how meaningful your relationship is? Are you in a primary relationship now that deepens as each year passes?

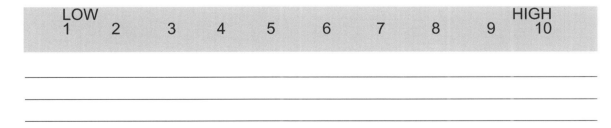

_____

_____

_____

Commitment—The ability to form a deep, meaningful, and satisfying relationship. Do you keep your commitments? Do you have difficulty forming close relationships that endure? Do you consistently take steps to honor and nurture your primary relationship? Are you in a deeply satisfying primary relationship? If not, what responsibility do you have in it not being satisfying?

LOW									HIGH
1	2	3	4	5	6	7	8	9	10

Reflections of Romance and Sex

At this point you should have a much greater understanding about yourself and your sexual addiction. We have provided a page for you to write a summary of what you have learned. Doing this will help you in the next chapter as you begin the work of your first step.

_____

_____

_____

_____

_____

_____

_____

_____

_____

_____

_____

_____

_____

_____

_____

_____

_____

_____

_____

_____

_____

_____

Understanding sexual compulsivity for most readers must include an appreciation of the role of cybersex. Seventy percent of sex addicts have problematic behavior online. Their behaviors parallel the ten types that have emerged over the decades of our research.

Consider what you now know from this chapter about the ten types and how these distortions of courtship can appear on-line. Table 3.2 summarizes how each type might emerge in online behavior.

Table 3.2

TYPE	COURTSHIP ISSUE	ONLINE BEHAVIOR
Fantasy Sex	Noticing, attraction	Email, chat rooms, instant messaging, fantasy stories
Voyeurism	Noticing, attraction, flirtation	Voyeur sites, mini-cam sites in dorms and dressing rooms, CUSeeMe acitivites, pornography sites
Exhibitionism	Flirtation, demonstration	Unwanted pictures, workplace exposure, CuSeeMe
Seductive Role Sex	Flirtation, demonstration, romance, intimacy, individuation	Email chat rooms, dating services, bulletin boards
Trading Sex	Flirtation, demonstration, romance, intimacy, individuation	Posting sexual services, chat rooms, escort and massage services
Intrusive Sex	Intimacy, individuation, touching, foreplay	Internet stalking, unwanted intrusion, hidden files
Paying for Sex	Intimacy, individuation, touching, foreplay, intercourse, commitment, renewal	Online strippers, phone sex contacts, booking prostitution
Anonymous Sex	Intimacy, individuation, touching, foreplay, intercourse, commitment, renewal	Chat rooms, screenname contacts, email cruising
Pain-Exchange	Touching, foreplay, intercourse, commitment, renewal	Pain sites, specialty groups and bulletin boards, specialty prostitution
Exploitive	All courtship dimensions	Chatrooms and emails; grooming and scouting

In effect, cybersex has become the great "accelerator" of sexually compulsive behavior.

Cybersex: The Great Accelerator

Cybersex is transforming our sexuality. It is now the number one profit center on the Internet, having passed sales in computers and software. Most sex education occurs on the web. It is the number one activity for kids while they do their homework. Most pornography is downloaded between nine and five, so it is a fact of life in the workplace. On the positive side, people are able to access information about sex in ways that are comfortable and helpful. People are able to connect with significant partners that they would never have met without the help of the internet. Recovery resources have become a great asset on the internet. Some of our best 12-step meetings are online meetings. For readers of this book, it is also important to understand that many people have trouble with sexual compulsion that would never have had the problem were it not for the internet. Consider the following examples:

• A minister discovered pornography on the internet. Within five weeks he had spent his family's savings and embezzled eight thousand dollars from his church

• The wife of a successful surgeon uses emails to contact her husband's friends and now has a nightmare of multiple affairs

• A base commander in the air force with full knowledge that information systems were monitored used a base computer to access prostitutes and was caught

• A hospital information filter picks up child pornography by two physicians who are pediatricians

• A parent discovers that her eighth grader is using his computer for sexual purposes on the average of sixty hours a week

The question is often asked, why does sex on the internet have this power? Among the answers, anonymity stands out. Internet users are lulled into thinking that no one is watching what they are doing. The facts are that our internet trails can be and often are carefully tracked by a variety of interested parties. Further, those trails are recorded for a long time. Yet, the illusion of being alone is seductive. It allows a person to think of sex on the internet as impersonal (hurts no one). It is more like a computer game – another in the panoply of virtual realities. It is very easy to access requiring little skill to do.

A strong case has emerged that internet sexual stimulation has the capability to go beyond our own biological limits. Researchers in this area such as Al Cooper have described cybersex as the crack-cocaine of sexual compulsivity. No partner can compete with the internet. People get so stimulated that sex feels more real on the internet than in their real lives. The marketing loops used by the marketers of pornography create so many options that they "access the unresolved" in net users. We all have parts of our sexual experience in which we were not able to explore. For example, we all were sexually attracted to children at one time in our lives – because we were children. As we mature, we look for adult partners and recognize that attraction to children is not appropriate. Yet on the net you can go back and explore that which you have always wondered about. So it is with all forms of sexual expression that is strange, forbidden, or beyond our reach. Some things we know for sure:

- Sexual addiction using cybersex once started can escalate quickly

- Sexual addiction on the internet will extend to non-internet behaviors (fantasies turn into behaviors)

- Those who already had a sex addiction problem find that internet sex magnifies both behaviors and associated problems

- Sexual compulsivity escalates to behavior that the addict has never done before or maybe never even knew existed

- Sex addicts in recovery report that internet sex is one of the leading factors in relapse

If sex on the internet has been part of your pattern, it is very important to become specific about how cybersex has affected you. The following is an inventory of your internet patterns. Please complete the inventory and then reflect on how cybersex has changed your patterns and maybe even your sexuality.

Cybersex Use Inventory

The purpose of this inventory is to review your internet sexual use. You will note that the focus is not specific behaviors but rather to discern the patterns. This will raise your personal awareness as well as assist you in your recovery and therapy.

Date you started _____

Estimate realistically the hours per week involved in some form of current sexual behavior:

_____times per week   _____hours per session   Weekly total_____

Have you ever had periods where you have "binged" sexually on the internet:

Yes   No   (circle one)

If yes, describe:_____

_____

_____

Were there periods of time when you made efforts to stop your behavior:

Yes   No   (circle one)

Please describe:_____

_____

_____

Has your behavior even been a problem so that you stopped the behavior for an extended period of time:

Yes   No   (circle one)

Please describe:_____

_____

_____

Over time have you noticed any of the following (place a check mark in front of all that apply:

_____   a pattern of taking greater risks

_____   seeking more violent, angry, or unusual pictures

_____   an attraction to underage persons (ages 12-16 years)

_____   an attraction to children (up to 12 years)

_____   an attraction to underage persons or children evolved as part of internet use

_____   attracted to sexual behaviors or persons you were not attracted to before your internet experiences

_____   attracted to sexual behaviors or situations you had not been aware of before your internet experiences

_____   taking sexual risks with others you had never taken before since your sexual experience on the internet

_____   starting new sexual behaviors because of things you saw or experienced on the internet

_____   engaging in old sexual behaviors you had stopped doing because of your internet use

_____   a declining ability to respond sexually to your partner because of internet sex

_____   anger or anxiety when unable to get online for sexual contact

Risk Taking and Unmanageability

When internet sex becomes compulsive, the user starts to take inordinate risks. Plus, cybersex starts to create chaos in one's life. The following is a list of risks and problems associated with cybersex addiction. Review the list and check all those which would be true in your experience.

_____ risk of being discovered at home

_____ was discovered at home

_____ risk of being discovered at work

_____ was discovered at work

_____ diminished or little sleep

_____ all night binges with no sleep at all

_____ failure to complete important or scheduled work

_____ spent money you could not afford

_____ sharing personal identification information with unknown persons

_____ misuse of personal information by internet sexual partners

_____ meeting unknown persons

_____ attacked or exploited by internet sexual partners

_____ entangled relationships started on the internet

_____ loss of primary relationship because of internet use

_____ inability to respond sexually off-line with real person

_____ computer compromised because of viruses or spyware contracted because of sexual sites

or contacts on the internet

_____ replaced hard disk or computer because of internet sexual behavior

_____ risk of arrest because of behavior

_____ was arrested because of behavior

The following rationales and self-talk are often used to explain or justify sexual behavior. Check any of these rationales if they were part of your thinking about sex on the internet:

_____ no one will know

_____ it is not really sex because it is just electrons

_____ not unfaithful because no one is touched

_____ no one is hurt by the behavior

_____ it is like a computer game, not real

_____ every one does it

_____ it is a good, safe, and fun way to escape my problems

_____ it does not affect anything as long as no one finds out

_____ it is better to do it online than in real life

_____ it has not changed me in any way

_____ it is a good way to learn

_____ my partner is not sexual enough and I deserve sex

_____ I feel controlled and it is a way to get my needs met

_____ it is a safe way to break the rules

_____ my partner is not interested in meeting my needs

_____ I can see and explore what I have always wanted to do

_____ I am making up for what I have missed

_____ I often feel lonely and it helps

_____ I am not very social and I can get my needs met

_____ Cybersex is a safety valve for me to let off steam

_____ I love the secrecy of doing something no one knows about

_____ I like "forbidden" territory

During your sexual episodes on the internet, were your orgasmic?

Yes   No   (circle one)

What conditions needed to be present for orgasm to occur? Please describe:

_____

_____

_____

Have you hurt yourself physically because of extended sexual stimulation on the internet?

Yes   No   (circle one)

If yes, please describe injuries: _____

_____

_____

Were there specific rituals you used to initiate your internet activity? There are ways to prepare for the internet episode. Or they could even be ways to talk yourself into doing the behavior, even though you did not feel like it. Consider these activities as a way to "seduce yourself" into your regular cybersex patterns. Please describe these rituals:

_____

_____

_____

During cybersex would you use any of the following substances? Check all that apply:

_____ alcohol
_____ cocaine
_____ amphetamines
_____ poppers
_____ hallucinogens
_____ Oxycontin or other pain killers
_____ nicotine
_____ caffeine

After cybersex, would you have any of the following? Check all that apply:

_____ despair over time wasted

_____ despair about secret life

_____ sexual unavailability to partner

_____ suicidal feelings

_____ shame because behavior does not fit your values

_____ vows to never do the behavior

_____ anxiety and obsession about risks taken

_____ use with alcohol, nicotine, or drugs to feel better

_____ compulsively eat to feel better

_____ masturbate to feel better

_____ use other online activities such as gambling, e-trading, gaming, or auctions to feel better.

In addition to problematic sexual behavior, were any of the following online behaviors problematic for you. Check all that apply:

_____ gambling

_____ e-trading

_____ gaming

_____ auction sites

Any others, please list:

_____ _____

_____ _____

_____ _____

_____ _____

_____ _____

Using the space below, create a map of the usual sites you visit as part of your pattern. Typically there are a few sites an addict prefers to start with. Then, depending on what is found, there will be specific directions they will pursue. Usually three to five patterns will emerge. Create the map using specific site names. As you label each direction, note what it is you are looking for. This may be an exercise that is difficult to do alone. Ask your therapist to help you if you find it difficult to do by yourself. Many therapists require this activity as a specific session for this reason. Use one color pen to list the sites. Use another color to note what it is you are seeking. Complete the map until you have the most compelling sites listed.

Cybersex: Part of Sex Addiction?

Having completed the previous pages, it is important to now reflect on whether cybersex is part of your sexual addiction. Below are listed criteria by clinicians to determine the presence of sex addiction. Review each criteria and then circle yes or no if this criteria fits for you. Space is provided for you to record examples for each dimension listed. If you have questions, talk to your therapist about each one that is not clear to you.

Addiction Criteria

1. *Preoccupation with sex on the Internet*
Fantasizing and thinking about your next cybersex forays. Planning and manipulating so that you will have your cybersex time. Reviewing in your mind your most recent activities.

yes   no

Examples:_____
_____

2. *Frequently engaging in sex on the Internet more often or for longer periods of time than intended.* It is common for you to give yourself a limit, such as how much time you are going to spend, but then fail to do so. The allotted time passes, but it does not matter. Or perhaps there are certain websites you do not want to be on, but you find yourself there anyway. Addicts find that it continues to take more -- time, risk, or money. Is it hard to stop once you have started?

yes   no

Examples:_____
_____

3. *Repeated unsuccessful efforts to control, cut back on, or stop engaging in sex on the Internet.*
Once you realized that the amount of time you'd been spending for sex online was excessive, you decided to set some limits. Perhaps you promised yourself that you would go online only once a day or week and only for thirty minutes at a time. Or maybe you decided to quit cold turkey for a week or to go online only on weekends. But whatever promise you made to yourself, you couldn't keep it. Maybe your attempts at control worked for a few days, a week, several weeks, or even a month, but eventually "something" happened and you "needed" to go back online. No matter what you tried, you eventually returned to the Internet for sexual activities.

yes   no

Examples:_____
_____

4. *Restlessness or irritability when attempting to limit or stop engaging in sex on the Internet.*
When planning to go online, and something happens to disrupt your plan, such as your spouse returns early, do you find yourself irritated and upset? During those periods in which you attempted to quit, were you quick to become angry? Do you get anxious and upset when your intended routine is changed?

yes   no

Examples:_____
_____

5. *Using sex on the Internet as a way of escaping from problems or relieving feelings such a helplessness, guilt, anxiety, or depression.*
Everyone has feelings of helplessness, sorrow, worry, depression, and anger. There are many ways to address or cope with these feelings. Do you turn to the Internet for a sexual release so you can feel better and function at home or work? Is internet sex a way to cover lonliness? procrastination? escape from painful events or duties?

yes   no
Examples:_____
_____

6. *Returning to sex on the Internet day after day in search of a more intense or higher-risk sexual experience.*
Your expectations of what you want out of the Internet continue to increase and become more elaborate. You might hope to find your true love via the Internet. At first, you may drop into chat rooms, remaining anonymous, just to see whether you could find a potential mate online. Eventually, being anonymous no longer does it for you. Your search of various chat rooms becomes more intense and frantic and time-consuming. After connecting with one man in particular, you begin corresponding privately with him via e-mail. Eventually, you arrange a meeting with him for sex in a hotel. The excitement and hope you feel in your search lead to more risky behavior both on and off the Internet. Do you keep returning to sites or situations you know are not good for you?
       What have you been looking for on the Internet? How has that changed from when you first started going online? Are you moving into areas you once told yourself you'd never explore?

yes   no
Examples:_____
_____

7. *Lying to family members, therapists, or others to conceal involvement with sex on the Internet.*
In our culture, most people are secretive about their sex lives, regardless of whether their behavior is normal or problematic. What is of concern is being dishonest about it when asked..
       Have you lied about using the Internet for sex-related activities? Have you downplayed your involvement or failed to be honest about your involvement to a spouse, partner, boss, or therapist? Have you used the "just curious" excuse?

yes   no
Examples:_____
_____

8. *Committing illegal sexual acts online (for example, sending or downloading child pornography or soliciting illegal sex acts online.*
Certain activities on the Internet have been declared illegal in many, if not all, states. As people

use the Internet for sex-related activities, and as they increase their time on the Net, some also move closer and closer to engaging in illegal behaviors. A forty-year-old male who'd fantasized about having sex with a teenager for several years eventually began visiting a teen chat room. He engaged in a conversation with a thirteen-year-old female for some time before moving the relationship to a point where he asked where he could meet her to have sex. Soliciting sex acts with minors online is illegal, just as sending, exchanging, or downloading child pornography is illegal. These are felony offences that, in many states, will result in mandatory prison time. Have you engaged in or are you thinking about such actions?

yes   no

Examples:_____
_____

9. *Jeopardizing or losing a significant relationship, job, or educational or career opportunity because of online sexual behavior.*
Online sex-related activities can have serious consequences. Ray downloaded a child pornography image to a chat room. As a result, he was arrested through an undercover operation. The shame of being charged with felony counts for sexual exploitation of a minor became overwhelming, and the consequences rippled through every aspect of his life. Because of escalating legal fees, he lost most of his savings and retirement funds. He was closing on his new home the day the search warrant was served. Consequently, he lived in his new home for only two days before he had to sell it as a result of this crime. He lost a well-paying, prestigious job with tremendous advancement potential in an excellent corporation. He endured house arrest and faced a potential prison term of 220 years. Ray had been respected in his community and was on numerous boards and committees. This all ended with his arrest.

What parts of your life are being affected by your online sexual behavior? Have you jeopardized or lost a significant relationship? What about a job, a career, or your health and well-being?

yes   no

Examples:_____
_____

10. *Incurring significant financial consequences as a result of engaging in online sexual behavior.*
While basic Internet access can be fairly inexpensive, many cybersex sites charge a monthly access fee. A thirty-two-year-old male client was shocked when he opened his credit card bill one day to find charges totaling more than twelve hundred dollars. He'd been registering to enter various cybersex sites and had completely lost track of how many he'd paid for. A twenty-three-year-old female client received an Internet server bill for hundreds of dollars. She'd spend six or so hours per day in chat rooms and had sailed miles past her free minute limit without having any idea of the charges that were accruing. Another male client spent forty thousand dollars in one month dating high-priced call girls and using cocaine. He'd arranged for both through an online prostitution service.

Have you felt the financial consequences of your time online? How many memberships are you paying for each month? What are your monthly Internet fees? Have you lost job or educational opportunities because of your time online?

                                           yes   no

Examples:_____

_____

Looking back over the criteria, consider the connection that cybersex and sex addiction may have for you. Record your thoughts below. This brings you to a point where you are ready to take on the challenge of the first step and accepting your problem.

Reflections on internet sex and sex addiction for you:

_____
_____
_____
_____
_____
_____
_____
_____
_____
_____
_____
_____
_____
_____
_____
_____
_____
_____
_____

Reading Assignments

Read and reflect on *Out of the Shadows,* pp. 133-160 and *Don't Call It Love,* pp. 181-258. Also, you may want to read *In the Shadows of the Net.*

CHAPTER FOUR: What Is a First Step?
Accepting the Problem

The tremendous fact for every one of us is that we have
discovered a common solution.
—ALCOHOLICS ANONYMOUS

SOME SEVENTY YEARS AGO, a stockbroker who was down on his luck because of his drinking problem sat in the kitchen of a house on Ardmore Street in Akron, Ohio. The house belonged to a physician who had the same problem. He simply could not stop drinking. They sat over a cup of coffee discussing a letter the broker had received from Carl Jung, the famous physician pioneer of psychotherapy. In the letter, Jung told Bill W. that if their new group was to achieve success, they had to pass on their stories. Essentially, the key to success was to help each other as opposed to acting alone. Thus was born the "telling of the story" that has been the cornerstone of Alcoholics Anonymous. The framework these men developed has helped millions of people. Not only alcoholics, but gamblers, compulsive overeaters, and sex addicts—and their partners—have all benefited from their original insights. The key outcome of telling the story is that the teller admits that he or she has a problem while the listeners affirm the teller by acknowledging that they had the same experience. This transaction reduces the shame for all involved and supports them in their common commitment to stay sober.

Storytelling is powerful. When parents, for example, tell family stories, the children always object if a piece is left out. One might ask why the children want to hear these stories again and again since they already know them so well. The answer is that the storytelling is not about passing on information. It is about bonding. The child feels bonded in that he or she is a part of the story. To return to our earlier discussion about addiction stemming from a failure to bond, Twelve Step groups actually begin a re-bonding process that helps people make up the deficits of the past. Members of a Twelve Step community are accepted for who they are.

Such bonding holds incredible importance, and this additional example will illustrate why this is so. When Amnesty International first attempted therapy to help torture victims, they got nowhere. Victims of torture, even though they were miserable, resisted help at a most profound level. Eventually, AI staff made a discovery. If torture victims could tell the story of their experience to a room full of other people who were also torture victims, an acceptance of the experience occurred. The victim was then able to bond enough to make therapy succeed. The same happened with drug addiction and alcoholism. Professionals tried to help for years, but it was not until AA provided a format for alcoholics to tell their stories that therapy could actually help. Most addicts have experienced deep trauma in their lives. What's more, being an addict of any type is traumatic in itself. These people need a safe place with other people who know the story before it is told.

Essentially, the storytelling details the way life used to be and how it is today. Put simply, the story is about change. The Twelve Steps, more than anything else, teach about profound change in a person's life. They essentially reveal a life stance—what psychologists and philosophers call an "existential position"—on how to live life. The Twelve Steps are actually sound principles about change and life that everyone can use, but they are especially useful for those who have to experience the radical changes of recovery. The spirit of these principles is best captured in what is called the Serenity Prayer, which asks for "the serenity to accept the things I cannot change, the courage to change the things I can, and the wisdom to know the difference." The internal acceptance of those ideas helps reduce anxiety dramatically. Addictions draw their power from anxiety and fear.

The First Step captures that principle. It reads, "we admitted we were powerless over our sexual addiction—that our lives had become unmanageable." People who do a First Step usually learn the following lessons:

- that you must accept totally that you have a problem
- that you recognize there are things happening you cannot control by yourself
- that to be successful you have to ask for help from others
- that you must focus on what you can do
- that you have to give up secrets and pretending to be something that you are not
- that addictive behaviors will continue until you truly learn this lesson

The following series of worksheets will help you prepare for a First Step. As you work through them, I encourage you to ask for help. A therapist can be a wonderful resource as you think about these issues. You also should select a couple of "consultants" from your Twelve Step group or your therapy group to help you. Whenever you feel shameful or discouraged or unsure about what to do, get a consultation. Talk to someone. Ask for help. Remember this is *exactly* what those guys did back in Dr. Bob's kitchen.

Your Sexual Addiction History

This section asks you to focus on the development of your sexual addiction. Because it may be difficult for you to recall specific events or details, respond to the following questions as best you can.

1. At what age do you believe your sexual addiction started (i.e., sexual obsession or behavior helped you to cope; you lost faith in yourself)? _____

2. What were some critical events during the early development of your sexual addiction (e.g., increase in frequency, unmanageability, abandonment, abuse)?

    _____

    _____

    _____

    _____

    _____

3. At what age do you believe your sexual addiction was firmly established (i.e. life priorities became reversed, your sexual preoccupation and acting out interfered with your life, job, family)? _____

4. What were some critical events during this period of your addiction (e.g., stressors, denial, impaired thinking)?

    _____

    _____

    _____

    _____

    _____

5. Were there periods during your life in which your addiction suddenly escalated in terms of frequency or types of sexual acting out behavior?

    _____ Yes _____ No

    If yes, at what ages (e.g., 15–18, 22–24, 30)? _____

    _____

6. Was there a seasonal (spring, summer, fall, winter) pattern in your sexual acting out?

    _____ Yes _____ No

If yes, please specify _____

7. What were some critical events during these periods of escalation?

_____

_____

_____

_____

_____

8. At what ages do you believe your sexual addiction was at its highest level? _____

9. What were some critical events that took place during this period when your addiction was at its highest level?

_____

_____

_____

_____

_____

10. Were there periods during your life when your sexual addiction de-escalated (i.e., was less intense, went underground, was controlled)? _____ Yes _____ No

If yes, at what ages? _____

11. What were some critical events that preceeded this de-escalation or that occurred during it?

_____

_____

_____

_____

_____

12. Were there periods during your life when it seemed that you had no life beyond the obsession and the predictable addictive cycle of acting out sexually (i.e., you had breaks in reality, you completely abandoned your value system)? _____ Yes _____ No

If yes, at what ages? _____

13. What were some critical events during these periods?

_____

_____

_____

_____

14. Are you currently working on limiting other compulsive behaviors or are you currently in recovery for any other addiction? _____ Yes _____ No

_____ compulsive use of alcohol or other drugs

_____ alcohol or other drug dependency

_____ co-dependency

_____ eating disorders (overeating, anorexia, bulimia)

_____ nicotine/tobacco addiction

_____ caffeine abuse or addiction

_____ compulsive gambling

_____ compulsive spending

_____ compulsive work

_____ other, specify: _____

15. How did your other addictions (if any) affect your sexual addiction?

_____

_____

_____

_____

_____

_____

_____

_____

_____

_____

_____

Powerlessness Inventory

List as many examples as you can that show how powerless you have been to stop your behavior. Remember, "powerless" means being unable to stop the behavior despite obvious consequences. Be very explicit about types of behavior and frequency. Start with your earliest example of being powerless, and conclude with the most recent. Generate at least thirty examples. By generating as many examples as possible, you will have added significantly to the depth of your understanding of your own powerlessness. Remember, you do not have to complete the list in one sitting. Add to the list as examples occur to you. When you finish this inventory, do not proceed until you have discussed it with one of your guides. The gentle way means you deserve support with each piece of significant work.

Example: Sarah said she would leave in 1988 if I slipped again, and I did it anyway.

1. _____
   _____

2. _____
   _____

3. _____
   _____

4. _____
   _____

5. _____
   _____

6. _____
   _____

7. _____
   _____

8. _____
   _____

9. _____
   _____

10. _____
    _____

11. _____
    _____

12. _____
    _____

13. _____
    _____

14. _____
    _____

15. _____
_____

16. _____
_____

17. _____
_____

18. _____
_____

19. _____
_____

20. _____
_____

21. _____
_____

22. _____
_____

23. _____
_____

24. _____
_____

25. _____
_____

26. _____
_____

27. _____
_____

28. _____

_____

29. _____

_____

30. _____

_____

The most recent examples will make you feel your powerlessness most strongly. Circle five recent examples.

Unmanageability Inventory

List as many examples as you can that show how your life has become totally unmanageable because of your dependency. Remember, "unmanageability" means that your addiction created chaos and damage in your life. If you need further ideas, return to chapter one and review your list of consequences. Again, when you finish this inventory, stop and talk to your guides. You deserve support.

Example: Got caught stealing in 1988 to support my addiction.

1. _____
2. _____
3. _____
4. _____
5. _____
6. _____
7. _____
8. _____
9. _____
10. _____
11. _____
12. _____
13. _____
14. _____
15. _____
16. _____
17. _____

18. _____

19. _____

20. _____

21. _____

22. _____

23. _____

24. _____

25. _____

26. _____

27. _____

28. _____

29. _____

30. _____

The most recent examples will make you feel your unmanageability most strongly. Which are your most recent examples? Circle five that have happened to you in the last ten days. Circle five that have happened to you during the past thirty days.

Financial Costs Worksheet

Sex addiction can be very expensive. Prostitution, gifts to lovers, medical costs, divorces, and lost businesses are just a few of the ways addicts pay a price for their addiction. Many sex addicts hit a point of no return when they add up just the financial costs of their sexual behavior. Usually the financial costs in no way approach the emotional and personal costs. Yet determining how much of your resources have gone into your sexual behavior provides one very clear index of how out of control you have been. For many, totaling up the bill is staggering because they have substantially deluded themselves about the costs. Most addicts spent more than they could afford.

The following worksheet will help you determine what the financial costs of your addiction are. Go through each section carefully and total each. You may have to use separate sheets of paper to make the calculations. Enter the description and provide your best estimate as to how much you have spent. Some of the costs may have to be approximate. The goal is to document what has happened to you, not survive an audit. You know more than anyone what the costs have been. Simply record what those costs probably were. Use your consultants if you are stuck or need support.

Direct Spending

Include money spent on prostitution, gifts to lovers, strip bars, swinging clubs, phone sex, travel with lovers, travel to places for sexual contact, pornography, memberships in Internet sex websites, and blackmail. Also include babysitting, clothes, makeup, exercise classes, and cosmetic surgery.

Item Amount Total _____

Business and Career Costs

Include lost earning time, sexual harassment lawsuits, sexual misconduct lawsuits. Consider costs due to bad performance or bad decisions because you were acting out. If a career has been lost or suspended, include the cost of training and what income has been lost. If a business has been lost, calculate not only the investment, but what potential earnings were lost. Include the misuse of other people's money, hush money, and bail money for self or others.

Item Amount Total _____

Medical Expenses

Include obvious direct expenses such as treatment for AIDS, hepatitis, or other sexually trans-mitted diseases. Specify medical costs for car accidents or other accidents that occurred while acting out. If major medical conditions occurred such as a heart attack due to the stress of your sexual behavior specify that as well. Include abortions and unwanted pregnancies.

Item Amount Total _____

Divorce or Family Support

Include divorce costs including attorney's fees, child support, and settlements. If you supported a mistress, additional families, or a sex partner, calculate related financial costs. Specify any ongoing support of those for whom you have felt guilt or have been legally required to support.

Item Amount Total _____

Legal Problems

Include money spent on attorneys for defense against legal charges, bail money, and court fees. Consider also lost time due to legal involvements, prison stays, or workhouse sentences. Any lawsuit not part of your business or career but a result of your sexual behavior should be recorded.

Item Amount Total _____

Add up all the total costs here _____.

Reflection on the Total

What insights or reflections do you have now that you have an approximate cost? If that money was available to you today, what would you be able to do with it? What role has money played for you in this process? Record your thoughts below:

_____

_____

_____

_____

Give five examples of denial about your spending: (example—I was always short of cash at the end of the month but never saw it as a result of my sexual behavior)

1. _____

_____

2. _____

_____

3. _____

_____

4. _____

_____

5. _____

_____

Give five examples of delusion (rationalization and justification) about your spending: (example—I told myself I would do my work better if I got relief)

1. _____

_____

2. _____

_____

3. _____

_____

4. _____

_____

5. _____

_____

Record your reactions to your denial or delusions about the costs to you of your addiction. Start with your thoughts and then record your feelings.

Thoughts:

_____

_____

_____

_____

_____

_____

Feelings:

_____

_____

_____

_____

_____

_____

Ten Worst Moments

List your ten worst moments as a sex addict. Think of events that were the most painful or catastrophic. For each event, record the feelings you had then and the feelings you have now as you look back on these moments.

1. Worst moment: _____

   _____

   Feelings then: _____

   Feelings now: _____

2. Worst moment: _____

   _____

   Feelings then: _____

   Feelings now: _____

3. Worst moment: _____

_____

Feelings then: _____

Feelings now: _____

4. Worst moment: _____

_____

Feelings then: _____

Feelings now: _____

5. Worst moment: _____

_____

Feelings then: _____

Feelings now: _____

6. Worst moment: _____

_____

Feelings then: _____

Feelings now: _____

7. Worst moment: _____

_____

Feelings then: _____

Feelings now: _____

8. Worst moment: _____

    _____

    Feelings then: _____

    Feelings now: _____

9. Worst moment: _____

    _____

    Feelings then: _____

    Feelings now: _____

10. Worst moment: _____

    _____

    Feelings then: _____

    Feelings now: _____

Now that you have completed the list, rank order the worst moments by putting a "1" next to the very worst, a "2" next to the second worst, and continue until you have ranked all 10. This will help you focus on what you will share in your First Step process.

Sharing Your First Step

You will share your First Step many times. Initially, it will be with your Twelve Step groups and in therapy. As you progress, you will share in other groups, with sponsers, and ultimately with those you love. This will be the part of your story about how bad it was. As we noted earlier, this "retelling the story" is not about relaying the facts. Rather it is done to create the deep bond that comes out of deep sharing. We have noted how telling the story teaches principles about change. As you make "multiple presentations," a life stance emerges about change and stress. This chapter and the next are designed to help you understand that "stance."

The First Step also breaks rules about always looking good and keeping secrets, and thus it helps destroy the secret life and the shame that perpetuates dishonesty. As that happens, addicts start to experience long-buried feelings. Obliterated and numbed by your obsession and behavior, these are feelings that have literally been haunting you. As you share your story, you will also be able to share your feelings. Not only is this important self-knowledge, but expressing these feelings will allow others to know your interior world. Those who listen can then provide feedback and support. That exchange is essential to the healing process. In short, you cannot share your First Step without sharing the feelings that go with it. Unexpressed feelings provide fuel for all addictions.

Addicts have years (even decades) of practice at ignoring feelings, containing feelings, and hiding feelings, so expressing them will feel very awkward at first. Yet it is how those who listen will know that you are really internalizing your First Step. A predictable pattern exists. It typically goes as follows:

Defensive explanation and manipulation—indicates addict is still in denial

Reporting the facts—shows intellectual understanding

Expressions of anger and fear—reflects addict taking *responsibility*

Describing shame and embarrassment—means *addictive pride lifts*

Sharing sadness and pain—shows *emotional understanding*

Admits depth of loneliness—indicates *acceptance*

Reaching the point of acceptance represents a profound turning point for most people in recovery. Here are some tips on how to get there. There should be two people from your group who know the whole story, along with your therapist. With these people, go over all the work that you have done, including your sexual behavior, your sexual history, your consequences, your examples of powerlessness, your examples of unmanageability, your costs, and your worst moments. When you present your Step, you will not be able to tell the whole story since there usually is a limited amount of group time. Your goal is to share your feelings. If you can get to your core feelings, they will not need all the details. Focus on the most painful and shameful parts for you. Your guiding question should always be how bad it was for you. Ask your consultants and your therapist for help deciding what parts of your story and feelings to present.

Many addicts find it difficult to feel. Here are some ideas that can help you do so. Select items that involve impact on your children, your spouse or partner's pain, your losses, or your public embarrassment. Ask yourself what would it be like if everyone knew everything. Use your "worst moments list" right at the outset to help you access your feelings. Your Twelve Step group or your therapist may ask you to put additional work into it until they see your complete acceptance. Asking you to work on it more is normal. It means two things. First, they are supporting you and pushing you to really get your needs met. Second, they know what acceptance looks like. Here is what they look for:

- no excuses or explanations (you acted out because you acted out)
- clear understanding of powerlessness, with good examples of efforts to stop
- clear understanding of unmanageability, with good examples of consequences
- knowledge of your own addictive system
- knowledge of how your behavior fit the criteria for addiction
- the worst expressed and the secrets exposed
- taking full responsibility for actions
- a range of feelings expressed
- feelings are appropriate for the events reported
- suffering including grief, pain, sorrow, and remorse
- ownership of loneliness
- a commitment to do whatever it takes to change

With Those Criteria in Mind You Then Tell Your Story

Sometimes addicts get confused about how one can be powerless and still take responsibility. A paradox does exist here, but it untangles if you remember this. Alone you are powerless. You were not able to stop your behavior. With help you can. You did the behavior. No one else is responsible for it. You chose your behavior. Now, by knowing what you know, you have a responsibility to use the tools you have and to get the help you need. There were forces at work you did not understand, but no longer.

Remember the advice from the *Big Book of Alcoholics Anonymous* when it described addiction as "cunning and powerful." Your "addict" will attempt to sabotage your First Step. Here are some things that might happen:

- you may be tempted to act out, even in some minor way
- you may want to keep a secret or protect someone
- you may want to procrastinate on this task
- you may find distractions and things to upset you
- you may find fault with your group, your therapist, or your treatment program
- you may find or create a family crisis
- you may find yourself craving in your other addictions
- you may find yourself mired in self-hatred and self-loathing

In other words, your "addict" may ask you to stay loyal to the old ways. Cunning and powerful! Yet if you persevere, you will find that the First Step teaches a new and more conscious way of life. Anxiety and suffering become guides rather than enemies. You will learn that change is the substance of life and that the unknown is for everybody. That which used to cripple you will become an extraordinary source of wisdom. Troubles will not cease, but your effectiveness will multiply. And you get to have problems that are not sexual ones. You will forge new bonds and be respected for how you handle yourself. No matter how big the fear or the challenge, a core of peace will pervade all you do. You start by getting this done. Just like those people back on Ardmore Ave.

Recommended Reading

Don't Call It Love, **pp. 258–327**; *A Gentle Path Through the Twelve Steps*, pp. 89–138.

CHAPTER FIVE: What Damage Has Been Done?
Responding to Change and Crisis

You choose your behavior, but the world chooses your consequences.
—PAT MELLODY

PAT MELLODY IS ONE OF THE PIONEERS in addiction treatment in this country. He often uses the phrase, "you choose your behavior, but the world chooses your consequences." This favorite maxim highlights the reality for most addicts that unmanageability may continue long after the recovery. Simply said, addictive behaviors often cause much damage. And addicts have little control over some of those consequences. Pat uses this phrase to remind addicts who are angry about how things are unraveling that their behavior brought on all these problems. This is a difficult moment for people who now realize they have an addiction and are working hard at recovery—but the problems continue. To them, this does not seem fair.

This chapter focuses on helping you face consequences using recovery principles. In early recovery, life usually seems to be spinning out of control. Arrests, health issues, job problems, money difficulties, and family complications all add up. Early recovery is hard, especially if you are out of work or fighting the AIDS virus or your partner has initiated divorce. That kind of problem compounding is typical. Then you have the problem of sorting out who you tell what. Disclosure to your therapist is going to be different than disclosure to your boss or spouse. Such problems require determining what you can control and what you cannot. This chapter is designed to help you determine what you can manage and to guide you in dealing with the areas that you cannot manage. First you have to understand what happens with change.

Understanding Change

Recovery is more than a shift of emphasis. It is a series of internal movements that alters one's life. How does dramatic change occur? It helps to understand the nature of change itself. Scientists have long noted that some changes are transforming and others are not. By looking at how systems work, including family systems, political systems, molecular systems, mathematical systems, and even computer systems, we have concluded that two types of change exist. They are first order change and second order change.

First order change is most accurately described with the French aphorism, "The more things change, the more they stay the same." They are concrete actions taken to quickly stop a problem and to address specific consequences. Consider the woman who marries three abusive alcoholics in a row. Each one is worse than the last. Yet, before each marriage, she was determined to do better than before. The harder she tried, the worse the marriage and life became. Did she change? Yes, she changed husbands, but her situation remained the same. That is first order change.

Second order changes are those steps that people take to actually change the dynamics of their life and the way they live. The story of the woman above did not end with her three marriages. She began to look at her own life. She found a therapist and began going to Al-Anon. She learned that she had felt dependent on men and had few relationships with women. She learned that the criteria she used for selecting partners were rooted in beliefs formed during an abusive childhood and in intense feelings of inadequacy. She made new plans for herself, took a break from dating, learned to set appropriate boundaries, and eliminated the people from her life who abused her. That is second order change.

Addiction is a first order phenomenon. The harder addicts try to stop addiction behaviors by themselves, the worse things get. Those who act out sexually lead double lives. They isolate themselves from others. They attempt to have their needs met through their addiction. The worst part is that the double life works for a while; the acting out is hidden and the addict is fairly successful in other areas of his/her life. This causes addicts to become very grandiose in their thinking. They operate believing they can always pull it off. Yet, chaos begins to close in.

The painful reality of negative consequences teaches recovering people insights that lead to new "programming." First, they learn that there really are no secrets. They realize that they are unable (powerless) to change their behavior on their own and by themselves; they need others. Finally, they begin to take a realistic look at themselves and discover the damage that has been done in every area of their lives and in the lives of their families and friends. Then comes a decision to put order back into their lives and to limit the damage. At this point, they begin therapy and join a Twelve Step or similar recovery program. The recovering person can either use willpower to try to make life different and stop the old behavior, or this same person can truly dig in and face the realities of life. In other words, recovering addicts can choose either first or second order change. Figure 5.1 will show you the difference between the two kinds of change and the requirements of each.

Figure 5.1

FIRST ORDER OF CHANGE Addicts Believe:	SECOND ORDER OF CHANGE Recovering People Know:
No one knows or will know.	There are no secrets.
I can change behavior by myself.	I am powerless to change without the help of others.
I can always figure out or force a way to handle problems.	Sometimes there are events that I can't control.
I work best alone.	I need contact with and the help of others.
No one is hurt by what I have done.	Damage has rippled through the lives of people I know.
I have not been hurt by what I have done.	My behavior has disconnected me from myself.

REQUIREMENTS OF EACH KIND OF CHANGE	
I must operate in secrecy.	I must make a full disclosure.
I must isolate from others.	I must create support networks.
I cannot give anyone the whole story.	Trustworthy people get the whole story.
A double life is the only way to get my needs met.	Integrity must become how I get my needs met with a lot less hassle.
I use grandiosity in thinking and in actions.	I exercise humility and embrace mistakes and needs.
Chaos is the norm.	I have a damage control plan and seek the help of others.

Your Turn

List five examples of first order changes that you have made in your life in an effort to control your behavior or make your life different. Include such examples as changing jobs, moving, and leaving relationships.

1. _____
_____

2. _____
_____

3. _____
_____

4. _____
_____

5. _____
_____

What were some of the beliefs that led you to attempt to change your life by first order change only?

_____
_____
_____
_____
_____

Since you have begun this program, list five steps you have taken that have led to or will lead to true second order change. Don't forget the effort you have put into this workbook.

1. _____
_____

2. _____
_____

3. _____
_____

4. _____
_____

5. _____
_____

Provisional Beliefs

Stephen Covey, who wrote *The Seven Habits of Highly Effective People*, talked about radical change. He pointed out that if you focus only on behavior, you will achieve only modest change. Significant change requires an internal "paradigm shift"— a change in the belief system that supports the addictive system. It includes all the personal perceptions that anchored the impaired thinking you learned about in chapter two. As in a computer system, you have to change the software to get a different result. You have to develop and "install" for new programming. Even if you can think of examples of both kinds of change and differentiate clearly between them, you may not be able to believe that true change is possible for you or that you have any idea of how to do it. Until you do believe such change is possible for you, you will need to adopt provisional beliefs. They are really an act of trust, held until your own recovery process takes over a bit more. Provisionally embracing the truths below will help you through the challenge that comes with starting change. They will help you as you begin to repair the damage caused by your addictive behaviors.

For the time being, you may not be able to trust your own perceptions. You will have to trust the perceptions of others, even as mistaken and unpleasant as you believe them to be.

For the time being, you will have to trust that you have been damaged far more than you know, but that time and recovery can work wonders in repairing this damage and in helping you become the person you were meant to be.

For the time being, you must remember that addiction is a form of insanity in which you are deluded about reality. You need to believe that you must pursue reality at all costs. The only way out of this insanity is to tell those who are helping you all that has happened. They can support you in reclaiming reality. You must do this without minimizing or omitting awkward details. And you may not make private deals with yourself about holding things back. Anything less than full disclosure lowers the probability of your recovery.

For the time being, you must allow people to care for you, even if you do not feel that you deserve anyone's love and care. You are important, valued, and appreciated in ways that are hard to accept right now. This means you must follow through on what is asked of you—to surrender control of your life to those who can care for you better than you can care for yourself at this time.

Damage Control Plan

Using these provisional beliefs, you are ready to create a new "order" in your life. You begin with a damage control plan. Most people at this point face problems and challenges as a result of their addictive behavior: arrests, public shame, loss of career, severe relationship complications, and disease, for example. The list may seem endless. Recovery teaches that it is important to get help and to keep things simple. Break all tasks into small component parts and tackle them one at a time and one day at a time.

Use the following pages to help you think through your damage control plan. Begin by making a list of the problems you are currently facing. You may wish to consult the problems list you made in chapter one. This list, however, should focus on your current problems that are caused by unmanageability, such as divorce, disease, unemployment, or an arrest.

Current Problem List

1. _____
   _____

2. _____
   _____

3. _____
   _____

4. _____
   _____

5. _____
   _____

6. _____
   _____

7. _____
   _____

8. _____
   _____

On the pages that follow you will find a form that allows you to think through each of the problems you just listed in an organized and logical way. Use one form for each problem that you listed above. If you need more space (and many people do) simply continue the exercise in your journal. You will find that this way of thinking through problems is not only helpful now, at the start of your recovery when things are chaotic and overwhelming, but that you also can use it on an ongoing basis as normal life difficulties arise.

For each problem, you will be asked to write the following:

Best possible outcome: What would be the best result of any actions you might take or plan you might devise?

Minimal acceptable outcome: What is the minimal result that is acceptable?

Possible solutions: Gather all the solutions that you and the people in your support system suggest. List each one, no matter how far fetched it may seem.

Best solution: From all possible solutions, combine and/or choose the ideas that might work for you.

Action steps with target dates: What concrete actions do you need to take? By what date will you take them?

Support needed: What do you need in order to take these steps and/or who do you need to help you with this solution?

By carefully laying out your action steps and including the support you need, the tasks will not seem so overwhelming. You will have also met the requirements of second order change. This process will help you build support systems and deal with problems in ways that can continue to help you throughout your recovery.

Damage Control Worksheet

Problem:

_____

_____

_____

_____

_____

Best Possible Outcome:

_____

_____

_____

_____

_____

Minimum Acceptable Outcome:

_____

_____

_____

_____

_____

Possible Solutions:

1. _____
   _____

2. _____
   _____

3. _____
   _____

4. _____
   _____

5. _____
   _____

6. _____
   _____

7. _____
   _____

8. _____
   _____

9. _____
   _____

10. _____
    _____

Best Possible Solutions:

_____

_____

_____

_____

_____

Action Steps:

1. _____

   _____

   Date taken by: _____

2. _____

   _____

   Date taken by: _____

3. _____

   _____

   Date taken by: _____

4. _____

   _____

   Date taken by: _____

5. _____

   _____

   Date taken by: _____

Support needed:

_____

_____

_____

_____

_____

Damage Control Worksheet

Problem:

_____

_____

_____

_____

_____

Best Possible Outcome:

_____

_____

_____

_____

_____

Minimum Acceptable Outcome:

_____

_____

_____

_____

_____

Possible Solutions:

1. _____

_____

2. _____

_____

3. _____

_____

4. _____

_____

5. _____
   _____

6. _____
   _____

7. _____
   _____

8. _____
   _____

9. _____
   _____

10. _____
    _____

Best Possible Solutions:

_____
_____
_____
_____
_____

Action Steps:

1. _____
   _____

   Date taken by: _____

2. _____
   _____

   Date taken by: _____

3. _____

_____

Date taken by: _____

4. _____

_____

Date taken by: _____

5. _____

_____

Date taken by: _____

Support needed:

_____

_____

_____

_____

_____

_____

_____

_____

_____

_____

_____

Damage Control Worksheet

Problem:

_____

_____

_____

_____

_____

_____

Best Possible Outcome:

_____

_____

_____

_____

_____

Minimum Acceptable Outcome:

_____

_____

_____

_____

_____

Possible Solutions:

1. _____

_____

2. _____

_____

3. _____

_____

4. _____

_____

5. _____

_____

6. _____

_____

7. _____

_____

8. _____

_____

9. _____

_____

10. _____

_____

Best Possible Solutions:

_____

_____

_____

_____

_____

Action Steps:

1. _____

2. _____

_____

Date taken by: _____

3. _____

_____

Date taken by: _____

4. _____

_____

Date taken by: _____

5. _____

_____

Date taken by: _____

Support needed:

_____

_____

_____

_____

_____

_____

_____

_____

_____

_____

_____

Damage Control Worksheet

Problem:

_____
_____
_____
_____
_____

Best Possible Outcome:

_____
_____
_____
_____
_____

Minimum Acceptable Outcome:

_____
_____
_____
_____
_____

Possible Solutions:

1. _____
   _____

2. _____
   _____

3. _____
   _____

4. _____
   _____

5. _____
   _____

6. _____
   _____

7. _____
   _____

8. _____
   _____

9. _____
   _____

10. _____
    _____

Best Possible Solutions:

_____
_____
_____
_____
_____

Action Steps:

1. _____
   _____

   Date taken by: _____

2. _____
   _____

   Date taken by: _____

3. _____

_____

Date taken by: _____

4. _____

_____

Date taken by: _____

5. _____

_____

Date taken by: _____

Support needed:

_____

_____

_____

_____

_____

_____

_____

_____

_____

_____

_____

Damage Control Worksheet

Problem:

_____

_____

_____

_____

_____

Best Possible Outcome:

_____

_____

_____

_____

_____

Minimum Acceptable Outcome:

_____

_____

_____

_____

_____

Possible Solutions:

1. _____

   _____

2. _____

   _____

3. _____

   _____

4. _____

   _____

5. _____
   _____

6. _____
   _____

7. _____
   _____

8. _____
   _____

9. _____
   _____

10. _____
    _____

Best Possible Solutions:

_____
_____
_____
_____
_____

Action Steps:

1. _____
   _____

   Date taken by: _____

2. _____
   _____

   Date taken by: _____

3. _____

_____

Date taken by: _____

4. _____

_____

Date taken by: _____

5. _____

_____

Date taken by: _____

Support needed:

_____

_____

_____

_____

_____

_____

_____

_____

_____

_____

_____

Damage Control Worksheet

Problem:

_____

_____

_____

_____

_____

Best Possible Outcome:

_____

_____

_____

_____

_____

Minimum Acceptable Outcome:

_____

_____

_____

_____

_____

Possible Solutions:

1. _____

   _____

2. _____

   _____

3. _____

   _____

4. _____

   _____

5. _____
_____

6. _____
_____

7. _____
_____

8. _____
_____

9. _____
_____

10. _____
_____

Best Possible Solutions:

_____
_____
_____
_____
_____

Action Steps:

1. _____
_____

Date taken by: _____

2. _____
_____

Date taken by: _____

3. _____

_____

Date taken by: _____

4. _____

_____

Date taken by: _____

5. _____

_____

Date taken by: _____

Support needed:

_____

_____

_____

_____

_____

_____

_____

_____

_____

_____

_____

Damage Control Worksheet

Problem:

_____

_____

_____

_____

_____

Best Possible Outcome:

_____

_____

_____

_____

_____

Minimum Acceptable Outcome:

_____

_____

_____

_____

_____

Possible Solutions:

1. _____

   _____

2. _____

   _____

3. _____

   _____

4. _____

   _____

5. _____
   _____

6. _____
   _____

7. _____
   _____

8. _____
   _____

9. _____
   _____

10. _____
    _____

Best Possible Solutions:

_____
_____
_____
_____
_____

Action Steps:

1. _____
   _____

   Date taken by: _____

2. _____
   _____

   Date taken by: _____

3. _____

   _____

                                    Date taken by: _____

4. _____

   _____

                                    Date taken by: _____

5. _____

   _____

                                    Date taken by: _____

Support needed:

_____

_____

_____

_____

_____

_____

_____

_____

_____

_____

_____

_____

Damage Control Worksheet

Problem:

_____

_____

_____

_____

_____

_____

Best Possible Outcome:

_____

_____

_____

_____

_____

_____

Minimum Acceptable Outcome:

_____

_____

_____

_____

_____

_____

Possible Solutions:

1. _____

_____

2. _____

_____

3. _____

_____

4. _____

_____

5. _____
   _____

6. _____
   _____

7. _____
   _____

8. _____
   _____

9. _____
   _____

10. _____
    _____

Best Possible Solutions:

_____
_____
_____
_____
_____

Action Steps:

1. _____
   _____

   Date taken by: _____

2. _____
   _____

   Date taken by: _____

3. _____
   _____
   Date taken by: _____

4. _____
   _____
   Date taken by: _____

5. _____
   _____
   Date taken by: _____

Support needed:

_____
_____
_____
_____
_____
_____
_____
_____
_____
_____
_____

Damage by Disclosure

The worst happens when disclosure is forced upon an addict. The family is unprepared. Spouses are outraged. Children are scared. Friends and colleagues often have no comprehension of what sex addiction is. The result? Everyone involved is disillusioned. Addicts themselves are filled with shame and despair. They have no support. If the disclosure becomes public, such as appearing on the front page of the newspaper, all involved are traumatized. Given that the issues are sexual, everyone has a great deal of interest but not always compassion or understanding. While it is through discovery of addictive sexual behavior by a spouse or boss that addicts often get help, this makes the discovery no less difficult.

Early in recovery, addicts sometimes feel so much better they want to tell everybody about their progress. In that early euphoria it is common to reveal something to someone you will later wish you had kept to yourself. In early recovery, partners can also demand to know details about what happened—only to become enraged by what they have learned. Further, many addicts come from abusive and dysfunctional families which do not respect boundaries, so they do not have the judgment they need to make good decisions. The metaphor that therapists use to describe their point is a zipper. When you live in shame, the zipper to yourself is located on the outside. Anyone can unzip and access information—or sex, or your commitment to do things you do not want to do. It is hard to say no. Healthy people have the zipper on the inside. They decide who gets access. They have boundaries—in other words they know where the line is between themselves and other people. Addicts suffer from boundary failure—especially in early recovery.

Here are some suggestions about talking to others about your sex addiction:

- Be careful. Tell only those you trust.
- Wait. Even after having decided to tell someone, take time to think over your decision before actually going through with it.
- Know your motives. What payoffs do you seek? Do you want support or are you seeking approval?
- Do it if you can help others with the same problem. Sharing with people who need to be in a Twelve Step program, or who already are, helps you, those people, and the group.
- Remember, it is not necessary to tell many people at all. You do not have to tell even when people ask or pry.
- When in doubt, talk with your sponsor and your group. They can provide the support you need to make safe decisions.
- Mistakes will happen. All addicts tell someone they later wish they had not told. It is okay to make mistakes.

You must tell your therapist, family, and the people closest to you. It would be unfair to them if you were not to share something this significant. Besides, these people will play a vital role in your healing process. The issue is not whether to tell, but when and how much to tell. Take each situation one by one.

Your Therapist—Your therapist must know everything. If you edit, omit, or filter information, you limit how effective therapy can be. Addicts, however, know they need their therapist. When they need someone, they use "impression management"—they try to look good or in control as a way to keep the therapist "on their side." The heart of success in both therapy and recovery is sharing the very worst secrets, allowing yourself to be seen as a "mess," and admitting how out of control you have been. Therapists are trained to help in such situations. Few things are more counter-productive than for critical information to be revealed in therapy after it's too late. Your therapist will in fact ask you in some way, "is that all?" You need to make full disclosure. We know from follow-up studies that sex addicts who made full disclosure do better in recovery.

Your Sponsors—In the Twelve Step program, you will ask key people to become ongoing consultants for you in your recovery. These sponsors will spend endless hours listening and helping you when things are hard. They will do this because it helps their recovery as well. It is part of passing on the story. They need to know everything—perhaps in even greater detail than your therapist. Impression management does not help here either. They need to have the whole story.

Your Spouse or Significant Other—To have secrets is to have shame. Addiction thrives in secrecy and shame. In addition, a committed relationship works best when each person "lays all their cards on the table." Talking to your partner about sex addiction is more difficult than talking about a gambling or alcohol problem. Nevertheless, it is very important to do. Just involving your spouse in early recovery increases your chances of successful recovery. Further, your spouse has to know what he or she is dealing with. When they do, they enter codependency recovery for themselves, which further increases the potential for success. Yes, they will be upset. But telling the truth is an important step in restoring trust. In an extended follow-up study by Debra Corley and Jennifer Schneider, 96 percent of spouses and 93 percent of addicts said that making full disclosure benefitted their recovery. The survey also revealed that it is best to make full disclosure in one setting. To dole out information a little bit at a time actually created further hurt and eroded trust. Remember that spouses only need general categories, not the details. The exception to that rule is that partners need all the data if it affects them directly. Examples would be if they were exposed to disease or if the sexual acting out was with a close friend of theirs.

Children—Carl Jung, the same man who told Bill W. about passing on the story—made an important statement about parenting. He said that the most important gift a parent can give children is to tell them about their dark side. Telling children about your struggles helps them developmentally to have a realistic picture of what it means to be human. They need this disclosure from you. The key issue here, however, is timing. Disclosure is best when they are old enough to understand sexual issues, and that means they should be at least in their teen years. Again, no details are needed, just general categories. You will find in most cases kids are very concerned about their parents, and they will be supportive. Disclosure also opens up the path of therapy and recovery for them. On many occasions I have sat in family sessions where parents and offspring have had more in common than they ever imagined.

Extended Family—Siblings, parents, cousins, and other extended family members can all be part of the disclosure process. In this case, your decision should be based on your sense of safety. If you think it would be useful for extended family members to know, and if you feel safe talking about your recovery, then tell them. One person getting into recovery has transformed whole families. You all may find that you have more in common than you know.

Business—Here the issue is more complicated and you have to exercise careful judgment as to whom it's safe to talk with. Many Employee Assistance Professionals are quite well trained in sex addiction and can actually help your process. A rigid, judgmental boss, however, might not be the best person with whom to disclose. If people you work with are to know, it's very important that they be educated about sex addiction first.

There are several principles that can guide your decision:

1. Always make sure you are feeling solid and supported. You do not have to do this alone. Make sure you can connect with someone in your group before and after disclosure.
2. Difficult disclosure is best done with a therapist you trust. A professional can help contain and focus the process so that it maximizes healing.
3. Expect that people will be upset and have strong reactions and feelings—especially spouses. Be prepared for this. And remember not to be reactive yourself. Your job is to supply information. Stay with your plan.
4. Be clear about what you wish to disclose and why. Make sure you review this with others so your expectations are realistic.
5. Disclosure works best when the person you are disclosing to also has support. Difficult disclosure does not go well for either party when done alone.
6. Disclosure also works better when there is at least a working knowledge of what sex addiction is, and this often requires some education prior to disclosure.

Disclosure teaches many lessons. First, you learn that you have control over what you disclose and when you disclose it. This means putting your zipper on the inside. Placing such boundaries is different than having a secret life. Boundaries allow you to be fully known by those close to you while still using discretion. Second, disclosure teaches you that you can prepare for conflict by getting support from those who understand you and sex addiction. You do not have to be driven into despair. Disclosure becomes a process, albeit painful, from which you can learn and grow. If you disclose from a solid position, you can also appreciate the harm you have caused. Finally, when you realize that people do not leave you, you begin to appreciate your own worth.

The following exercise will help you clarify whom and what to tell. Complete it and share with your therapist and your consultants.

Disclosure Plan

List ten persons to whom you need to disclose facts about your sex addiction. After each, be specific about what you wish to tell and what your goal is in telling them. Review your secret list (chapter 1) and your First Step information (chapters 2 through 4) to see if you need to do more. Record when you will do this and where your support will come from. Remember you do not have to complete this whole list. Rather, just use the format for those appropriate for you. You may need additional paper for some individuals.

1. Person: _____

   Material to be disclosed: _____

   _____

   _____

   Payoff: _____

   Timing: _____

   Support from: _____

2. Person: _____

   Material to be disclosed: _____

   _____

   _____

   Payoff: _____

   Timing: _____

   Support from: _____

3. Person: _____

   Material to be disclosed: _____

   _____

   _____

   Payoff: _____

   Timing: _____

   Support from: _____

4. Person _____

   Material to be disclosed _____

   _____

Payoff: _____

Timing: _____

Support from: _____

5. Person: _____

    Material to be disclosed :_____

    _____

    _____

    Payoff: _____

    Timing: _____

    Support from: _____

6. Person: _____

    Material to be disclosed: _____

    _____

    _____

    Payoff: _____

    Timing: _____

    Support from: _____

7. Person: _____

    Material to be disclosed: _____

    _____

    _____

    Payoff: _____

    Timing: _____

    Support from: _____

8. Person: _____

    Material to be disclosed: _____

    _____

    _____

    Payoff: _____

    Timing: _____

Support from: _____

9. Person: _____

   Material to be disclosed: _____

   _____

   _____

   Payoff: _____

   Timing: _____

   Support from: _____

10. Person: _____

    Material to be disclosed: _____

    _____

    _____

    Payoff: _____

    Timing: _____

    Support from: _____

Review your plan with your therapist, your sponsor, and your group. Solicit suggestions about your plan. Remember that you are doing all that you can. The rest is beyond your control.

Restoration of Trust

Addicts ask "how do I restore trust?" First, let's look at what you should not do. Making protestations of how much you love your partner will not get you much at this point. Nor will fervent promises of good behavior. Nor buying or doing things that had long been asked for. Promises and "I love yous" can in fact bring ridicule and shame. The most important step you can take now is to be truthful and to listen. Acknowledging how sorry you are is appropriate. Being defensive or blaming is like pouring gasoline on the fire. It works better to really understand how deeply you have hurt people. The goal is not to fill yourself with shame, but rather to develop resolve for change.

What makes a difference to people is what they see you do. If they see a deep commitment to change, they will most often join you and eventually take pride in what you have done. Begin by stopping your behaviors. They will see the change as you go to meetings, work on your therapy, and make sacrifices to make recovery work. That is when they will start to trust. Therein lies the tremendous irony in this process. People start to trust addicts when the addicts start to trust themselves. Those in your life intuitively know the process is working.

Most people who ask about how to restore trust are concerned with a marriage or primary relationship. Within these relationships, trust starts to be earned with the pain of disclosure. When partners realize they are hearing the truth, credibility begins to return. Here are some guidelines drawn from the experiences of many people who have gone through this process:

- *Give it a lot of time.* Most recovering people say this is the most difficult, but also the most important, thing they learned. Phrases like "patience," "go slow," and "a day at a time" were very useful. This reflects the old Al-Anon adage, nothing major the first year.

- *Be willing to lose it in order to get it.* Both partners must resolve not to give up parts of themselves in order to keep the other from leaving. If you can be fully who you are and your partner does not leave, you have something truly valuable. Fidelity to self is the ultimate act of faithfulness to the other.

- *Restore self first.* If you do the repair work that you yourself need, your perceptions of the relationship will change dramatically. Most people's unhappiness in their relationship is about themselves and not about their partners. You have to trust yourself before you can trust the other.

- *Accept the illness in the other.* Start by acknowledging at the deepest level of yourself that you both are powerless and fully involved in the illness. This will be as difficult for your partner as it will be for you.

- *Admit mistakes promptly.* Avoid blame. Work to be honest and accurate, not to prove who is right. Self-righteousness inevitably kills intimacy.

- *Share spirituality.* Explore ways to be spiritual together. You have to find the meaning in your suffering, and doing so together can dramatically shift your perspective as a couple.

- *Use the amends steps.* Steps Eight and Nine of the Twelve Steps teach us to make amends by expressing regret for what we have done and doing something to make up for it. Use this approach as a model for daily living. Reverse the blame dynamic by taking responsibility for pain you have inflicted on the other. Do what you can to make up for it.

- *Remember, it's never going to be perfect.* **Just** as the ultimate partner does not exist, neither does the ultimate relationship. Accepting human limits in ourselves helps us in being generous with our loved ones.

- *Be with other recovering couples.* **Attend** open meetings together. Join fellowships of couples such as Recovering Couples Anonymous. Go on couple's retreats and workshops. Support other couples and socialize with them.

- *Have fun together.* **All** work (on recovery) with no play makes for great intensity, not intimacy. Closeness comes from shared common experiences—especially the fun ones. Remember, play is, in its own way, an act of trust.

The Trust Process

Addicts experience despair after acting out. It was not worth it. And they promise themselves that they will never do it again. When they act out again, they have not even kept the promise to themselves, let alone promises made to others. This repeated disappointment undermines the trust addicts have for themselves. They simply are not doing what they intend. They can even tell themselves that this will have a bad end. And it does. Then they say, "I wish I would have listened to myself." Because we look at others with the same lens with which we view ourselves, addicts will believe no one else is trustworthy either.

Things start to change in recovery with damage control and disclosure. Addicts are taking responsibility for personal behavior. In addition addicts stop acting out and go through the pain of withdrawal. Literally the line is drawn in the sand. No more slipping. Once they have success doing those things, the shame dissipates. They start to trust themselves. Robert Bly once remarked that growing up is making your body do what it does not want to. Most addicts have not been able to develop normally and so the normal maturation process starts. They start doing what they say they will. And they feel good about themselves. Up until this point they have been filled with shame and have made decisions on the basis of what people will think of them. Now they are making decisions on the basis of what is right for them.

This is the turning point. Henri Nouwen, the famous theologian, described this process as the "conversion of loneliness to solitude." Addicts who spent years running from themselves now start to have a relationship with themselves. This means they have a compassion for themselves which results in self care. Nouwen further points out that this ability to be true to self creates a new trust of others. They now can let others care for them. Once they trust others, they then also start to trust a higher power. People who have trouble trusting a God often have significant trust issues. Nouwen says there are essentially three movements in a spiritual life starting with trust of self, followed by trust of others, which transforms into a trust in God.

The Twelve Step program also mirrors that process. When addicts first come, they admit how wounded they are. This is in the form of the first step. By doing this, they also break the old rules of the addictive paradigm that say never admit how bad it is and never ask for help. As you will remember this is part of the rule set that kept the addict in first order change. While sponsors and group mates cannot reparent the addict, their care and constancy do accelerate the healing of the relationship deficits of the family of origin. The second and third steps ask the recovering person to trust that a higher power will help them. For many at first the group becomes the higher power.

Eventually they start to "trust the process" and recognize there are larger forces at work in their recovery. This is how the second order change starts, which radically alters the rules (belief system or paradigm) the addict lives by. The second and third steps help the addict move from the provisional beliefs with which we started the chapter to a new life based on a recovery paradigm.

This transition also lays the foundation for a new sexuality. Although sex addicts have tremendous amounts of sexual experience, it was sex that was not about who they were. It was simply sex. Passion really extends from the self and requires a level of trust and letting go that is very much in the spirit of Steps One, Two and Three. Sex is a nurturing experience which can only happen when you allow people to know you and to care for you.

Use the steps. They are a proven recipe for spiritual wholeness. Remember that the program started with the realization that without the spiritual component, recovery could not happen. Decide a spiritual life is essential, not an option. While there are lots of resources for doing a Second and Third Step (some of which are listed in the recommended reading for this chapter), here are some suggestions for sex addicts who wish to cultivate a new spiritual life:

- *Find guides.* Listen to others share their spiritual experiences and ask how healing happened in their lives. Brokeness, failure, and tragedy have helped many find parts of themselves they had not known. Most also started with anger or fear, skepticism or detachment.

- *Separate religion from spirituality.* Many come with "baggage" about religious institutions that damaged or constricted their growth. Resentment about these experiences can cast shadows over genuine spiritual development. Organizations and institutions are not ends in themselves, but should be designed to help you have a spiritual life and build a spiritual community. Use only those which help.

- *Connect with nature.* Spirituality starts with a sense of marvel at our existence and at the wonders of creation—other living things, the oceans and mountains, forests, deserts, and weather. Go for a walk. Watch stars. Take care of a pet. Notice your body. Play with children. Then connect these miracles with what else you see around you.

- *Make a daily effort.* Key to spiritual life is constancy. Daily rituals that anchor your sense of stability help you achieve incremental spiritual growth. Then when leaps of faith are required and stress overwhelms you, a reservoir of accumulated strength awaits.

- *Find ways to promote reflection.* Spirituality is about what is meaningful to you. What gives your life value. Find strategies that help you to reflect on meaning and value. Inspirational writing, daily meditation books, liturgy, prayer, journals, yoga exercises, and letter writing are the kinds of things that need to be part of your daily rituals. These also help you make sense out of special spiritual events.

- *Surrender.* All inner journeys start with an "emptying" of self—a fact reflected in all religious traditions. Addicts begin recovery with an admission of powerlessness and live their lives according to the principle of "letting go." Serenity, according to the prayer, is doing all you can and accepting that that is enough.

- *Heal the sexual/spiritual split.* Much damage has been done on sexuality in the name of religion. The result inhibits progress on both planes. To heal, start by acknowledging that sexuality is about meaning and that spirituality is about meaning. Search for areas of commonness between the two. Be gentle with yourself about old torturous conflicts. They are not about you. They never were.

Recommended Reading

Out of the Shadows. 2nd edition, pp. 115–164. *Sexual Anorexia,* pp. 103–132.

Additional Reading

Gary Zukav, *The Seat of the Soul,* New York: Simon and Shuster, 1989. Especially the chapter on addiction, pp. 148–179.

John Bradshaw, *Healing the Shame that Binds You.* Deerfield Beach, Florida:Health Communications, Inc. 1985.

Ralph Earle, and Gregory Crow, *Lonely All the Time: Recognizing, Understanding, and Overcoming Sex Addiction, For Addicts and Co-Dependents.* New York: The Philip Lief Group, Inc., 1989.

Henri Nouwen, J.M., *Reaching Out.* New York: Harper and Row Publisher, 1983.

CHAPTER SIX: What Is Sobriety?
Managing Life without Dysfunctional Sexual Behavior

"I will take the ring although I do not know the way."
—FRODO IN TOLKIEN'S LORD OF THE RINGS

IN ONE OF THE BEGINNING SCENES of Tolkien's great epic, *Lord of the Rings*, the wizard Gandalf challenges the hobbit Frodo to bring back peace to the land by returning the magic ring back to the land of Mordor. The return of the ring is the key to freedom from the tyranny of the evil magician Sauron. Gandalf holds out the ring for Frodo to accept the quest. Frodo feels a penetrating chill, which he immediately knows has been sent from Mordor to distract him from accepting the challenge. This evil sent by Sauron is designed to paralyze Frodo and render him incapable of responding to Gandalf. He musters all the courage he can and slowly raises his hand to accept the ring. He hears his own voice though it seems far away. He says to Gandalf, "I will take the ring although I do not know the way." Then begins Frodo's great quest that brings so much good to so many.

All the great stories of human courage start with the hero or the heroine not knowing how to do it, but starting anyway. So it is with recovery. In the Big Book of Alcoholics Anonymous, there is a famous phrase, "some of us exclaimed, "What an order! I can't go through with it." That is roughly akin to the cold chill from Mordor. It is the addiction trying to paralyze the addict from taking action. The people who succeed are the ones who start even though they do not know the way. Part of the benefits of the quest is what they learn as they do it. The point is they start by taking action.

Taking action here is establishing sobriety. Another famous phrase from the Big Book is being willing to "go to any lengths" to get sobriety. I remember two guys in the early days of sex addiction recovery. They lived on the coast of Louisiana where there were no Twelve Step groups for sex addiction. They decided to start a group in their own town. One of the guys went off to treatment because he was so depressed. The other man put the word out through local churches and therapists. Every Sunday night he would put on the coffee and set up the chairs in the meeting room of a local church. No one came. He did that for five Sunday nights. Still no one came. On the sixth Sunday the other man returned from treatment and came to the meeting. That night a third man also came. Today that group has grown so much, it has split many times. They have an annual retreat on an island off the coast. It started with one man who wanted recovery so bad he kept coming even though no one else was there.

Sobriety rests on the internal decision that you are now going to do what it takes to make it different. It helps to understand sobriety as a boundary problem in order to make the decision work. Addicts typically have poor boundaries that result in poor impulse control. They learned in their families somehow to take an easier and softer way. When the addiction took over, it became habitual. The other part of the boundary problem is that they ended up doing things they did not intend or even want to do. Lack of boundaries also made them easily exploited by others. For many, sobriety is the first concrete expression of meaningful boundaries. Having a clear statement about your abstinence allows you to start the journey back to being yourself.

In the previous chapter you learned the importance of having boundaries as part of damage control. "Having the zipper on the inside," "staying with a plan," and "doing what you said you would do" are all part of developing good boundaries. They are also key to the process of reclaiming yourself. Sobriety is the next phase of boundary development and reclaiming yourself. Your sexual acting out is really about boundary failure. Learning to set limits becomes a revolution in a recovering person's life. A clear sense of what matters to you governs your life. Self-respect returns. A new toughness emerges that gains the respect of others. And ironically, the toughness brings a sense of peace never before experienced in your life.

There are a number of factors in the boundary failure. First, the addictive system has a power and momentum of its own. Beliefs and delusion propel the addictive cycle. The resulting unmanageability just intensifies the downward spiral. In the next chapter, we will explore how your biology (and specifically your neurochemistry) has been altered by the addictive process. But, for the moment, just consider that there also is a biological "momentum" once the addiction cycle is engaged. All those sexual behaviors, which have kept you so driven, have a power of their own. So all the promises you made to yourself to set limits (boundaries) failed. Part of recovery is to accept that even the most disciplined people are powerless when they have an addiction.

In addition, most addicts have issues that compound the problem. They are principally family-of-origin issues, but they often serve to strengthen the addictive system. They all impact the ability of a person to set limits. They also are critical issues for being a healthy person: achievement, self-esteem, self-care, accountability, realism, conscience, self-awareness, and relationships. In therapy, professionals routinely see recurring patterns for sex addicts in each of these areas that affect their ability to establish a relapse-free sobriety. Before exploring the basic elements of sobriety, you need to understand how these issues might undermine your efforts. While all these patterns might not be true for you, chances are some of them will fit.

Achievement. Two patterns of achievement stand out in sex addicts. One is a very accomplished person who works extremely hard and is quite successful. These addicts are doctors, attorneys, executives, clergy, and entrepreneurs. They share a commitment to excellence and success that is so potent that they become driven people. Minimally, they are constantly so stressed, they live in chaos and depletion. Maximally, they may have a problem with compulsive working. They never have time for family or friends. Nor do they have time to reflect much on why they are trying so hard. Their sense of worth is measured only by money, power, and recognition. They often are reacting to parents who were very successful and they are trying to match it. Or they are attempting to be better than others—such as their parents— or they're seeking a special kid status or even are trying to settle some score. Whatever, their frenetic life usually is rooted in some crazy loyalty to the family that results in overextension.

The recovery challenge is that they approach recovery as a "to do" list as opposed to a process that does not have goals or outcomes. It is a better way to live. I once counseled a physician who spent the first three days of treatment using every spare moment filling out the exercises in the *Gentle Path through the Twelve Steps*. He even did a couple all-night efforts to complete the work. Of course this is how he would study for medical school. He thought he could fill in the blanks and he would have completed the work. He presented us with the completed book and said he was ready to go home. It took him weeks to understand that he had relationships to build, decisions to make, and feelings to express. At the end of treatment, he laughed about how he had planned to make therapy a matter of filling in the blanks. But if you are goal oriented, learning that it is just as important to look at how you get there is a major accomplishment.

The further trouble is that sex addicts are used to living depleted and exhausted lives, which leads to entitlement and poor self-care. Addiction is fueled by deprivation. Overextension, chaos and constant stress lead to depletion. Thus, when success is achieved, the addict starts to crave an inordinate reward. Your values, consequences, reality—all that goes out the window. "I did it, so now I deserve it" is the refrain. And when you are constantly pulling things off, "you deserve it" becomes one of the anchors of the addictive system.

Underachievers are the flip side scenario of this pattern. Often, they come from families that are very successful. Surrounded by success, the only way to succeed or even be noticed is to fail. These addicts become the family "problem." School, jobs, relationships, and responsibilities go badly. The addict feels lots of shame and a curious loyalty emerges. As long as the addict is the problem, no one has to notice the emptiness or the abuse in the family. So being a scapegoat serves a function. In recovery, addicts with this pattern realize that the family is actually invested in the addict staying in trouble. What would happen if they became very successful and happy? Who in the family would suffer? In other words, as long as the fingers are pointed at the addict, no else has to look at his or her behavior. Some even find their marriages have elements of the addict being "a problem child."

The further trouble here is that the pattern revolves around failure, problems, and disappointment. In all the chaos, pain, and despair, addicts feel they deserve some relief. They feel betrayed and victimized. And that is often true because they have not taken care of themselves, so are vulnerable to exploitation by people both inside and outside of the family. The net effect is "Things are so bad, I deserve it." Or maybe "So much has happened to me, I deserve it." Or "I feel so bad, I deserve it." No matter what, you deserve it. The overachievers and the underachievers have the same result: they deserve it. In fact, some report having periods in life in which they combined both—when something bad happened, they deserved to act out and when something good happened, they deserved to act out. Finally, it reaches the point where something only has to happen and you feel you deserve it. The constant is convincing yourself you deserve it. Feeling that you deserve it is one of the surest roads to relapse. Sobriety will require you to look at how you respond to achievement and success and where that fits in to your recovery.

Self-Esteem. Children should be made to feel special. Yet in some families specialness becomes problematic. A child can become favored over others, or be protected from consequences, or exempted from rules or tasks. The child can become what therapists call a "surrogate spouse," which means being a confidant or helper to the parent in things a spouse should do. The other parent may be absent, abusive, addicted or deceased. The kid becomes "the man of the house" or "my little woman." Ken Adams' book *Silently Seduced* (see suggested readings) has been very helpful to recovery from this form of emotional incest. Because of this specialness, addicts may have been catered to and, as a result, are not conscious of others. They can become very self-absorbed with meeting their own needs. They have a minimal sense of their impact on others. They place themselves consistently at the center of things. In its most extreme forms, we call this narcissism or narcissistic personality disorder. Remember Narcissus was the Greek mythological figure who became obsessed with his own image. From a sex-addiction-relapse perspective, it is very difficult to maintain sobriety if you are not aware of your own limits or your impact on others.

The flip side is also true. Some kids did not feel special. In fact their self-esteem was eroded through abuse and neglect. Because they feel unworthy, they sabotage things when they could go well. They do not believe that they deserve success or attention. They are programmed for failure. Their attempts to do well are mined with self-fulfilling prophecies about not making it. We do become what we envision. If you do not believe that you can make sobriety work, it will elude you.

Either being self-absorbed or filled with shame causes the same result: a distorted picture of your place in the universe. For sobriety to occur, you must develop an appreciation for yourself that is not overinflated or overdeflated. If you fit in either category try this: Take one hour and make three lists. Start with a list of events in your life in which you genuinely could take pride. Compare that with a list of times you programmed or "talked yourself" into failure. These are times when your own feelings of worthlessness kept you from doing what you needed. Also draw up a list of events when your preoccupation with self hurt those you care about. On the basis of these lists, make a quick list of your strengths and your limitations. You will eventually do this very thoroughly in the Fourth Step. Here, it is to provide perspective on what risks exist to your staying sober. You might wish to learn about using "affirmations." Essentially, affirmations help reprogram you so you can accept the lovable person you are. The path out of this is to find a way to affirm yourself from within so you have a realistic and confident sense of yourself. (See suggested readings.)

Accountability. Addicts typically resist being accountable. They resist being accountable because of how rigid or controlling their families were. Most feel that if they caved in to others' demands, they would lose their identity. That probably is an accurate perception, because in most families they would have a hard time developing a separate sense of themselves. Good parents accept the fact that kids do not want to do what their parents tell them, and they love them anyway. They are willing to struggle and show kids the benefits of doing what you have to do. Part of being grown up is making your body do what it does not want to do. Kids learn the meaning of "no." They can do this for themselves and they can do it with others. And they know their parents love them. And these parents are also accountable to their kids. For example, they admit their mistakes to their children. Children grow up knowing that it is ok to be imperfect, that it is important to be responsible, and that saying no is the first step in learning self-limitation.

Many addicts miss these core lessons. First, there are those who are never accountable. They do not do what they say they will. They do not admit their mistakes. They do not let anyone know what they really do with their time, their money, or their actions. Another category includes those who are accountable in appearance. In fact, many addicts are very disciplined publicly with reputations for hard work and integrity. Yet they have a secret life. They may have learned this is a way to escape the control and shaming ways of their family. Or maybe they learned it by watching the adults in their family. The net effect is that on the outside they are accountable, but if no one knows what they do, they are willing to do things that violate what they truly value. In business, the phrase is "keeping a separate set of books"—one for show and the secret one.

Sobriety works only if there is total accountability. Your group, your therapist, and your sponsor become important links to accountability. A second set of books simply will not work. There have to be people in your life who know everything and who will challenge you.

Self-Care. Neglect is a common problem in the history of sex addicts. Busy or uncaring parents who do not take the time to help kids and show them how to live life really are neglecting their children. The children, in turn, fail to internalize skills in taking care of themselves. They do not do things to protect themselves from harm and so are vulnerable to be exploited by others. They often see things they should do or prevent—and when disaster occurs, they kick themselves saying, "Why didn't I do something about that when I knew better?" They neglect their own bodies and welfare. In short, they do not love themselves enough to go the extra lengths for good self-care. For these people sobriety is difficult because it requires a whole reorientation. They have to take care of themselves or relapse will happen.

Other addicts lived with parents who did everything for them. They did not learn how to do things for themselves, expecting it to be done for them. I have seen this in very wealthy families, in which "nanny kids" have every whim met—but still were not convinced of their parents' love. I have also seen parents of very modest means who protect and cater to kids, who, ironically, also feel unloved. The bottom line is grandiose entitlement. Everything is negotiable. No consequences really hit. No matter what the addict does someone rescues him or her. They may even be outraged if no one does rescue them. They also are upset, when things are not done for them. If they do not do what they need to do for themselves, they always say they tried. Recovery is a rude awakening here as well. No one can do your sobriety for you. Like Yoda says to Luke Skywalker in the movie *The Empire Strikes Back*, "Do or not do, there is no try." Sobriety requires self-care. And you must do it for yourself.

Self-care means you do not put yourself in jeopardy. You do the regular things that maintain your health, including flossing when you brush your teeth. You consistently exercise. You avoid depletion. You let your friends do kind things for you. You figure out nice things to do for yourself. You take your recovery very seriously, let your sponsor help you, go to meetings. Neither neglect nor entitlement works in sobriety.

Conscience. Some define conscience as the ability to follow the rules. To some degree that is true. Some addicts have no remorse for their behavior even though they clearly hurt others. In its most extreme cases, we use the term "sociopath" when there is no empathy for victims. Usually this term is used with sex offenders. Yet many sex addicts have this quality. Often, sex addicts talk about not wanting to see someone again after seducing him or her. Or in prostitution or anonymous sex, part of the deal is no entanglements. Bottom line, this means no regard for the other. This is not sociopathic behavior, *but,* does mean having no remorse for behavior that contributes harm to others. Recovery means taking responsibility for your behavior.

Part of the pain of sex addiction for many sex addicts is that they have violated their value system, and they are guilt driven. One of the essential drivers of the addiction cycle is the despair after doing behavior you feel bad about. Addicts act out further in an effort to blot out the despair. Torturing yourself for your behavior that was exploitive or thoughtless adds power to the addictive process. The Twelve Steps help guide you through a process in which you do all you can to make amends and learn how to make peace with yourself.

Conscience is really more than following the rules. We call that compliance. A conscience determines that for which you will fight. If someone attacked someone you love, you would immediately put everything at risk to protect your loved one. A conscience asks what you are willing to put everything at risk for—because it matters so much. A person with a conscience comes to recognize that which matters. A recovering person draws a line in the sand, saying this is what matters to me. I will do everything for this.

Reality. People describe a person who is realistic and pragmatic as having "common sense." In short, people who have common sense learn from their mistakes. One of the most famous lines to come out of self-help literature is by M. Scott Peck in his book *The Road Less Traveled*, in which he writes, "Mental health is a commitment to reality at all costs." A frequently quoted aphorism complements that statement: "Insanity is doing the same self-destructive behavior over and over, and expecting different results." Common sense is the ability to see what works and what does not. Learning from your mistakes is essential to your mental health.

I am not talking about delusion and denial here, although impaired thinking certainly affects this issue. I am referring to a deeper problem—that some people do not develop the ability to learn from mistakes. Usually they come from families in which kids were not allowed to experience consequences. They never had to figure out that many of their problems they brought on themselves. We do make our own happiness. And unhappiness. Some never learn common sense. Recovery, however, is built on common sense.

Others do have common sense but choose to ignore it. This is the problem of willfulness. Along with entitlement and grandiosity comes the addicts' "I want what I want when I want it." To paraphrase an old Navy adage, "Damn the consequences, full speed ahead." Addicts are creative, resourceful people who shrewdly figure out how to overcome intrusive reality. Yet, sooner or later you have to learn from your mistakes and not rely on your damage-control skills. Recovery brings the additional reality of your addiction, which means you have to be realistic and accepting of your own limits.

Self-Awareness. Typical addicts do not know much about themselves. In part, it is because of their beliefs around their own unworthiness. They feel so defective, they are uncomfortable being in their own presence. So they distract themselves with compulsive busyness, filling their lives with so much activity that there is no real interior life. They get uncomfortable with being alone—minimally having to have the TV on or some distraction. Many addicts have reflected that a fear of being alone was a significant factor in their behavior. Some addicts would either avoid or procrastinate on anything that would have meant delving into their feelings, motivations, and patterns. They even report mocking therapy and self-help. It simply was too painful. It was easier to dismiss any type of self-reflection as silly or useless.

Sobriety comes only with painful self-realization. Addiction is fundamentally a means to escape the internal turmoil. The core of therapy and Twelve Step work is developing a functional relationship with yourself. It is "the conversion of loneliness into solitude" referred to in the earlier chapters. In order for that to happen, you must use ways of reflecting on your recovery work. Readings, meditations, journaling, Step work—whatever you do, you must have sources of personal reflection built into your life. Further, there must be regular periods of down time to do the reflecting. Rest. No activity. Just being with yourself. These "windows of time" are incredibly important to your ability to sort out. Recovery groups use a phrase that John Bradshaw popularized about becoming human beings versus human "doings." There is an essential rhythm to life you have to observe that is part of accepting your human limits. Rest. Stephen Covey refers to it as one of the essentials of effective people. He calls it "sharpening the saw." One of the best books on this part of life is by Wayne Mueller, called *Sabbath: Restoring the Sacred Rhythm of Rest*. Rest and reflection are key to an "examined" life.

Relationships. Addicts have incomplete relationships at best. Most addicts struggle with isolation. They have to handle things on their own. No one knows how much they struggle. No way out of the shame exists for the addict who lets no one in. Ironically, many addicts are very social, but they hide the vulnerable parts of their lives. No one gets the whole picture. Along with accountability, one has to experience the acceptance and help of others in order to heal. It is the experience of other people that makes your self-acceptance work. One way to make sure sobriety is second-order change versus first-order change is to stay connected with people who know the whole story.

Affect. Therapists use the word "affect" to describe our emotional lives. Just as we need intellectual skills such as problem solving, we need emotional skills such as handling anxiety and expressing our feelings. Addicts have "disordered affect," which means they do not handle their emotions well. People who are new to recovery often tell me that they struggle to have feelings. In many ways, they were punished for having feelings. In some families it simply was not acceptable to have an emotional life. So to survive, your feeling life was shut down. Or it may have just been the family norm not to express feelings. Or some people who are very smart learned to rely only on their ability to think and neglected the development of their feelings and intuitions. Perhaps the biggest reason is that life was just so painful, it was simply easier to numb everything. Numbing out is one of the benefits of addiction. It keeps the feelings at bay.

Others overreact. Simple things escalate into intense emotional drama. Addicts are particularly prone to using rage to manipulate and intimidate. This rage becomes a self-indulgent extension of "I deserve it" or "I want what I want when I want it!" Volatile, romantic, and intense relationships become a venue for emotional roller-coaster scripts of disappointment and excitement. The turmoil obscures the anxiety and the emotions underlying the dramatic scenes.

Whether high drama or numbness, the core feelings remain unacknowledged. Recovering people often have to start by labeling the most basic feelings of joy, pain, sadness, anger, and fear. That way they start to have clarity about what they are feeling. They learn basic strategies around anxiety, such as learning to stay in the here and now, as opposed to stirring themselves up by obsessing about the past or the future. The principles of "letting go" summarized in the Serenity Prayer become a life stance to deal with anxiety and control.

The Sobriety Challenges

Underachieving despair	Distorted Achievement	Overachieving depletion and chaos
Self-defeating shame	Compromised Self-Image	Self-absorbed obsession
Not accountable	Lack of Accountability	Secret life
Profound self-neglect	Problematic Self-Care	Grandiose entitlement
No remorse	Impaired Conscience	Guilt driven
No common sense	Faulty Realism	Common sense ignored
Avoidance/procrastination	Limited Self-Awareness	Compulsive busyness
Isolation	Incomplete Relationships	Hidden parts of self
Shutdown feelings/ numbness	Disordered Affect Feelings	Indulgent rage, drama, intensity

Figure 6.1

The Sobriety Challenges

Figure 6.1 summarizes challenges to sobriety. Notice that each issue can fundamentally affect a person's ability to set limits and boundaries. You may have also noticed that you fit in more than one category and that sometimes you fit both extremes within a category. That would be very normal for addicts. These are the most common issues. Addicts tend to come from dysfunctional families. As they grow up, they learn to cope in the extremes. By working on these issues, addicts notice that the very groundwork of their lives change. They start to see that sex is not the enemy—it is the underlying dynamic that provides the addictive system with its power. Part of recovery will be discovering what sexuality is. For all the endless diversity and sexual experience sex addicts have had, they actually do not know much about themselves sexually. Remember that if it was not sex, more than likely it would be something else. In fact, it is usually a collage of addictions and deprivations, as we shall see in the next chapter.

The proven recipe to deal with these issues is quite simple. Summarized, the recovery essentials are

Do only what is important.
Reward yourself for good work.
Affirm yourself.
Be accountable.
Take care of yourself.
Know what matters.
Learn from mistakes.
Rest and reflect.
Connect to those who know your story.
Allow pain, joy, fear, and anger.
Stay present.
Accept that sex is not the enemy.
Seek your sexual self.
Have boundaries with self and others.

I am often approached by people having difficulty achieving sobriety. They tell me that they have a relapse prevention plan, that they go to meetings, and that they work the program. First I verify whether that is true—i.e., they have a sponsor, have been given and are working steps, are doing service work and other signs of active involvement. Usually what I find is that the inability to stop is rooted in one of the above challenges to sobriety. All the plans in the world will not help if you do not see the underlying challenges. However, by clarifying those underlying issues and how they might limit your ability to establish boundaries in sobriety, you will be ready to define what sobriety is. That is our next task. Before starting, complete the following sobriety challenges worksheet and discuss it with your therapist and sponsor.

Also consult the suggested readings at the conclusion of this chapter.

Sobriety Challenges Worksheet

Listed below are each of the challenges addicts have to establishing sobriety. Within each challenge there are extremes listed with a scale of one to five. One means not a problem and five means a severe problem. Rate yourself in each category. In some categories you may find yourself high on both extremes. Beneath each scale, record examples of your behaviors and specify how this behavior pattern might sabotage your sobriety process.

DISTORTED ACHIEVEMENT

Underachieving despair	Overachieving Depletion and Chaos
1. 5	1. 5

COMPROMISED SELF-IMAGE

Self-Defeating Shame	Self-Absorbed Obsession
1. 5	1. 5

LACK OF ACCOUNTABILITY

Not Accountable	Secret Life
1. 5	1. 5

PROBLEMATIC SELF-CARE

Profound Self-Neglect	Grandiose Entitlement
1. 5	1. 5

IMPAIRED CONSCIENCE

No Remorse	Guilt Driven
1. 5	1. 5

_____

_____

_____

FAULTY REALISM

No Common Sense	Common Sense Ignored
1. 5	1. 5

_____

_____

_____

LIMITED SELF-AWARENESS

Avoidance/Procrastination	Compulsive Busyness
1. 5	1. 5

_____

_____

_____

INCOMPLETE RELATIONSHIPS

Isolation	Hidden Parts of Self
1. 5	1. 5

_____

_____

_____

DISORDERED AFFECT FEELINGS

Shutdown Feelings/Numbness	Indulgent Rage, Drama, Intensity
1. 5	1. 5

_____

_____

_____

Reflections on the Recovery Essentials

The following worksheet will help you more clearly understand just what the "recovery essentials" can mean for you. Respond to the questions in the space provided.

Do what is important. What important matters are being neglected in your life? What distractions from important priorities do you currently allow in your life?

_____

_____

_____

_____

Reward yourself for good work. What have you done well lately that you have not yet rewarded yourself for? Why have you allowed this to happen?

_____

_____

_____

_____

Affirm yourself. Write down some affirming statements from you to you. Make the statements a genuine compliment for tasks you are doing well. How does it feel to do this? Why those feelings?

_____

_____

_____

_____

Seek your sexual self. List one thing you've learned about your sexuality since starting recovery. What do you think is the "next frontier" for you sexually?

_____

_____

_____

Have boundaries with self and others. Has there been a recent boundary collapse in your life? What did you learn as a result?

_____

_____

_____

_____

Be accountable. In what ways have you been accountable recently? In what ways have you had lapses in accountability?

_____

_____

_____

_____

Take care of yourself. What recent examples of self-care can you report? What recent opportunities for self-care have you missed?

_____

_____

_____

_____

Know what matters. Have you recently gone out of your way or taken an unpopular stand because something mattered to you? Or, have there been times when you did not stand up for something important to you? Explain.

_____

_____

_____

_____

Learn from mistakes. Are there certain mistakes you still make? Why?

_____

_____

_____

_____

Rest and reflect. Do you have regular periods of rest in your life that you and others can count on? If not, why not?

_____

_____

_____

_____

Connect to those who know your story. Who are the people in your life who truly know everything that is going on with you? When was the last time you were in touch with each of them?

_____

_____

_____

_____

Allow pain, joy, fear, and anger. Have you avoided any feelings lately? Which ones? What was the occasion? Why did you avoid them? What can you do about this now?

_____

_____

_____

Stay present. Are there any recent occasions in which you missed what was currently happening because you were absorbed by thinking about the past or the future or by preoccupation with work, stress, or sexual fantasy? What sense do you make of those moments now?

_____

_____

_____

_____

Accept that sex is not the enemy. Have you had any moments of sexual self-hatred lately? Regrets about being a sexual person? Wishes that you did not have sexual feelings? What do you think caused these feelings?

_____

_____

_____

_____

Establishing Sobriety

Curt would start with pornographic videos. Once he was somewhat excited, he would get in his car and start cruising the part of his city in which many of the strip clubs were concentrated. Curt would stop at adult bookstores and buy videos. Then he would stop at several of the clubs. While watching the dancers, he would call an escort service and arrange to meet a woman in a motel. After sex with her, he would think of the risks he took as a married man and as a professional person (Curt was an elected official). He would promise himself never to do it again. Yet within a few days, he would tell himself that he just wanted to look at the videos for a little bit. Watching the videos were not public or risky—just entertaining. And sometimes he would just watch and masturbate. Yet inevitably watching the videos led to a desire to cruise in his car—just to see what was happening in the street. Curt would rationalize that he could simply not go into the strip clubs. Yet he always would. Sometimes in the strip club, he would hold out before making the phone call. He held on to the delusion that he was still in control. There were even occasions when he would tell himself he would give the woman money and simply go home. That never happened either.

Eventually a bunch of things happened all in one day. First, from his family physician he received a diagnosis of hepatitis C—a serious sexually transmitted disease. In the afternoon, he was called by the outcall/escort service he used most often. They had his name, phone number, and address. They wanted to talk business, which turned out to be a blackmail threat. And the worst, his wife, Joan, was listening in on the conversation. This was a bad day for the addict but a good day to begin recovery. Curt started by being partially honest with his wife. The prostitute was a one time event that he did because their sex life had been so sparse. Further, he revealed his hepatitis C diagnosis, telling her he had contracted it during this one time event.

Curt knew he was in enough trouble to seek help. He went to see a therapist named Jack. His therapist listened to the whole story and then very carefully reconstructed how many times this had happened over the previous year. Curt was very surprised to realize he had been sexual with forty-seven women in the previous year, or about once every week. Further, Jack pointed out that the masturbation with videos occurred every two to three days. Together, Jack and Curt figured out that he was averaging about four hundred dollars on each prostitute and about sixty dollars a video. Net cost for the year was in the neighborhood of twenty-seven thousand dollars.

Jack asked Curt to agree to bring in all of his videos and not to use them anymore. Nor was he to go into the parts of town where the strip clubs and adult bookstores were. If he had to be in that area, he had to arrange for someone to be with him. Jack was helping Curt develop boundaries for himself. In one of their sessions, they did a ceremony around destroying the videos. Curt was caught in predictable addictive cycles. Eliminating the videos and cruising bypassed the triggers for the acting out. Curt was beginning to establish sobriety.

Curt came to accept that he was a sex addict, disclosed everything to his wife, went to meetings, and had a sponsor. Jack surprised him in session one day by asking Curt to consider a period of celibacy. He said it would help Curt learn about himself and his sexuality. Curt found it very upsetting. So did his wife, who had been stung by Curt saying that he had acted out because they were not sexual enough. She was afraid that if they stopped, Curt would use it as an excuse to start again. So they came in to talk to Jack together. Jack explained that to take a vacation from sex would enhance both their sexuality and their therapy. Being celibate awakened interest in each other sexually for both Curt and his wife, Joan. That is when they started learning about what sex really was.

Usually sobriety starts with a sponsor or therapist asking the addict to stop a specific dysfunctional, destructive, or dangerous behavior. As in Curt's case, this usually takes the form of a contract that the addict refrain from specific sexual activities. Fairly early in recovery, addicts will also commit to a period of celibacy. Usually this lasts from eight to twelve weeks and includes all forms of erotic activity, including sex with self. Some recovering people extend that time because the lessons are so useful. Here are the reasons for a celibacy period:

- Often times there are so many complications due to the addict's unmanageability, it provides a cooling-off period in which to do damage control.
- The addict who learns to handle emotions without any sexual crutch becomes more available for therapy.
- Therapists have noticed that repressed childhood memories start to emerge during a period of celibacy.
- A celibacy period has long been used by therapists as a way to stimulate healthy sexual

interest.
- Celibacy provides an important context for defining what sobriety is, what relapse is, and what healthy sex is.

The goal of celibacy is not to create sexual anorexia, but rather to provide important perspective on reclaiming sexuality, which has been lost amidst the cycles of addiction and anorexia. Curt discovered the impact his dad had on his sexuality by sharing his pornography with Curt, starting when he was eleven. He learned to label that as a form of child abuse. Joan discovered that she had shut down sexually starting with a series of date rapes in her teens. When Curt became distant because of work and addiction, he paralleled the experience she had had with the man who had assaulted her. But she thought this happened to all women. Both had "normalized" these events. Now they had to face the deeper issues in their lives, including what it meant to be a man and a woman.

When beginning a period of celibacy, the following suggestions may help:

- View it as a time-out, not an end. A celibacy period will provide you space to refocus on other needs. It is not a sentence, not the end of your sexuality. On the contrary, celibacy will make you fully aware of your sexual self.
- Work through commitment issues with your partner. The decision to be celibate will affect your partner. Respecting your partner means involving him or her in your thinking, so you can commit together to the celibacy period.
- Get support from your therapist, sponsor, and group. You will need their guidance and help to maximize the experience. Being open with those in your support network will help you to implement your plan.
- Expect that it will raise issues. For many, this change is drastic and places life issues in sharp relief. Make this a goal and not a surprise.
- Understand that resistance is typical. You may experience anger and resentment at first. This isn't surprising. We seldom embark gracefully on any ordeal that involves significant change and insight.
- Prepare yourself to experience new feelings. The new feelings that emerge will be guides to parts of yourself you need to reclaim. As uncomfortable as these feelings may be, they will serve as significant allies in helping you become all that you are.
- Plan active tasks to enhance the experience. Select a specific Step to work on, work on assignments from your therapist to help you accept nurturing and develop spiritual and sexual awareness, and keep a journal about the experience.

Defining What Sobriety Is

Karen started being sexual on the Internet in the early nineties. She used e-mail to talk with friends of her husband and neighbors. The e-mail relationships turned into affairs. Karen loved the romance and intrigue of cybersex. That her wealthy husband was preoccupied with business and civic activities made her angry, which added the momentum of getting even. One way to get even is to have affairs with your spouse's friends. She expanded her activities to trading nude pictures. From there she started to collect pornography. All this came crashing down when her husband discovered one of her affairs.

Karen entered recovery and did most of the right things: meetings, therapy, workshops and sponsor. Yet she left out parts—like her compulsive masturbation. She did not want to give it up nor did she consider it as hurting anyone. She also stayed in touch by e-mail with a lover—the very one her husband had told her that if she saw again, the marriage was over. Karen rationalized contact by believing that it was not sexual. They were not sleeping together, so technically she was sober. There came an evening when she was going to attend an event that her old lover was at. Her group had suggested she take a friend with her so she would not be at risk. The group did not know about the e-mail contact. Karen reported that even though the friend was there, she had eye contact with the old lover. From that moment on she was lost. The next day they saw each other and had sex. Her husband also found out about their being together. He was already distrustful of this recovery stuff and this blew all trust forever.

Karen's e-mails were like Curt's videos. They were the beginning of her acting-out scenario. It is imperative to have the total picture of your addictive cycle in order to define your sobriety. To simply say "I will not have sex outside of marriage" is not enough. You have to map out carefully the most likely ways you will act out and eliminate the roads that lead there. This process is called "relapse prevention planning." It starts with identifying the most likely scenarios of relapse and then you specify what your sobriety is. Then you develop a plan to prevent relapse. Start by describing the chain of events that go into your acting out.

Relapse Scenarios

The following worksheets are designed to help you identify the most likely way you would act out again. If stuck, it might help you to review the work you did on your addictive cycles in chapter two. Select the most probable ways you would set up acting out. In figure 6.2, the relapse scenarios for both Curt and Karen have been laid as if they were steps downward. Recorded on each step is a behavior, event, or action that leads toward sexually compulsive behavior. Underneath each step is an example of Curt's or Karen's self-talk. These are phrases they would tell themselves to justify taking the next step. On page 169, map out each potential scenario you know could bring you to relapse.

When you have completed each scenario, title the scenario. For example, Curt's might be "Path to Prostitution." Karen's could be "E-mail Nightmare." We will use these titles in a later chapter. Also complete the section in each scenario that calls for you to list the probable preconditions. Include such factors as depletion, anger at spouse, completion of project, or overwhelmed at work. Then return to the earlier section in this chapter on sobriety challenges. List whatever issues you have identified as potential problems within yourself that could contribute to this scenario. Thus, you would list such things as entitlement, compulsive busyness, isolation, or ignoring common sense.

Finally, in the lower left-hand corner of the worksheet, there is a place for you to list the probable outcomes. On the basis of your experience, what is most likely to happen because of these events? Further, you are asked to specify what the risks are. What is the worst that could have happened? When you have completed this analysis, share your work with your therapist, group, and sponsor. After you complete the worksheet, do the exercise on "fire drills." Then you will be

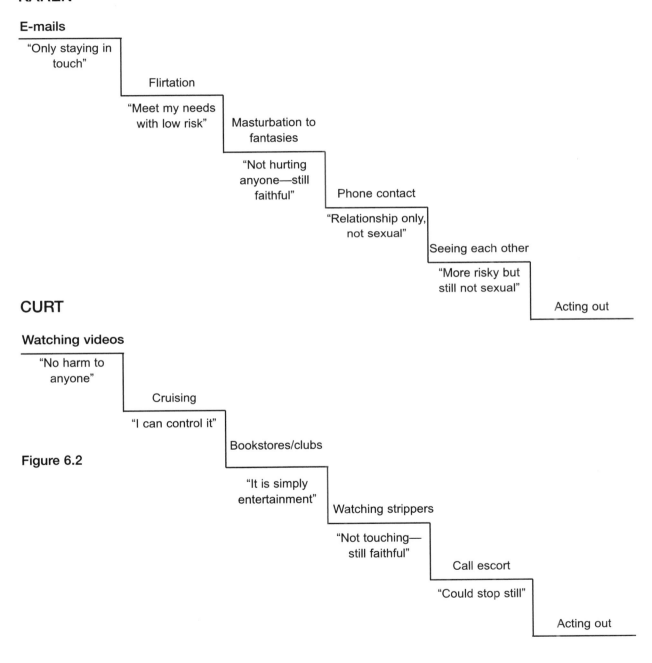

KAREN

E-mails
"Only staying in touch"

Flirtation
"Meet my needs with low risk"

Masturbation to fantasies
"Not hurting anyone—still faithful"

Phone contact
"Relationship only, not sexual"

Seeing each other
"More risky but still not sexual"

Acting out

CURT

Watching videos
"No harm to anyone"

Cruising
"I can control it"

Bookstores/clubs
"It is simply entertainment"

Watching strippers
"Not touching—still faithful"

Call escort
"Could stop still"

Acting out

Figure 6.2

ready to proceed to the next section in which you will write your sobriety statement. Use extra sheets of paper if necessary.

Scenario Worksheet 1

Scenario 1: _____

Probable preconditions present

1. _____
2. _____
3. _____
4. _____

1.

Self-talk _____
_____
_____

2.

Self-talk _____
_____
_____

Personal sobriety challenges present

1. _____
2. _____
3. _____
4. _____

3.

Self-talk _____
_____
_____

Worst possible consequences:

_____
_____
_____
_____

↑

Probable consequences:

_____
_____
_____
_____

4.

Self-talk _____
_____
_____

5.

Self-talk _____
_____
_____

6.

Scenario Worksheet 2

Scenario 2: _____

Probable preconditions present

1. _____
2. _____
3. _____
4. _____

1.

Self-talk _____
_____
_____

2.

Self-talk _____
_____
_____

Personal sobriety challenges present

1. _____
2. _____
3. _____
4. _____

3.

Self-talk _____
_____
_____

4.

Self-talk _____
_____

Worst possible consequences:

_____
_____
_____
_____

↑

Probable consequences:

_____
_____
_____
_____

5.

Self-talk _____
_____
_____

6.

Scenario Worksheet 3

Scenario 3: _____

Probable preconditions present

1. _____

2. _____

3. _____

4. _____

1.

Self-talk _____
_____
_____

Personal sobriety challenges present

1. _____

2. _____

3. _____

4. _____

2.

Self-talk _____
_____
_____

3.

Self-talk _____
_____
_____

4.

Self-talk _____
_____
_____

Worst possible consequences:

_____
_____
_____
_____

↑

5.

Self-talk _____
_____
_____

6.

Probable consequences:

_____
_____
_____
_____

Fire Drill Planning Sheet

A fire drill is an exercise in planning what to do in an emergency. In relapse prevention, fire drill means what you will do if it looks as if you are about to relapse. To use the fire drill metaphor, you see and smell the smoke and you know the fire is about to start. The fire drill is a routine set of steps put into action immediately, should trouble be near. This is an automatic protection plan. The success of the fire drill depends on three elements:

- a clear alarm (a good sign of trouble)
- very concrete steps to be taken
- a routine way to practice the concrete steps.

Review the scenarios you have just completed. Complete the following exercise by listing symptoms or signs of trouble, specific action steps you can take, and ways you can practice (or drill) for resisting relapse. Show this worksheet to your group, sponsor, and therapist. Ask them to critique the steps you have listed. Encourage them to be honest, and be willing to listen. It could make a huge difference later. This extra effort on your part, along with the scenario worksheets, will help you to be thorough in your sobriety definition.

Fire Drill Planning Sheet

First, enter specific signs that there may be a relapse problem. Then describe action steps you will take and indicate how you can practice the action steps. The success of the plan depends on how specific you can make it.

Symptom or Sign of Trouble	Practice or Drill Steps	Immediate Action Steps
Crusing in risk area	*Call my sponsor regularly*	*Call my sponsor*
1.	1.	1.
2.	2.	2.
3.	3.	3.
4.	4.	4.
5.	5.	5.
6.	6.	6.
7.	7.	7.
8.	9.	8.
9.	9.	9.
10.	10.	10.

Sobriety Definition

A sobriety statement has three components. First, there is the abstinence list. These are the behaviors, that are part of your addiction. Part of your sobriety then is to abstain from these behaviors. Curt, for example, would list watching pornographic videos, going to strip clubs, and calling prostitutes. Second is the boundaries list. Here are the things you do not do because they create a hazard to your recovery. It is best if these are very concrete. Curt simply does not go into the part of town where he would act out—unless he is accompanied. If he does, that does not mean he has relapsed. But to go there does not add to his recovery. Karen might include in her boundaries list that she does not use e-mail. Later she may revise it to using e-mail only with women.

Finally, there is the sex and relation plan that asks what you are working toward sexually. Sobriety does not mean anorexia. It means to explore your sexuality in healthy ways. One often hears a recovering person say jokingly "That isn't in my plan." More than likely, they are referring to some behavior on their abstinence list. Yet the plan is not intended to be restrictive. It is designed to map out sexual and relational areas to explore. This is a big project that will go far beyond your initial list. In fact, when we wrote *Sexual Anorexia: Overcoming Sexual Self-Hatred*, more than half the book is dedicated to the process of developing a healthy sexuality for addicts and anorexics. It becomes an ongoing process. Yet you have to start with an initial description of what you would like to work on. As with the abstinence and the boundaries lists, your work needs to be very specific.

Taken together, these three lists become your sobriety statement. It is reviewed and discussed by your therapist, your group, and your sponsor. It becomes an agreed-upon contract about how you will conduct your life. It can change. For example, you may discover new behaviors that you need to add to the abstinence list or remove boundaries that are no longer necessary as you become healthier. Your sex plan will definitely expand as your recovery matures. Over the years, your sobriety statement (all three lists) will become a well-worn document that will serve you well.

Your sponsor or therapist may ask you to use the three-circle method of making these lists. To do so, the addict takes a large piece of newsprint and draws three concentric circles. The inner circle is the abstinence list, the middle circle is the boundaries list, and the outer circle is the sex plan. Figure 6.3 illustrates what this looks like.

Using a big piece of paper has the advantage of having it all in one place so it is easy to show to others. It is a very helpful way to do the work, affording a lot of space to work in. Other people can write comments and encouragement on it as well.

In this workbook we separate the components out. You will find on the following pages worksheets for each segment of your sobriety definition. Feel free to choose either method. Or do the three circles on the big sheet of paper as a worksheet, and distill it over the next pages.

Three-Circle Method
Figure 6.3

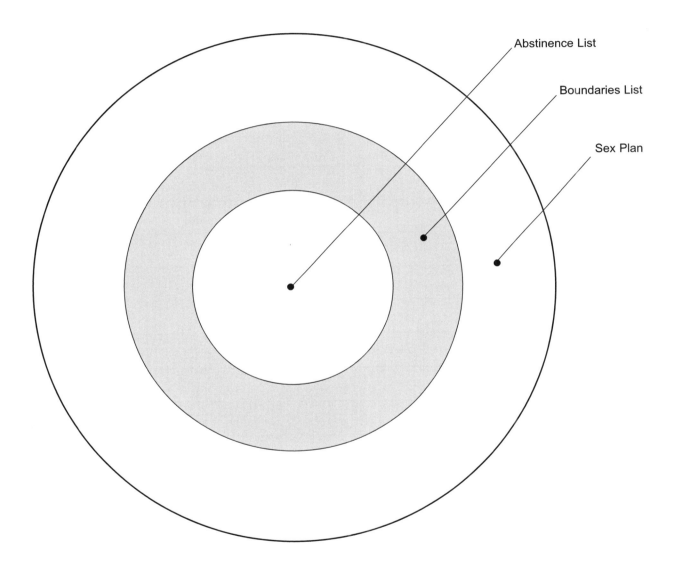

Abstinence List

Boundaries List

Sex Plan

Abstinence List

"Abstinence" means concretely defining behaviors that you will abstain from as part of your recovery. To use one of these behaviors again means a slip; to continue it over a period of time means a relapse. You identify these behaviors when you admit your powerlessness over them and you specify your unmanageability. List as many behaviors as you need to. Be very specific and concrete. Remember that addicts often amend, add to, or delete from their lists as circumstances and recovery warrant. No change should be made, however, without consulting with your group, sponsor, or therapist.

Example: No visits to strip joints, prostitution or outcall services, or pornography stores or theaters.

Your Abstinence   As of (date): _____

1. _____

2. _____

3. _____

4. _____

5. _____

6. _____

7. _____

8. _____

9. _____

10. _____

11. _____

12. _____

13. _____

14. _____

15. _____

(Continue as required)

Boundaries List

Boundaries are self-imposed limits that promote health or safety. They may involve situations, circumstances, people, and/or behavior that you avoid because they are dangerous, jeopardize your abstinence, or do not add to your recovery or your spirituality. Boundaries are guides to help you toward health. Crossing over a boundary does not signify a relapse but, rather, a need to focus again on priorities. List below boundaries that will help your recovery. Be as concrete as possible.

Your Boundaries   As of (date): _____

1. _____

2. _____

3. _____

4. _____

5. _____

6. _____

7. _____

8. _____

9. _____

10. _____

11. _____

12. _____

13. _____

14. _____

15. _____

16. _____

17. _____

18. _____

19. _____

20. _____

21. _____

22. _____

23. _____

24. _____

25. _____

26. _____

27. _____

28. _____

29. _____

30. _____

Healthy Sexuality and Relationship Plan

Start by listing ten sexual and relationship goals you have. If you have difficulty—and most addicts do—get a consultation from your sponsor, group members, or therapist. After you have identified your goals, go back and list specific steps you can take and resources you might use. Remember, you are looking for areas you wish to improve. These are uncharted waters for many. If you do not have a partner, you can still work on various dimensions of your sexuality. Consult *Sexual Anorexia: Overcoming Sexual Self-Hatred.* All of the activities have a relationship version and an individual version.

Example:

Goal: I would like to be present emotionally with my partner during sex. All the activities have a relationship version and individual version.

Action Steps: Practice being here and now in general. Talk to partner about it. Make an effort to share feelings every time we are sexual. Identify ways I disappear. Make a list of reasons I disappear. Discuss in therapy.

Resources: Get help from partner. Ask therapist for strategies. Find books that can help. Go to workshop on sexual recovery. Do couple's exercises on sexuality. Talk to RCA group about what other couples do.

Goal: _____

_____

Action Steps: _____

_____

Resources: _____

Goal: _____

_____

Action Steps: _____

_____

Resources: _____

Goal: _____

_____

Action Steps: _____

_____

Resources: _____

Goal: _____

_____

Action Steps: _____

_____

Resources: _____

Goal: _____

_____

Action Steps: _____

_____

Resources: _____

Goal: _____

_____

Action Steps: _____

_____

Resources: _____

Goal: _____

_____

Action Steps: _____

_____

Resources: _____

Goal: _____

_____

Action Steps: _____

_____

Resources: _____

Goal: _____

_____

Action Steps: _____

_____

Resources: _____

Preventing Relapse

Imagine a boulder on top of a hill. You have been given the job of keeping that boulder there. If it rolls down the hill, it will cause all kinds of damage. At the bottom of the hill is a large lake. If the boulder hits the water, it will be much more difficult to retrieve. The boulder serves as an important stabilizer for all that is around it, so it would be important keep it up there. And if it were to fall, it is your job to return it.

As this big rock rests there, it takes little or no effort on your part to keep things in balance. But let us say that the land becomes unstable and the boulder starts to roll down the hill. Where is the best place for you to intervene? At the top it might take only 20 percent of your strength to stop the boulder's momentum. By the time it is halfway down the hill, it might take 100 percent of your ability to stop it. At the bottom of the hill, it may have so much speed and power, you may not be able to stop it. Figure 6.4 illustrates the principle of the boulder gaining momentum.

Obviously, it is best to keep the rock stable in the first place. But if you have to intervene, it is far better to do it at the top of the hill, than "last ditch" efforts at the bottom. So it is with recovery. It is better to keep stable or intervene early. Using the rolling-boulder analogy, let us construct how the addictive cycle can reassert itself in your life. A very predictable sequence of events occurs in relapse. These events follow the basic components you already know: obsession and preoccupation, ritualization, sexual compulsion and despair. By following the cycle, we can create an anatomy of relapse.

Obsession and Preoccupation—Relapse typically starts with lifestyle imbalance. Stress and neglect take their toll. Sobriety challenges start to appear. "I deserve it," "I want what I want when I want it," and "Damn the consequences, full speed ahead" become the refrains. Urges and cravings appear, feeding obsession and preoccupation. The addict starts to distort reality and impaired thinking creeps in. Denial and delusion become partners with the obsession.

Ritualization—Boundaries start to collapse when addicts start to test themselves: Cruising in acting-out neighborhoods. Calling the massage parlor or escort services to "ask for prices" just out of curiosity. E-mailing the old lover because you were thinking about him. These tests are really at the edge of the old ritualized patterns. Typically, active addicts do not have coping strategies in place to stop ritualized behavior. Remember, the purpose of ritual is to alter awareness and go into trance. Once there, reality becomes fully distorted and loss of control is almost inevitable.

Sexual Compulsion—Once there is an initial slip, addicts tend to say, "I have gone this far, I might as well do the whole thing." A famous pioneer in relapse prevention, G. Allen Marlett, called this the "abstinence violation effect." In addictive thinking, the situation is now hopeless, which leads to ongoing use.

Figure 6.5 uses our boulder analogy and the addictive cycle to graphically show the progression of a relapse. The more the cycle engages, the harder the relapse is to stop. The obvious place to start is to keep the boulder from starting to roll in the first place. You have to build up a barrier that keeps you from going down the classic "slippery slope." Here are some suggestions about how to build that barrier:

Resisting Addictive Cravings
1. *Develop spiritual strategies.* Meditation, yoga, prayer—whatever strategies help you con-

Figure 6.4

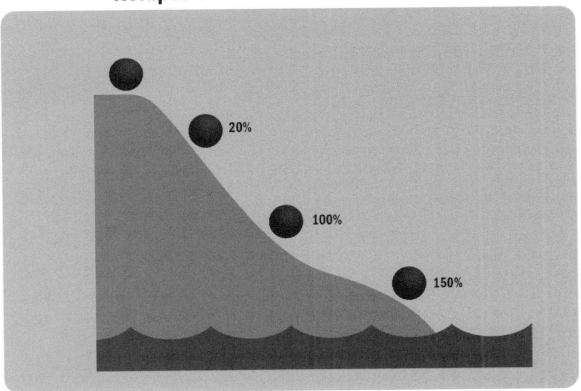

Relapse Prevention: Loss of Control

©2005 Relapse Prevention: Loss of Control, Dr. Patrick Carnes, Ph.D.

nect with yourself and the rhythm of the universe—need to be deepened, strengthened, and practiced. Number one on almost everyone's list is the development of a spiritual base—a calm center, which helps you resist turmoil on the periphery.

2. *Decode feelings.* Sex that is about addiction and not sexuality is usually accompanied by feelings of shame, loneliness, fear, pain, or anger. Always check for these feelings. Remember that to act out a feeling sexually does not resolve the feeling. If you cannot decode your feelings, consult with a sponsor, a therapist, or group members. Remember the old Twelve Step aphorism: "Horniness equals loneliness."

3. *Avoid trigger situations.* Identify situations, persons, and circumstances that can trigger addictive responses. Respect your powerlessness and avoid those triggers. Remember, when in doubt, don't.

4. *Forgive yourself for slips.* If a slip occurs, turn it into a learning experience. Be gentle with yourself. Your shame will cause you to beat up on yourself, which will make you even more vulnerable.

5. *Work on nurturing yourself.* Exercise. Walk. Eat well. Rest. Enjoy massages, baths, and safe indulgences. Seek out nature, music, art, humor, and the companionship of good friends. Find time to take care of yourself. Make your living space a cocoon for your transformation. Buy yourself a teddy bear. You deserve this treatment.

6. *Avoid keeping cravings secret.* Keeping your cravings secret will add to their power. When you feel like acting out, go to the people you trust so you are not alone. In general, secrets are about shame, and shame always makes you more vulnerable. Secrets will separate you from others in recovery.

7. *Find alternative passions.* Practice hobbies, sports, and activities you enjoy. Cultivate these parts of your life so compulsive patterns in working, obsessing, or acting out have to compete with activities and interests that are rewarding. Alternative passions become new arenas for growth.

8. *Acknowledge your choices.* Avoid the feeling that you are a victim. You are powerless about your addiction, but you are in charge of your program of recovery and your lifestyle. In most areas you have choices, which can help you achieve the balance needed in your life. Be proactive instead of reactive, by acknowledging to yourself and to others what your choices are.

The most important strategy is to create a recovery zone. The recovery zone is a lifestyle that if you stay within certain parameters, you will be safe. The trick is creating those parameters.

Creating Your Recovery Zone: The Personal Craziness Index

Most of us have had the experience of being really "on". Everything clicks together. Complicated challenges seem effortless. Problems are simply problems. And you feel great. There is an optimum zone of psychological and physical health for each of us. An essential task in life is to figure out how to stay in that zone. Recovery in many ways is the reclaiming of that zone as you emerge from addictive illness. Sometimes recovery is perceived as an effort to avoid stress, when in fact good recovery means resilience. We will always have stressors and challenges. Recovery is much like training for athletes. Olympic competitors or professional athletes know that to succeed, they will experience great stress. Therefore, what they do is train for it. They work every day

Relapse Prevention: Addiction Cycle

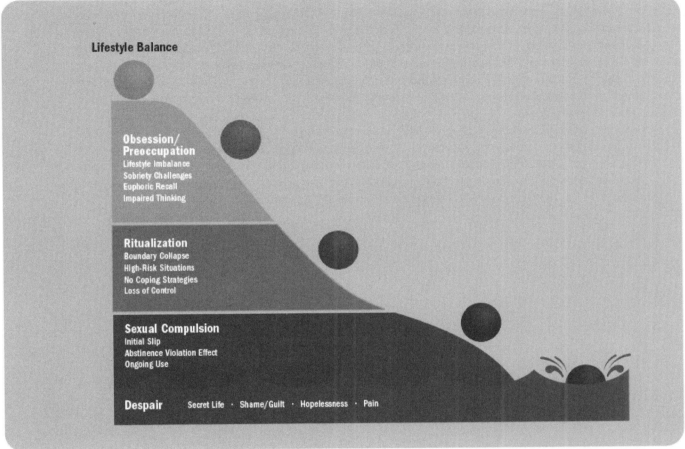

©2005 Relapse Prevention: Addiction Cycle, Dr. Patrick Carnes, Ph.D.

Figure 6.5

to prepare for the stressful event, be it a game or tournament. Similarly, recovering people prepare every day so that a stressor will not be overwhelming. They plan, they practice, they develop skills and strategies. They build their stamina and reserves so they can perform consistently. Sponsors and therapists coach and mentor so that when the challenge comes, they are prepared.

Some years ago we developed a self-assessment process called the Personal Craziness Index or the PCI (pronounced pick-key). Over the years it has really helped many people establish basic parameters of their recovery zone. It starts with the very basic practices that help us be "on." Put another way, it keeps the boulder in place. When addicts actually observe and work their PCI process, it dramatically reduces the potential for relapse. To do it well takes time—and you may wish to refine it as you go. But the daily self-assessment of your PCI keeps you very mindful of your recovery zone.

There are two ways to do the PCI. You can complete the one in this book, which is specifically adapted for sex addicts, or you can go to recoveryzone.com, a Web site dedicated to helping recovering people establish the parameters of their recovery zone. There is an interactive personal craziness index on that site that will help you focus each day. Other resources reside there as well. Either "pick-key" can make a real difference in establishing balance in your life.

Personal Craziness Index

The Personal Craziness Index (PCI) is based on two assumptions: 1) craziness first manifests itself in routine, simple behaviors that support self-maintenance, and 2) behavioral signs will occur in patterns involving divergent sectors in our lives. Thus, we can be caught up in issues of cosmic importance and not notice that our checking account is overdrawn. If our checking account is overdrawn, we are probably out of socks as well because we have not done our laundry. If this pattern is pervasive, there is risk that our lives will become emotionally bankrupt as well—cosmic issues notwithstanding.

Addicts are particularly vulnerable to the "insanity" of loss of reality due to neglecting basics. "Keep it simple" and a "One day at a time" are not shopworn clichés but guidelines borne by the experience of many recovering people. The PCI serves as a reminder each day of what we need to do. Without a process for such reminders, "cunning and baffling" self-destructive behavior returns.

The process of creating your own PCI is designed to be as value-free as possible. Each person uses the index by setting his or her own criteria. In other words, generate behavioral signs (or as they are termed, "critical incidents"), that, through your own experience, you have learned to be danger signs or warnings that you are "losing it, "getting out of hand," or "burnt out." The boulder is ready to roll. Thus, it will be by your own standards that you will prepare yourself. The following are twelve areas of personal behavior suggested as sources of danger signs. You may substitute one of your own if you wish.

1. Physical Health—The ultimate insanity is to not take care of our bodies. Without our bodies we have nothing, yet we seem to have little time for physical conditioning. Examples are being over a certain weight, having missed regular exercise for two days, smoking more cigarettes than normal, being exhausted from lack of sleep. How do you know that you are not taking care of your body? (at least three examples)

_____

_____

_____

_____

2. Transportation—How people get from place to place is often a statement about their lifestyles. Take, for example, a car owner who seldom comes to a full stop, routinely exceeds the speed limit, runs out of gas, does not check the oil, puts off needed repairs, has not cleaned the back seat out in three months, and averages three speeding tickets and ten parking tickets a year. Or the bus rider who always misses the bus, never has change, forgets his or her briefcase on the bus, etc. What are the transportation behaviors that indicate your life is getting out of control? (at least three examples)

_____

_____

_____

_____

3. Environment—To not have time to do your personal chores is a comment on the order of your life. Consider the home in which the plants go unwatered, fish unfed, grocery supplies depleted, laundry not done or put away, cleaning neglected, dishes unwashed, etc. What are ways in which you neglect your home or living space? (at least three examples)

_____

_____

_____

_____

4. Work—Chaos at work is risky for recovery. Signs of chaotic behavior are phone calls not returned in twenty-four hours, chronic lateness for appointments, being behind in promised work, an unmanageable in-basket, and "too many irons in the fire." When your life is unmanageable at work, what are your behaviors? (at least three examples)

_____

_____

_____

_____

5. Interests—What are some positive interests besides work that give you perspective on the world? Music, reading, photography, fishing, or gardening are examples. What are you doing when you are not overextended? (at least three examples)

_____

_____

_____

6. Social Life—Think of friends in your social network who constitute significant support for you and are not family or significant others. When you become isolated, alienated, or disconnected, what behaviors are typical of you? (at least three examples)

_____

_____

_____

_____

7. Family/Significant Others—When you are disconnected from those closest to you, what is your behavior like? Examples are silent, overtly hostile, passive-aggressive. (at least three examples)

_____

_____

_____

_____

8. Finances—We handle our financial resources much like our personal ones. Thus, when your checking account is unbalanced, or worse, overdrawn, or bills are overdue, or there is no cash in your pocket, or you are spending more than you earn, your financial overextension may parallel your emotional bankruptcy. List the signs that show when you are financially overextended. (at least three examples)

_____

_____

_____

_____

9. Spiritual Life and Personal Reflection—Spirituality can be diverse and include such methods as meditation, yoga, and prayer. Personal reflection includes keeping a personal journal, completing daily readings, and pursuing therapy. What are sources of routine personal reflection that are neglected when you are overextended? (at least three examples)

_____

_____

_____

_____

_____

10. Other Addictions or Symptom Behaviors—Compulsive behaviors that have negative consequences are symptomatic of your general well-being or the state of your overall recovery. When you watch inordinate amounts of TV, overeat, bite your nails— any habit you feel bad about afterward—these can be signs of burnout or possible relapse. Symptom behaviors are behaviors that are evidence of overextension, such as forgetfulness, slips of the tongue, or jealousy. What negative addiction or symptom behaviors are present when you are "on the edge"? (at least three examples)

_____

_____

_____

_____

_____

11. Twelve Step Practice—Living a Twelve Step way of life involves many practices. When done consistently, they can be key to staying in your recovery zone. Group attendance, Step work, sponsorship, service, and Twelve Step calls become the foundation of a good recovery. Which recovery activities do you neglect first when you are leaving your recovery zone? (at least three examples)

_____

_____

_____

_____

_____

12. Sexuality—For sex addicts, monitoring yourself sexually becomes very important. You must notice if there are sexual signs that you are not doing well, such as cravings for old behaviors, feelings of shame around sexual issues, or sexual aversion toward your partner. Also, there are the things you may be working on to improve your sexual life. What do you notice that happens (or doesn't happen) sexually that tells you things are not going well? (at least three examples)

_____

_____

_____

_____

Recording Your PCI

The PCI is effective only when a careful record is maintained. Recording your daily progress in conjunction with regular journal-keeping will help you to stay focused on priorities that keep life manageable; work on program efforts a day at a time; expand your knowledge of personal patterns; provide a warning in periods of vulnerability to self-destructive cycles or addictive relapse.

From thirty-six or more signs of personal craziness you recorded, choose the seven that are most critical for you. At the end of each day, review the list of seven key signs and count the ones you did that day, giving each behavior one point. Record your total for that day in the space provided on the chart. If you fail to record the number of points each day, that day receives an automatic score of seven. If you cannot even do your score, you are obviously out of balance. At the end of the week, total your seven daily scores and make an "X" on the graph. Pause and reflect on where you are in your recovery. Chart your progress over a twelve-week period.

My seven key signs of personal craziness:

1. _____

2. _____

3. _____

4. _____

5. _____

6. _____

7. _____

Personal Craziness Worksheet

DAY/WEEK	1	2	3	4	5	6	7	8	9	10	11	12
Sunday												
Monday												
Tuesday												
Wednesday												
Thursday												
Friday												
Saturday												
Weekly Total												

PCI Graph

50 — VERY HIGH RISK	
40 — HIGH RISK	
30 — MEDIUM RISK	
20 — STABLE SOLIDITY	
10 — OPTIMUM HEALTH	
0 —	

Interpretation and Use of the PCI

The PCI is useful in early recovery as recovery habits are established. Also, the PCI becomes helpful during periods of stress and vulnerability. Many simply use it as a daily reminder of their progress. These users change the items as they progress in their recovery.

To use the PCI, select seven items from the "critical incidents" you have already listed. Then following the worksheet instructions, you can generate a weekly score ranging from 0 to 49. A guideline for understanding your score follows:

OPTIMUM HEALTH 0–9	Very resilient. Knows limits; has clear priorities; congruent with values; rooted in diversity; supportive; has established a personal system; balanced, orderly, resolves crises quickly; capacity to sustain spontaneity; shows creative discipline.
STABLE SOLIDITY 10–19	Resilient. Recognizes human limits; does not pretend to be more than he or she is; maintains most boundaries; well ordered; typically feels competent, feels supported, able to weather crisis.
MEDIUM RISK 20–29	Vulnerable to relapse. Slipping; often rushed; can't get it all in; no emotional margin for crisis; vulnerable to slip into old patterns; typically lives as if he or she has inordinate influence over others and/or feels inadequate.
HIGH RISK 30–39	Relapse potential. Living in extremes (overactive or inactive); relationships abbreviated; feels irresponsible and is; constantly has reasons for not following through; lives one way, talks another; works hard to catch up.
VERY HIGH RISK 40–49	Relapse probable. Usually pursuing self-destructive behavior; often totally in mission or cause or project; blames others for failures; seldom produces on time; controversial in community; success vs. achievement-oriented.

Tools for Staying in the Zone

In the story of Ulysses, there were mythical figures called the sirens. They were female and partly human characters who sang captivating songs that would lure mariners so they would crash their boats on the rocks. Sailors would have to plug their ears or tie each other to the masts of their ships so they would not founder in the siren's traps. The Greek stories of the siren's songs always depict the songs themselves as intensely sexual, filled with the promise of quenched desire. But the lesson was never to trust the siren's song—no matter how promising or believable.

As an addict you know the siren song of addiction. There was a promise of sexual fulfillment that always turned out to be as disappointing as the last time. Addiction specialists use the term "euphoric recall." In alcoholism, the alcoholic remembers the fun of the party but suppresses memories of the vomiting, the hangover, and the car accident. Similarly, the sex addict remembers pleasurable parts of the experience and blots out the risk, the disease, the feelings of betrayal, the arrest, and the despair. Like the mariner following the siren's song, the addict founders on the rocks following the illusion of addictive promise. One of the hardest lessons addicts learn is that they cannot trust their judgment about these matters. They must ignore, silence, or distance themselves from the song. It will always betray you.

So how do you do that? Boundaries. Two people who have really taught us a lot about boundaries are Pat and Pia Mellody. The book *Facing Co-Dependence* emerged out of their essential collaboration on the importance of boundaries. Pat Mellody tells the story of how he learned about boundaries. He was in a Catholic elementary school with some very abusive nuns. He was troubled with how they treated people and their verbal abuse. His mother told him that it was about them and not about him. He simply had to notice what they did but refuse to let it affect him. Pat's mother gave him the core advice about how to create a psychological boundary and not be affected by what other people say or do. In other words, intentionally create psychological distance. The same process applies to those people or situations that seduce you down the path of relapse. You will notice the presence, but you know the false promise. You simply do not respond.

What follows is a series of tools that will help you keep that distance.

A Letter from You to Yourself...

Imagine you were your own sponsor writing a letter to yourself just at the time you want to act out. What would you say? By writing the letter and carrying it with you, you have a significant resource to pull out at the last minute. Simply writing it creates the psychological distance you need. Take it to your group. Have sponsors and group members write notes on the letter itself. Then when you read it, you will have their support as well. It may help you keep your sobriety.

Instructions:

Address it from you to you. Include the following:

1. What are the probable circumstances under which it is being read?
2. What are the consequences if you ignore the letter?
3. What would you really need at the time of a slip?
4. Give criteria for behavior that is real clear for yourself.
5. What is the hope if you don't act out?
6. What is at stake if you do—what is the plea you need to hear at this moment?

The following is a model letter to give you some ideas.

Dear Chris,

When you feel the urge, pull out this letter. Chances are if you are reading it, there is a pleasurable thrill of the thought of doing something. Please read to the end because if the thought is about acting out, chances are you are alone in contemplating it. So please read.

Each time is the same. There is the thought—the pleasure. There is the anger, the loneliness, the feelings of entitlement. But remember, every time is the same; you will regret terribly what you now want to do.

- You will have to worry about being caught.
- You will wonder if you will get a disease.
- You will despair over your broken commitments.
- You will feel pain at the people you use.
- You will have to tell lies to cover up—always there are lies.
- You will have suicidal feelings.
- You will place all your career success in jeopardy.
- You will never enjoy it—you are always disappointed.
- You will lose yourself for days thinking about God's punishment, even though you know that isn't true.

Right now your addict is seducing you with promises that won't work. So figure out what you need:

- Are you hungry or tired?
- Are you angry?
- Are you overextended?
- Are you needing care?

Find whatever you need and get it. Do not do the one thing that will make all of the above worse.

The question is, if everybody could see what you are about to do, would you still do it? You are lovable and worthwhile. You deserve getting your needs met in a way that respects your wonderfulness. Imagine spirituality that is peaceful, graceful, vibrant, and growing—not what you are about now.

Please listen to yourself. You know that it won't happen for you by acting out. Think of all the faces of those in the past. Remember how you would have to front in order to get out. Do not kid yourself. Instead, love yourself enough to let it pass—let go. Call someone.

Love,

Chris

Emergency First-Aid Kit

Make yourself a psychological emergency first-aid kit. It can be a bag, a "medicine pouch," an envelope, or even a box. Place in it things that provide your life with meaning. Suggestions include

- symbols of recovery, including medallions, tokens, sponsor gifts, and other articles that remind you of significant moments in your recovery
- pictures and mementos of loved ones
- spiritual items
- copies of pages out of this book
- letters
- favorite affirmations, meditations, quotes
- phone numbers of peers and sponsors
- any items that represent personal meaning to you
- tapes of special music

Keep this kit in a place that is easy for you to get to. If you feel you are about to relapse or already have slipped, pull out the kit to get support for what you need to do.

Relapse Contract

Use the following contract as a way to talk to people important to you (i.e. sponsor, therapist, clergyperson) about what you will do if you do slip. Make a copy of the contract for that person, and keep a copy for yourself.

I (your name), _____ , do contract that if I have a slip in my sexual sobriety, to do the following:

I will make my very best effort to limit what I have done.

I will call you and let you know what my situation is.

I will also do the following (fill in whatever you and your support person think should be the first steps):

_____

_____

_____

_____

My sobriety date is: _____

Agreed to on this date: _____

Signed, _____

Resisting Relapse

Let's return to the experience of being "on"—when everything you do seems to be exactly right. All performers—singers, speakers, actors, or athletes—have had the experience. You intuitively know what to do with no thought. You just seem to be able to excel. This can happen in business or with hobbies. Even in simply exercising, times occur when your body performs above normal. Athletes will talk about playing "over their heads," meaning far above their normal capabilities. Authors experience moments when words just flow and ideas come seemingly from nowhere. Artists speak of ideas taking form easily and businesspeople refer to deals "coming together." There are days when you are simply unbeatable. We have called this the recovery zone

Neuroscientists tell us that this does not occur accidentally. Typically, these situations are the result of three factors: vision, practice, and resilience. Whether it be a fighter pilot rehearsing combat scenarios or an athlete using guided imagery for peak performance, there usually is a guiding vision. Being able to image a specific result and focusing on that image adds tremendously to bringing that vision into reality. A growing body of evidence shows that following a vision can effect corporate success in business and even accelerate healing in our bodies. You have to have a picture of it. Unfortunately, from a recovery perspective the reciprocal is also true. If you do not believe in recovery, let alone have a picture of how it looks, your chances of being relapse-free decline. Then the familiar, destructive sexual fantasies will provide your image, virtually guaranteeing the relapse process. In the next chapter, we will explore more precisely how that works when we describe the arousal template.

In addition to having a vision, there needs to be practice. When athletes are "in training," they prepare daily for essentially a stressful event, such as a tournament, game, or marathon. Each day they build their strength, push themselves to improve their skills, and practice strategies for winning. When they prepare for the stress, they are in essence activating the vision. As they train, however, they are careful not to "overtrain." They "cross train" so that the demands on one muscle set are not too much. They find regular patterns of rest. They take care of themselves, making sure they not only marshal their resources, but also give themselves real rewards. In short, they cultivate resilience. Resilience means they have reserves, so when they meet the inevitable stressors, they are not pushed beyond what they can do. Rather, the reverse occurs. They perform beyond even their own expectations.

The Greeks had a term for this process. They would describe someone who achieves being "on" as having "virtú"—meaning excellence. During the Middle Ages, the word "virtue" picked up moral connotations. Originally, it was about preparing yourself intellectually, emotionally, and physically to be the best you could be. In this sense, we can look at recovery as the equivalent of creating "virtu"—the cultivation of excellence. Often, people who have successful recoveries talk about how easy things have become and how they are doing things they never thought they would be able to do. Sobriety allowed them to have a new vision for their lives, and using recovery tools and principles every day created the practice and the resiliency necessary to meet the inevitable stressors. We call this living in the recovery zone. Think of a zone as a specific set of parameters or boundaries; by staying in the zone, you are optimizing your performance. By identifying that area of life including work, relationships, body, sex, and spirituality in which you thrive, the goal is to live within that area or zone.

Inevitably you will have stress in your life. As we noted earlier, lifestyle imbalance (translation = stressed out) is the beginning of relapse. The key to relapse prevention is to stay in your recovery zone. In part, you already have started to define that through your sobriety definition and your personal craziness index. The remainder of this workbook is devoted to helping you get clarity about living in your recovery zone. To summarize how far we have come, look at figure 6.6 that illustrates the basic stance for resistance to relapse. Notice that the boulder now is nestled in a hollow supported by lifestyle balance. Addicts can live in a recovery zone being "in training," doing more than they ever thought they could and being all they can be. When they experience challenges, they have prepared themselves for that. So there is a barrier of resilience that keeps them from even starting down the slope of relapse. If events happen that overwhelm the addict and they do start down the slope, four barriers exist to prevent disaster.

Barrier One—Living the recovery essentials (to review go back to page 157) can immediately pull you back into the recovery zone. Your personal craziness index provides concrete measures that you are at risk. The healthy sexuality and relationship plan tells you what you are working for. If successful, you are not living in deprivation. You have the stabilizing experience of knowing what you want sexually and as your recovery matures, you will experience fulfillment. Finally, what anchors all this is a sturdy, enduring decision to commit to recovery. Using the classic language of the Big Book of Alcoholics Anonymous, it is the willingness "to go to any lengths." Most recovering people know that moment when they said to themselves that they simply had to do whatever it took to make their lives different. That commitment is the cornerstone of the first barrier.

Barrier Two—If the stone does get past the initial barrier and a momentum toward relapse does start, we have barrier two. This barrier starts with reality checks. This means that recovering people check out questionable thinking and ideas with the support network. Therapists, sponsors, and other recovering people can quickly spot impaired thinking. If your old sobriety challenges such as grandiosity or entitlement should reappear, they can remind you that you have been down this road before. Most important, your support network helps you remember that it is important to everyone that you maintain your sobriety. What you do does matter to your group, friends, and family. Also, your boundary definitions serve as a very clear guide to staying out of trouble. By this time you have learned to reward yourself appropriately and have competing passions so that you are not operating out of deprivation. Rather than struggling with shame, your basic Step skills (developed in chapters 3 through 5) can help you with your sense of being worthwhile. You are not a bad or sinful person for having to struggle with this addiction. A path exists out of despair that would give momentum to the boulder.

Barrier Three—Further down the slope, you check in about boundary violations. The abstinence list becomes the guide to your behavior. It tells you what you have committed not to do. Moreover, you have the letter to yourself to help bring you back to reality. If you should have a slip, it does not mean that you have totally relapsed. Your fire drills should kick in, as if you were on automatic pilot. You have recovery rituals, such as your daily meditations and meetings, that serve as an alternative to your acting-out rituals. You have learned new coping strategies in dealing with stress. All the resources exist to stop the momentum here.

Barrier Four—If relapse does occur, it does not mean total immersion in the addiction. To begin with, there is a sobriety statement that is a map to where you need to be. Second, you have your first aid kit and all the resources of the twelve step process to bring you back. You have a contract with people to whom you matter about what you will do now. You signed it when you were relatively sane. Just follow the steps you agreed to take when you made the agreement. And if none of this works, you now have people who truly know about your illness and can intervene on your behalf.

By getting this far in this process, you can never really be in your addiction without knowing how to get back. In effect, you have now spoiled it. You will find the delusional thoughts just do not

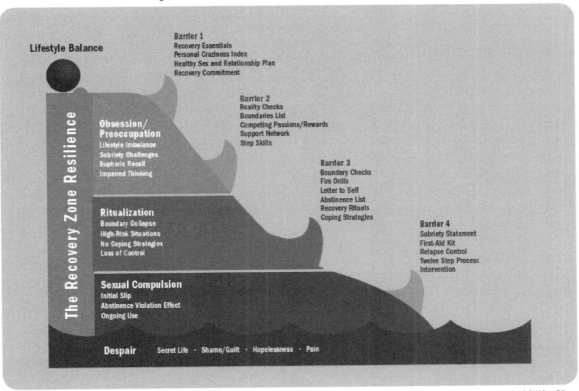

Figure 6.6

work the way they used to. You know that the addiction is the false siren and that you basically are avoiding yourself. You used to wonder if it was at all real. Now you know the unreality. What remains to start recovery for yourself is to look at the deeper issues of sexual arousal and what happens to your body. And that is the focus of the next chapter.

Resisting Relapse Reflection

The critical elements of being in your recovery zone are vision, practice, and resilience. In the following spaces, record your thoughts about each. Start by imagining recovery three years out and what that would be like. Then list what "ways" you can practice. And then specify how you can build resilience into your recovery.

Vision of recovery in three years:

_____

_____

_____

_____

_____

Strategies, skills, and practice now:

_____

_____

_____

_____

_____

Ways to build resilience in my life:

_____

_____

_____

_____

_____

Recommended Reading

Sexual Anorexia, pp. 103–216; *In the Shadows of the Net*, chapter 9, "Preventing Relapse: Maintaining the Changes You've Made."

Pia Mellody. *Facing Co-Dependence.* New York: Harper San Francisco, 1989.

Additional Reading

Ken Adams. *Silently Seduced: When Parents Make Their Children Partners.* Deerfield Beach, FL.: Health Communications, 1991. The best book we've seen on the problem of "specialness."

Claudia Black. *A Hole in the Sidewalk: The Recovering Person's Guide to Relapse Prevention.* Bainbridge, WA.: MAC Publishing, 2000.

Wayne Mueller. *Sabbath: Restoring the Sacred Rhythm of Rest.* New York: Bantam, 1999. One of the best books on the logic of self-care.

Stephen Covey. *The Seven Habits of Highly Effective People.* New York: Simon and Schuster, 1990. A classic that should be required reading for everyone.

M. Scott Peck. *The Road Less Traveled.* New York: Harper and Row Publishers, 1983. The classic guide for participating in therapy.

For Affirmations

Answers in the Heart: Daily Meditations for Men and Women Recovering from Sex Addiction. Center City, Minn.: Hazelden, 1990.

CHAPTER SEVEN: What Has Happened to Your Body?
Managing the Physical Impact of Your Addiction

> The paraphilic solution is one in which love and lovebonding are
> compromised because the genitalia continue to function not in the service of lust, but according to the specifications of a vandalized and redesigned lovemap, and often with compulsive frequency.... Sexual addictions, like drinking and eating addictions, are extremely particular. The sexual addict is always addicted to something sexually specific.
> —JOHN MONEY, LOVEMAPS, 1985

ADDICTION HURTS THE BODY. The stereotypical image of an addict is usually one of an emaciated heroin addict who can no longer find viable veins for injecting or a red-faced alcoholic expectancy steadily declines as their waistlines expand and the terribly emaciated food anorexics whose bodies are little more than flesh and bones. Sex addiction can leave a physical legacy as well, though sadly, it is often unnoticed until more severe damage is done. In this chapter we will look at the physical effects of sex addiction, including sexually transmitted diseases, depression, and withdrawal.

One of the greatest impacts of this disease is on sexual arousal; neuropathways and arousal patterns can be profoundly affected by compulsive sex.

Having a Physical

Sex addicts often have medical complications, so to begin, we strongly urge you to have a thorough physical examination. Thirty-eight percent of the sex addicts we studied in *Don't Call It Love* actually went to an emergency room or emergency physician because of some physical problem related to sexual acting out. Here are some other things we learned:

- 38 percent of the men and 45 percent of the women had contracted venereal disease through their addictive behavior
- 64 percent of addicts continued their sexual behavior despite the risk of disease or infection
- 16 percent of the men and 60 percent of the women were victims of physical abuse during sex
- 19 percent of the men and 21 percent of the women were involved in vehicle

accidents while acting out

- Almost a third of the study participants had serious health problems such as ulcers or high blood pressure which they attributed to the stress of their sexual activities

- 65 percent reported some type of sleep disorder (trouble going to sleep, staying asleep, or waking early)

- 70 percent of the women routinely risked unwanted pregnancy, 40 percent had unwanted pregnancy, and 36 percent had abortions

Pregnancies, abortions, injuries, accidents, AIDS and other diseases, other addictions, major health problems—no one knows how high the cost of sexual addiction is to our health care system. It took decades for us to understand the extraordinary health care costs of alcoholism, and even now, alcoholism professionals have difficulty convincing health care providers that many physical problems can be traced to compulsive drinking. We are at an even more primitive stage with sex addiction, though data like that above are beginning to document the cost for all to see.

Sex addicts often have physical problems and illnesses, but for various reasons they resist seeking help. Consider the following:

Joanna had a chronic sore throat. She had it for so long that she had actually became used to it. When she started recovery, her therapist insisted that she get a physical. During her exam, Joanna was surprised to learn that her sore throat was caused by a sexually transmitted disease called chlamydia. She had it in her throat rather than in its more common location in the vagina. If undiagnosed, the disease would have created serious problems.

Frank learned that he had HPV (Human Papillomavirus) when his wife was diagnosed with the disease. She had been infected by Frank. Sadly, as a result, she was no longer able to have children and now had a chronic debilitating illness. Early intervention would have prevented both problems.

Martin, a physician, a recovering sex addict and drug addict, had contracted AIDS. Living with AIDS, he focused his medical practice on helping others with AIDS. Because he was such an expert on this disease, Martin provided himself with needed medical care, believing that he could do for himself what any other doctor would be able to do, if not more. Prescribing for oneself is an activity that doctors are strictly prohibited from doing, yet Martin prescribed medication for his own depression. He did not do well, became more depressed, relapsed into drug use, and had unprotected sex. His self-medicating cost him his ability to practice medicine for five years.

Do you see the common thread in these examples? None of the persons involved sought appropriate medical help for themselves. In part, such resistance lies in addicts' own "sobriety challenges." Following this behavior that stems from childhood neglect, addicts will not even come to their own aid in times of profound distress, let alone deal with a matter so mundane to them as their own bodies. Another factor in such willfulness can be seen through the phrase, "I can do it myself." Such resistance to get help is further intensified by shame. Many times I have heard the stories of individuals who have damaged their genitals or their anus and were simply too embarrassed even to tell a physician. Instead, they would try to heal themselves only to have the situation worsen. Others attempt self-healing and still continue to act out. It's hard to find a better example of denial.

You must understand that at its core, having a physical is an act of caring for yourself. You can expect your therapist to ask you to make such an appointment. The truth is that you may not know if something is wrong with you that needs to be addressed. Also, you may have to return for further visits because some diseases do not manifest symptoms right away. Table 7.1 shows a list of sexually transmitted diseases, their symptoms, and the problems that will ensue if the illness is left untreated. Review each one to give yourself at least a working knowledge of the potential problems. Even being in a Twelve Step group or serving as a sponsor requires that you know what problems the people you are close to are facing.

Table 7.1

SEXUALLY TRANSMITTED DISEASE	CAUSE	SYMPTOMS	FOLLOW-UP PROBLEMS
Chlamydia	Chlamydia Trachomatis Bacterium	• painful urination • vaginal discharge in women • urethral discharge in men • eye infections possible (most common cause of blindness worldwide) • women often have no symptoms	• women-urethral infection, cervical and pelvic inflammation • men-urethral and epididymal inflammation • newborn-conjunctivitis, chlamydial pneumonia
Genital Herpes	Herpes Simplex Virus (genital HSV-2) (oral HSV-1	• pain, itching in genital areas • vesicles or open sores • dysuria • swollen groin lymph nodes • flulike symptoms (headache, fever)	• newborn infection in passing through the birth canal-brain damage, blindness, or death • herpetic eye infections • herpetic encephalitis
Gonorrhea	Neisseria Gonorrhea Bacterium	• thick, puslike discharge from urethra • burning, frequent urination • women are often asymptomatic for weeks or months • pharyngeal gonorrhea with sore throat after oral sex	• epididymitis in men • pelvic inflammatory disease (PIG) in women-can lead to fallopian tube scarring and infertility • fever, rash, joint pain • arthritis, meningitis, endocarditis
HIV	Human Immuno-Deficiency Virus	• persistent unexplained fatigue • soaking night sweats • shaking chills and fever—over 100 degrees for several weeks • unexplained weight loss-10 percent of body weight in 1-2 months • unexplained enlarged lymph nodes for 3 months • persistent dry cough • bruising blotches in mouth or under skin • chronic diarrhea • persistent headache • white spots on tongue	• opportunistic infections—Pneumocystis carinii • cytomegalovirus • constitutional disease • neurological disease (dementia) • neoplasm (Kaposi's Sarcoma) • death

SEXUALLY TRANSMITTED DISEASE	CAUSE	SYMPTOMS	FOLLOW-UP PROBLEMS
Scabies	(Crabs) Sarcoptes Scabiei Parasite	• severe itching (worse at night) • thin, pencil-like lines (burrows) on skin	• contact dermatitis • secondary skin infection • urticaria

Syphilis	Tyreponema Pallidum Spirochete (Bacterium)	**Primary:**
		• painless sores (chancres) on genitals, rectum, tongue, or lips
		• enlarged lymph nodes (in groin)
		Secondary:
		• rash on body, especially palms and soles
		• aching joints
			• second stage—aching bones and joints
			• tertiary syphilis
			  -general paresis
			  -tabes dorsalis (ataxia, etc.)
			  -joint degeneration
			  -optic atrophy
			  -cardiovascular aortitis

Trichomoniasis	Trichomonas Vaginalis Protozoa	• labial pruritis • vaginal discharge (yellow-green) • dyspareunia • dysuria	• persistent vaginitis • reddened, inflamed cervix • men are often asymptomatic but may have non-specific recurrent urethritis
Venereal or Genital Warts	Human Papilloma Virus (HPV)	• warty growth around vulva, anus, vagina, cervix, penis, scrotum, groin, or thigh • can be microscopic (not seen with the naked eye) • occasionally itching, pain, bleeding	• women with cervical HPV lesions have higher risk of cervical cancer • occasional delivery problem with warts blocking birth canal • shame • other forms of HPV can lead to pelvic inflammatory disease (PID) and sterility in women

Talking with Your Physician

Because so much is asked of them, physicians may be unfamiliar with addictive disorders, particularly sex addiction. The following references can provide useful overviews to help them better understand the problem.

For family practioners, internist, urologists, gynecologists, and emergency medicine physicians:

Carnes, Patrick, Ph.D., and Schneider, Jennifer MD, Ph.D. "Recognition and Management of Addictive Sexual Disorders: Guide for the Primary Care Clinician." *Primary Care Practice* 4, no. 3 (May/June, 2000): 302–318.

For practicing psychiatrists:

Carnes, Patrick, Ph.D., "Sexual Addiction and Compulsion: Recognition, Treatment, and Recovery." *CNS Spectrums: The International Journal of Neuropsychiatric Medicine* 5, no. 10 (October, 2000): 63–72.

You may also call 800-708-1796 for physician material packets, or review the information at the Web site: http://www.sexhelp.com.

Withdrawal and Other Mental Health Issues

At a Boston workshop on sexual addiction, a recovering professional stated in clear terms: "I have now experienced withdrawal from four addictions, including cocaine. By far the worst was from my sexual addiction." This is a common refrain among sex addicts with other addictions. The withdrawal period seems to be difficult for all sex addicts. The SLAA "Big Book" describes it this way: "This unraveling was wrenching. We found it necessary to live through withdrawal in day-at-a-time, twenty-four-hour compartments. We would waken in the morning, sometimes very early, and inwardly exclaim, 'Oh God! Another day of THIS!'" The same source also provides some of the best advice available about withdrawal:

We cannot go through your withdrawal for you, nor would we, if we could.
Who would knowingly volunteer to go through it again? Certainly none of us!
Yet the pain of each withdrawal is unique and special, even precious (although you probably

don't think so). In a sense, the experience is you, a part of you which has been trying to surface for a long time. You have been avoiding or postponing this pain for a long time now, yet you have never been able to lastingly outrun it. You need to go through withdrawal in order to become a whole person. You need to meet yourself. Behind the terror of what you fear, withdrawal contains the seeds for your own personal wholeness. It must be experienced for you to realize, or make real, that potential for you and your life that has been stored there for so long.

In a hospital study, we found there are fifteen symptoms addicts readily identify as characteristic of the early weeks of recovery. Listed by frequency of mention, these symptoms are:

> **fatigue**
> **tenseness, nervousness**
> **insomnia**
> **headaches**
> **shakes**
> **high sexual arousal**
> **low sexual arousal**
> **body aches**
> **increased food appetite**
> **genital sensitivity**
> **itchy skin**
> **chills, sweats**
> **nausea**
> **rapid heartbeat**
> **shortness of breath**

Usually, physical reactions last fourteen to fifteen days, but for some people, they may last for as long as eight to ten weeks. Many who have withdrawn from cocaine report parallels in the withdrawal experiences. These parallels are intriguing, since cocaine appears to be one of the top drugs for sex addicts. Researchers in cocaine have noticed a high incidence of sexual addiction in cocaine addicts.

Speculation exists about whether medication can alleviate severe withdrawal symptoms. Drugs ranging from lithium and Prozac to Depo-Provera have been used for sexual addiction withdrawal. Physicians working with patients who are confronting severe withdrawal also need to take into account the impact of concurrent mental health issues such as depression. Some leaders in the field of addictive disorders neurochemistry urge the use of amino acid compounds to ease the transition period of recovery. Because there is not yet consensus in the field, decisions are currently made on a case-by-case basis.

For most addicts, one of the most disturbing symptoms is insomnia. Given that over two-thirds of sex addicts struggle with sleep disorders, it is not surprising that this problem intensifies in the early weeks of recovery. There are, however, simple lifestyle adjustments and concrete strategies that are very helpful for dealing with sleeplessness. Many of them are described in a book called *Natural Sleep,* written by Philip Goldberg and Daniel Kaufman and published by Rodale Press. Addicts need to review their sleep patterns, determine their body rhythms, watch food intake, develop relaxation strategies, and exercise. Those with more severe sleep disorders may need professional assistance.

Another problem that can be anticipated is appetite changes. In one study, 38 percent of sex addicts who went through treatment had eating disorders. One-half of these people found that their urges to binge-eat increased, while the others actually found their urges decreased. There is no way to predict who will be in which group. We can predict, however, that recovery from sexual addiction will have some impact—positive or negative—on other compulsive behaviors.

How, then, does one deal with multiple addictions? Some typical comments addicts made when asked this question are listed below. Several principles emerge. To begin, the addictions that are the most life threatening should be dealt with first. Generally, this means that if chemical dependency is involved, the addict should begin by detoxifying from chemicals. Then, if sexual addiction is the next most perilous addiction, sexual recovery becomes the priority. This process should continue until each area of compulsivity is addressed. Once recovery is established, a different hierarchy comes into play: the core addiction becomes the primary emphasis of recovery work. Recovery work transfers, however, in that a good recovery program in one area supports progress in others.

Most addicts, were they to go to every group they qualified for, would not have a life outside of group. In other words, it is important not to be obsessive about recovery. Gentleness and progress are vital. Priorities should be set.

When we asked what sustained people during early recovery, the responses were simple and clear:

Once in recovery, many had a lower tolerance for pain and simply did not want to go back to active addiction.

Many felt their emerging spirituality was key.

Some knew that to return to their addiction would mean death.

For a majority, the beginning of renewed self-esteem helped them resist cravings.

Many felt it important to keep their commitment to their Twelve Step group efforts.

Addiction Neuropathways

All addictions use three basic road maps to activate the brain. A fourth, which is based on deprivation, often intermingles with the first three. These physical processes are the neurochemical basis for addictive disorders, and scientists use the term "neuropathways" to describe them. We started to learn about them in the mid-1970s when a series of breakthrough studies helped us understand that addiction was really a problem of the brain. When an alcoholic ingests alcohol, this drug eventually metabolizes into a chemical called dopamine. Another, sometimes faster, route to activating dopamine in the brain is through sexual activity. While the means of activating dopamine varies, the result is the same: you feel better. Exactly how you feel will vary depending on the means you used to activate dopamine production in the first place.

It is important to understand the basic concept of neuropathways for two reasons. First, it will help you understand how the physical component of your addiction works. Second, neuropathways are critical to understanding your own sexual arousal patterns—what we will eventually call the "arousal template." The fundamental fact of sex addiction is that your arousal template may have undergone profound changes as a result of your addiction. Knowing how such a change happens can profoundly affect your ability to remain relapse free. If you wish to learn more about this area, review Milkman and Sunderwirth's book entitled *Craving Ecstasy: The Chemistry and Consciousness of Escape*. It is a well-written and entertaining introduction to the very serious problem of how addictions work. Here is a summary of the neuropathways:

Arousal. The arousal neuropathway is about pleasure and intensity. The most common methods of stimulating arousal pathways are high-risk sex and high-risk relationships, compulsive burglary and shoplifting, "on the edge" business occupations such as day trading or "merger mania," and anything to do with violence. Certain chemicals, including amphetamines, cocaine, and ecstasy, also amplify the arousal neuropathway. Often times, these chemicals enhance or combine with high-risk behavior. We see sex addicts who will be sexual only on cocaine and vice versa. When a chemical and a high-risk behavior are combined, we call this fusing. That means they become a "package" experience. Many chemically dependent people do not recognize that their high-risk behavior is neurochemically part of their "package." They assume it happened *because* they were using.

Usually, addictions specialists call this the "opponent process of addiction"—meaning that high arousal becomes a way to deal with pain. For example, a heroin addict goes through pleasure and ends up in pain just as a long-distance runner goes through pain and ends up in pleasure. The brain always compensates. Addicts exaggerate this "compensation" because their pain is so overwhelming. Some people actually incorporate pain into their pleasure. For example, trauma victims who move into sadomasochism and then escalate it dramatically often are replaying "tapes" of early sexual abuse that was dangerous. Fear may also become part of arousal. For example, some female sex addicts can achieve orgasm only when a man is hurting them, and there are men who find someone arousing only if the encounter in some way puts them at risk. Thus pleasure and danger are fused. Throw in some chemicals and you have a way of amplifying and escalating the experience.

Numbing. This neuropathway produces a calming, relaxing, soothing, or sedative process. It creates an analgesic experience in the brain. While drugs and alcohol are obvious leaders in this sedation process, behaviors such as compulsive masturbation, gambling, shopping, and overeating can also numb worries. The hole to be filled, however, is bottomless. Chemicals typically used for numbing are alcohol, depressant drugs, and heroin. Again, they can be combined with certain behaviors into "packages." Thus can the alcoholic, compulsive overeater binge into oblivion. Whether it is "comfort food" or the mind-numbing repetition of the slot machine, this neuropathway tries to satisfy the insatiable. Milkman and Sunderwirth refer to these practices as the "satiation addictions" whose goal is to keep anxiety at bay.

Addictions used as an analgesic act alone or they can interact with other neuropathways. Gambling of any sort can be mind numbing, for example, but high-stakes gambling or e-trading can also produce a state of very high arousal. An alcoholic uses alcohol just to bury her trouble, or she may also use alcohol to disinhibit herself to take part in high-risk sex. There are sex addicts who uses anonymous sex because of its high risk and excitement, though at other times they use that same behavior to relax. Addicts are constantly wandering in and out of neuropathways, depending on what they need. In terms of recovery, it may be more important to know which neuropathways are involved than which addiction is being used to access it, because knowing the neuropathway reveals the internal problem.

A common scenario we see in sex addiction is the sex addict who spends the evening cruising and taking part in high-risk sex. When he returns home and is too zipped up to sleep, he turns to alcohol, food, TV, or compulsive masturbation to calm down. This pattern of arousal followed by numbing is a common combination in addictive disorders. In fact, this pattern is extremely common for all trauma survivors—from survivors of the Holocaust to natural disasters such as tornadoes and earthquakes. High adrenalin, and excitement followed by efforts to slow down are among the most common subsets of behavior seen in all trauma survivors. The obvious role of numbing to block memories of bad experiences is actually only part of the situation. Another way to combine is to use mindless numbing as a way to trance out—and this brings us to the next neuropathway.

Fantasy. Escape is the goal of this neuropathway. One can alter the perception of reality by using such chemicals as marijuana or psychedelic drugs like LSD. Behaviors like obsession and preoccupation, when combined with the right rituals, can actually create a trance state—the addict literally enters an altered state. Sex addicts are familiar with this trancelike state from experiences with cruising in a car or bar, watching porn, doing cybersex on the Internet, or sitting in a strip bar. Go into a casino and notice how many people have left their cares behind and are preoccupied only with their next win. The doctor who checks his trades between almost every patient has an obsession with money. The alcoholic who becomes a wine connoisseur legitimizes his preoccupation with drinking. The search for the fix becomes an end in itself.

At the core of such obsessions is a governing fantasy. In gambling, that fantasy is the "big win" that will make everything all right—thinking about what you would do with all that money, running mental scenarios about how to spend the money, and imagining what you would say to people. For those with a money obsession (the key to all financial disorders), it is the "windfall" fantasy that gets played over and over. With drugs, the fantasy is the right high with the right stuff. In sex addiction, it involves the right situation and person or the "cosmic relationship" (the windfall man or woman who makes everything good and right). Preoccupation and obsession are about shame and the desire not to be in your body. As a result, addicts create—and inhabit—another reality.

Children who are traumatized or who come from dysfunctional families (and thus are traumatized, too) learn how to "dissociate" from reality. They prefer fantasies and daydreams. Sometimes they act as if their made-up reality is real. They also discover the technique called compartmentalization—the ability to create separate "compartments" in their life into which uncomfortable internal realities can be placed and thus ignored. Many addicts tell us that it seems as though they have "more than one person" living inside them. There is the "real" self as well as another self who enters and takes over. This "secret life phenomenon" is well known to sex addicts. When Robert Louis Stevenson described Jekyll and Hyde, he was describing this phenomenon in alcoholism. Ultimately, exploiting the fantasy neuropathway is a solution to which people turn when acknowledging and living with their "real" self seems too much to bear.

Deprivation. Control is the goal. Anorectic spending, sexual anorexia, and food anorexia share a common assumption: doing without is the surest way to defend against the terror. From this worldview stems a sense of euphoric release—release from the burden of having to deal with deep-seated fears of insufficiency. What is "insufficient?" They believe that there is not "enough" (money, food, sex, and so on), or they fear that they themselves are not "enough," that they are lacking in some way (such as being too fat, too thin, or not attractive, for example). Part of the terror felt by these individuals stems from the belief that something really bad will happen if their needs *are* met or satisfied. Fear of fat, fear of sexual success or of further sexual exploitation, fear of intimacy, fear of financial loss—the list of terror can be endless for some people. They find that if their needs can be controlled, however, they can actually create a feeling of superiority and elation. Much research exists to show that the body prepares itself for starvation by releasing endorphins—a physical effect that produces a feeling of elation in those who starve themselves. Therapists notice a sense of righteousness in these individuals which manifests through rigid and judgmental attitudes toward others—and which provides comforting thoughts when you feel you are in control.

Deprivation serves as a kind of "twin" for excessive behavior—thus creating the phenomenon of "binge and purge." Consider the dieter whose extreme eating patterns are manageable for a while—until they "fall off the wagon." They view this as "failure" and feel ashamed at not measuring up to their own inhuman standards. Taken to its worst extreme it becomes what we call bulimia nervosa—the term used for people who eat and then purge. It's also possible to binge and purge with money. There are people who are caught up in endless cycles of buying and returning goods. In the sexual arena, you have, for example, the preacher who publicly "purges" by proclaiming the evils of promiscuity while privately bingeing with prostitutes. Those with addictions are often caught up in extreme deprivation. This neuropathway becomes the balance wheel for extreme behaviors—either acting out or acting in. It creates an alternative extreme to out-of-control behavior, wobbly though it might be. It also creates a predictable cycle of neuropathic bingeing and purging. This cycle can also involve different deprivations and addictions. The physician who works a hundred hours a week (deprivation) and who is sexually compulsive because he feels so entitled (addiction) serves as an example of how the deprivation and addiction behaviors can cross over. Figure 7.1 summarizes how the binge-purge cycle works.

Figure 7.1

ACTING OUT

OUT OF CONTROL
Eating
Sex and Romance
Alcohol
Drugs
Spending, Debting
Risk Taking
Work
Gambling

EXTREME CONTROL
Dieting
Sex Avoidamce
Alcohol Avoidance
Drug Avoidance
Saving, Hoarding
Risk Aversion
Compulsive Athleticism

ACTING IN

summarize, each neuropathway provides a solution to specific uncomfortable feelings. For arousal, it is about pain. Numbing behaviors are usually about anxiety. Fantasy, preoccupation, and obsession are about shame. And deprivation stems from terror. Notice that each pattern is driven by a typical fantasy. To understand sexual addiction, we need to both understand the type of pain involved and to identify the governing fantasy. To do this, we must look at what happens in the brain when humans are sexual.

Sexual Neuropathways

Eons ago when we evolved as a species on the African plains, we learned to stand on two legs. Some experts believe that when that occurred, a significant change occurred in male-female relationships. Women started carrying children in their arms as opposed to transporting them on their backs. Up to that point we could be mobile and protected in a pack. It became more functional for a woman carrying a child in her arms to have a male as a protector and provider. Those who survived were those who developed attachment for one another. Essentially, researchers believe that because of this shift in human mating, three distinct sexual neuropathways evolved.

The first to develop was libido or lust, the drive to mate. It was functional for both men and women to spread their genes for species survival. Men would experience desire for many women and attempt to have children by them so that their genes would survive. Women would be receptive because the gene variation would ensure the maximum survival of their children. We still experience these feelings today when we are attracted to people with whom it makes no sense emotionally or intellectually to be involved. It is very normal to be struck by another person's desirability. We see attractive people in shopping centers, in airports, in the car next to us, in magazines, and on television. In chapter 5 when we talked about courtship stages, we noted that we first notice that someone is attractive, but we do not then necessarily experience desire. We are, however, attracted to some of these people and this creates a physical reaction. Our hearts beat faster, we focus on them, our bodies become aroused, and we think about sex with them. Craving sexual gratification is driven by chemicals called estrogens and androgens. We use terms like lust, horniness, and libido to describe this reaction. What we mean is that the body becomes aroused by a reaction that has nothing to do with who that person truly is.

The second neuropathway to evolve was that of attraction or romance. Who the person is to whom we are physically attracted becomes very important. We crave being with this person and we become exhilarated in his or her presence. We often smile when we see couples in the "temporary insanity" we call romantic love. Physically, such couples are experiencing heightened amounts of dopamine and norepinephrine as well as depressed amounts of serotonin. Scientists hypothesize that this lack of serotonin is the physical cause for obsessing about one's partner during romantic attachment. Serotonin deficiency is in part the source of intrusive thoughts and preoccupation in general. Within six to eighteen months after the inception of romantic love, dopamine and norepinephrine levels drop and serotonin levels return to normal; thus the "temporary insanity" subsides. Couples then draw upon those neurochemicals that support attachment and bonding, which is the third neuropathway.

The neurochemistry of companionship lies at the core of being with a mate. The physical manifestations of companionship are shared chores, parenting, mutual grooming, nesting, and company-keeping. The feelings involved are those of intimacy and trust. Being with the person means feeling better, calmer, happier, and, according to recent evidence, physically healthier. The feelings of well-being come from two neuropeptides: oxytocin and vasopressin. If this companionship is disrupted, the person experiences what psychiatrists call "separation anxiety," which means they are upset until the partner returns. This threat of loss is actually a mini-withdrawal from the source of comfort. It is very functional for us to have these feelings, as they are essential to the ability to affiliate. In fact, this neurochemistry is part of the larger process of human bonding in general. Parental bonds, friendship bonds, sibling bonds—all critical relationships draw on some of the same physiology.

These three neuropathways often work in concert. First you are attracted and aroused, then you become romantically involved, and, finally, you attach and commit. In the context of that committed relationship, you will re-experience sexual arousal and romance, though it may ebb and flow. To put this idea in courtship terms, the dimensions of courtship literally draw their power from these neuropathways. Figure 7.2 graphically shows how each neuropathway contributes to the courtship process.

Sometimes the neuropathways act independently of each other. You can be sexual without romantic or relationship involvements. Some relationships are not particularly sexual or romantic. Other relationships are not overtly sexual and never achieve a level of commitment. Problems arise, however, when the neuropathways work at cross-purposes. While it is more functional to be in a pair bond, the desire for sex outside the partnership remains. Helen Fisher, one of the pio-

Figure 7.2

COURTSHIP DIMENSIONS AND SEXUAL NEUROPATHWAYS

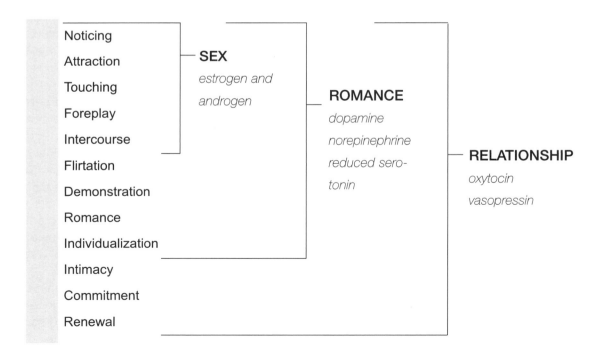

neers in developing a better understanding of the neurophysiology of sex, writes, "The vast majority of human beings around the world marry one person at a time." Humans have come to the realization that long-term, monogamous relationships seem to work best for families and societies. She also observes that divorce is also common across the planet because of, in part, the interplay of these three distinct emotional systems.

Sexual Neuropathways and Addiction

Many sex addicts take comfort in knowing that everyone can experience tension amongst their various desires. It is not just the sex addicts who struggle with desire for others when they are in a committed relationship; we are all subject to the brain circuitry we have inherited. The problem for sex addicts is that the chemicals produced in our brains are the most powerful substances we make. A classic experiment demonstrates just how powerful. In it, rats were first habituated to heroin and then given the choice between an electrical impulse that stimulated the sexual pleasure centers of their brains and another dose of heroin. They consistently chose sexual stimulation over heroin. John Money, a famous sex researcher at Johns Hopkins University, said it succinctly: "Being love-smitten may even be the prototype of all addiction."

Think about this in terms of what we now know about neuropathway physiology. To sit for many hours each day in front of a computer stimulating yourself with pictures of women you do not know and will never know is not what the sexual neuropathway evolved to do. Rather than helping to ensure the propagation of the species, such individuals become isolated, withdrawn from those whom they love, and are unable to do their work. Next, consider romance. There are those who are constantly falling in love simply to experience the rush and intoxication of having found their "cosmos-chosen" partner. I say cosmic because they expect each new "conquest" to bring a lifetime of meaning and happiness. As a result, they bring heart and soul to the relationship. They find each new partner and relationships so exciting and intimate—until they meet the next one. Their relationships never evolve into anything durable because they can't bear to be without the excitement a new relationship brings. Some seek a solution through multiple simultaneous romances, which insulate against withdrawal but create many problems. Some people become so obsessed sexually with their partners that they are constantly jealous and suspicious to the point of stalking. In addition, they demand sex very often. Such intensity flies in the face of the comfort and security that grows out of a healthy relationship bond.

How can we make sense of all this? We must match the four addiction neuropathways with the three sexual neuropathways.

Figure 7.3 (page 223) shows a matrix we have created from the three sexual neuropathways and the four addiction neuropathways that models ways people mix and match neuronal pathway interactions. It can serve as a guide to all the ways we can take our natural inclinations and turn them into problems. We will review the three sexual neuropathways by each addictive pathway.

Arousal. This neuropathway is about intensity, pleasure, and excitement, but not necessarily courtship. When problematic, addicts become so pleasure driven, they are unable to function in their daily lives and sex becomes a self-destructive priority. All focus is on erotic behavior with little attention paid to self or others. This behavior, in addition to being high intensity, is often high-risk or dangerous. If the addict is a trauma survivor, violence may even serve as an escalator of sexual arousal. For some, pain or even the trauma itself becomes part of the arousal pattern.

When addictive arousal stems from romance, the roller coaster of new love itself becomes the intensity fix. Romance junkies are constantly looking for the cosmic person who will make everything in life right. Falling in love repeatedly or simultaneously becomes the antidote to their inner pain. For these individuals, romance is often highly volatile and intensely sexual. They are often attracted to people who are dangerous, unreachable, unavailable, or incomprehensible (aloof or unreadable)—or all of the above. When relationships do emerge, they also tend to be volatile, intense, and somehow dangerous. Movies like *War of the Roses, Fatal Attraction*, and *Disclosure* depict how such relationships escalate. Traumatic bonding (attraction to a person who hurts you), stalking (obsession with a sexual partner), and codependency (out-of-control loyalty to another person) thrive in these relationships because of fear and terror. Often these relationships cycle through periods of intense sex after risky events or breakups.

Numbing. In any relationship, sex can serve as a way to relax or feel better. Problems occur, however, when sex is used compulsively to reduce anxiety. Sex addicts seek sexual release as a way to cope with the stress of daily living. They have a desperate need to achieve the feeling of post-orgasmic euphoria and calm just to get through the day. Having sex to the point of exhaustion as a routine path to sleep, numbing sex after high-risk behaviors (typical of trauma survivors), or compulsive sex to the point of self-injury or pain are examples of sex that is no longer about pleasure and connection with another. It has instead become a way to manage internal discomfort. Sex can be highly ritualized for these addicts, and if their rituals are disturbed, they can become very anxious.

Romance and falling in love become a "fix" as well. Addicts become anxious if they are not with a partner; they believe that something is wrong. If no romantic feelings occur or if the feelings go away, anxiety rises. Nurturing and comfort become more important than the person providing them. Being in love is preferable to the internal distress of loneliness. In healthy relationships, attachment brings comfort. Love addicts, however, will tolerate not liking how they are with that person or not liking the person with whom they're in the relationship because this state of affairs is better than being alone. Thus, love addiction often means tolerating the intolerable and accepting the miserable. Worse yet, for many it means accepting the improbable. Love addicts will accept elaborate distortions of reality rather than face abandonment in any form. They may stay in a relationship no matter what the costs, even when they include battering, addiction, abuse, and deprivation. Many codependents struggle with compulsive relationships.

Fantasy. For some sex addicts, obsession and preoccupation with sex, in and of themselves, become a solution to a painful reality. Their use of sexual stimulation to maintain pleasurable feelings creates long periods of time during which they have little connection with or interaction with the world around them. They can procrastinate over difficult tasks, ignore grief, and escape unbearable feelings by cruising for endless hours, by going into the trance of cybersex, or by continually plotting to gain a glimpse of nudity. Living in such a fantasy world allows sex that is divorced from reality.

Romantic preoccupation can serve the same function. Researching and planning intrigues takes time and provides an escape from life. E-mail and Internet chatroom relationships often become more real and more important than real relationships. Some romance addicts have romantic fantasies so complete that the person with whom they are having an affair has no idea of the addict's feelings; to them, no romance exists. Compulsive relationships can also be based on fantasy life. In such cases, the relationship focus grows out of imagined qualities in the partner. The partner's charisma, or an excessive feeling of gratitude toward the partner, can propel the addict to stay in an unhealthy relationship and dismiss reality. Cults, sexual misconduct, and betrayal often have a mystique built on a fantasy life. And there always seems to be a unique reason why the "secret" cannot be revealed. All of this is intensely sexual. Compulsive fantasy, whether sexual, romantic, or relationship, can lead to stalking behaviors in which the obsession is enhanced by gathering information or discovery.

Deprivation. Deprivation is compulsive avoidance of a need as a way to deal with terror or fear. Anything erotic or sexually suggestive is rejected. Sex is perceived as threatening, not pleasurable, and at best, it is humdrum or tolerable. People who have a history of sexual abuse often have an internal rule that says they cannot have sex with people who matter to them. As a result, important relationships become compulsively nonsexual.

Extreme distrust of romantic feelings or initiatives may also exist. For some, romance is, at best, seeking an arrangement. In her book *Facing Love Addiction*, Pia Mellody describes people in this situation as being "avoidants." These people compulsively avoid relationships, and in so doing, they are isolated, lonely, emotionally restricted, and have poor to nonexistent communication skills. Sexual and emotional anorexics can have deep attachments but they will never admit this.

Deprivation becomes something of a balance wheel for sex addicts. Some are sexually out of control in general, but they are compulsively deprived with those with whom they are intimate. Other sex addicts live a binge-purge existence.

Figure 7.3 summarizes the four addiction neuropathways and the three sexual neuropathways. Together they form a matrix of the neuronal pathways that make up sex addiction and its deprivation counterpart. This chart can help you identify the fundamental rhythms of your addiction. Moreover, it can help you understand that the signals your body is giving you have become distorted, and this distortion helps reduce their strength and makes them easier to ignore. The key to recovery is learning how to separate such distortions from the true expressions of your sexuality. In order to start that process, you will need to explore your arousal template—which we will do in the following section.

Before proceeding, however, please review the sexual addiction matrix and personalize it by identifying those areas in your life in which your sexual activity has become addictive. An empty matrix is provided for you below. In each square in which you think your behavior fits, record examples of the behavior and rate how powerful it has been in your life. Completing this task will prepare you to look at your arousal template.

Figure 7.3

THE SEXUAL ADDICTION MATRIX

	SEXUAL NEUROPATHWAY		
	EROTIC	**ROMANCE**	**RELATIONSHIPS**
AROUSAL	All focus is on erotic behavior, excitement, and orgasm. High intensity, risk, and danger are often associated. Trauma survivors may incorporate pain and trauma into behavior.	Romance junkies turn new love into a "fix." They fall into love repeatedly or simultaneously. Roller-coaster romances are highly sexual, volatile, and dangerous. Partners are often unreachable, unavailable, or incomprehensible.	Volatile, intense and often dangerous relationships. Traumatic bonding, stalking, and codependency thrive in abandonment or dangerous collaborations. Cycles of sex and breakups.
NUMBING	Sex is used to soothe the anxiety and stress of daily life. Sex is used to sleep, to calm down high-risk takers, or to manage internal discomfort. Anxiety occurs when highly ritualized behavior is frustrated or disturbed.	Romance becomes a way to manage anxiety. Person becomes anxious if not in love with someone. How you are and who the other is does not match. The only goal is to be with someone.	Compulsive relationships include tolerating the intolerable-battering, addiction, abuse, and deprivation. Person will distort reality rather than face abandonment.
FANTASY	Obsession and preoccupation become the solution to painful reality. Fantasy is an escape used to procrastinate, avoid grief, and ignore pain.	Person avoids life problems through romantic preoccupation. Planning, intrigue, and research fill the void. Emails and chats, magical romance, and stalking are more real than family.	Compulsive relationships are built on distorted fantasy. Charisma, role, cause, gratitude play role in cults, sexual misconduct, and betrayal. Mystique is built on secrecy and belief in uniqueness.
DEPRIVATION	Anything erotic or suggestive is rejected. Sex is threatening and not pleasurable. Sex may be OK if the other does not matter.	Extreme distrust of romantic feelings or instincts. At best, person seeks "arrangement."	Avoids relationships. Isolated, lonely, restricted emotions, and poor or nonexistent communication skills.

ADDICTION NEUROPATHWAY

Matrix Exercise

Review the Sexual Addiction Matrix and identify which "squares" fit your behavior. Make your own matrix by listing behaviors in the squares that fit for you. Leave squares empty that do not fit. In the ones you have listed behaviors, rate yourself from one to five in terms of power with one being low and five being high. When finished, share with your support group, sponsor or therapist.

ADDICTION NEUROPATHWAY	SEXUAL NEUROPATHWAY: EROTIC	SEXUAL NEUROPATHWAY: ROMANCE	SEXUAL NEUROPATHWAY: RELATIONSHIPS
Example AROUSAL	Using prostitutes on trips. One night stands. Low 1 2 3 4 5 High	Having sex with employees and professional "relationships." Office romances. Affair with a neighbor. Low 1 2 3 4 5 High	High involvement with Jane who stalked. Kept trying to break it off. Seen with her in public places. Low 1 2 3 4 5 High
AROUSAL	Low 1 2 3 4 5 High	Low 1 2 3 4 5 High	Low 1 2 3 4 5 High
NUMBING	Low 1 2 3 4 5 High	Low 1 2 3 4 5 High	Low 1 2 3 4 5 High
FANTASY	Low 1 2 3 4 5 High	Low 1 2 3 4 5 High	Low 1 2 3 4 5 High
DEPRIVATION	Low 1 2 3 4 5 High	Low 1 2 3 4 5 High	Low 1 2 3 4 5 High

Sexual Health Matrix

Addicts who are in early recovery tend to view all things sexual as bad or dangerous. After you complete the Sexual Addiction Matrix, you may find it useful to keep in mind our discussion of the neuropathways and think of them from the perspective of sexual health. Yes, these same neuropathways can also be life-enhancing. When have the same neuropathways had a significantly positive effect on your life? For example, rather than addictive arousal, when have you experienced life-giving passion? Rather than mindless numbing, think of reflective calming. Instead of obsessive escapism into fantasy, think of focus. Finally, have there been times in your life when being nonsexual had a positive effect on your life rather than detracting from it. (We call these times "moments of asceticism"—i.e., going without for higher purpose.) Out of this reframing we can construct a new matrix that focuses instead on sexual health. Go through each square and record examples of times when sex, romance, or relationships added to your life. Again, leave squares blank if you have no examples. Rate each square in which you have made an entry from one to five in terms of life enhancement. Ask yourself if this event made your life a little bit better (one on the scale) to dramatically better (five on the scale). After completing the task, use the questions provided to reflect on both matrixes.

	SEX	ROMANCE	RELATIONSHIPS
PASSION	Low 1 2 3 4 5 High	Low 1 2 3 4 5 High	Low 1 2 3 4 5 High
CALMING	Low 1 2 3 4 5 High	Low 1 2 3 4 5 High	Low 1 2 3 4 5 High
FOCUSED	Low 1 2 3 4 5 High	Low 1 2 3 4 5 High	Low 1 2 3 4 5 High
ASCETIC	Low 1 2 3 4 5 High	Low 1 2 3 4 5 High	Low 1 2 3 4 5 High

Matrix Reflection Questions

The following questions will help you reflect on how your matrix works:

What are the differences between your addictive behavior and your healthy sexual behavior? Was it difficult to differentiate between the two? If so, what does that teach you about recovery?

_____

_____

_____

_____

_____

Are there parallels between the two matrixes? What do you notice about what is left blank?

_____

_____

_____

_____

_____

Which matrix was harder to do? What do you think the reason for this is?

_____

_____

_____

_____

_____

Contrast your highest ratings for addiction power with your highest ratings for life enhancement. What are the implications of this result for your recovery?

_____

_____

_____

_____

_____

The Arousal Template

As a child matures, an arousal template is formed. Family messages, early sexual experiences, church influences, childhood abuse, magazines, television and movies, and a variety of other factors flow together to create an internal process called sexual arousal. Part of the arousal template is formed intentionally by church, culture, and family while other parts are formed quite accidentally, as we shall see. Remember that arousal is a physical phenomenon. As such, it will operate using the same principles your body does. Your immunological system scans for patterns of threatening microorganisms that fit the pattern of a threatening bacteria and it immediately organizes an attack on cells. Likewise, your brain constantly searches for patterns that are familiar in order to make sense of them. There is a sexual scan that occurs to see if a pattern fits. The arousal template for each person can be unique and quite specific. Here are some recent stories I have run across:

Jake's mom often walked nude in front of him when he was a child and an adolescent. As an adult, Jake developed a problem with voyeurism and in fact had two major relationships with strippers who took care of him and then left him for someone else.

Freddie's dad had a large pornography collection that he allowed his son to use. As an adult, Freddie took a part-time job for a time working as a bartender in a strip club. Often, he would have one-night stands with women who worked in the club. Soon thereafter, he discovered the Internet and began to access pornography Web sites. He was soon downloading pornography three hours a day and most of every weekend.

As a youngster, Sam became sexually fascinated with lingerie ads he stumbled across in a department store catalog. He would tear out the lingerie pages and stuff them under his mattress. When he learned to masturbate, he used these pages to stimulate himself. As an adult, Sam discovered the Internet and was soon spending about two hours every day downloading pictures of women in lingerie. When he came into treatment, he had more than a hundred superdisks full of pictures of women in lingerie. He had met his then-current girlfriend in church. Her occupation? A sales representative for lingerie companies.

All three of these men had a problem with voyeurism, or visual sex. Did you notice, however, that the route each followed into his problem was different? They were each seeking out and following a different sexual pattern that had started early in life. Jake's preoccupation with women who strip and with abandonment started with his mother's behavior. Freddie learned at a young age about hoarding pornography. And Sam's fixation with lingerie really started in a family that never talked about sex—the catalog provided his only access to sexual "information." They each formed a template that filtered all sexual stimulation, allowed only certain patterns to enter, and thus limited their sexual options. Then came obsession and ritualization, and the addictive cycle was born. Disrupting this cycle starts with understanding the pattern-seeking characteristics of your body and how the arousal template was formed. In so doing, you can begin to broaden your sexual stimuli and to introduce new sexual options that are more functional and healthy.

The arousal template can already be discerned between the ages of five and eight; hence events early in life can have a profound impact on the emerging sexual self. Cybersex has already taught us that adults can experience significant alteration of their arousal template under the hypnotic influence of electronic sex. Thanks to cybersex, people rapidly form new obsessions that become so fixed, they have the power of early childhood experiences. This fact is very important because for many years we believed that the arousal templates were firmly fixed and unalterable. Now we realize they can be supplemented or even replaced. The downside is that the template can still lead to obsession. The upside is that change is possible. For change to take place, however, you must understand your current template, beginning with feelings, especially anger.

Sexualized Feelings

Consider the following:

Many Web sites dedicated to voyeurism frequently post nude pictures of spouses, ex-girl-friends, and ex-spouses submitted by men who report that these women do not know about the posting. To post a nude picture for others' sexual gratification without that person's knowledge or permission is an angry and vengeful act. The opposite also occurs. Angry "ex's" post nude pictures of themselves to retaliate for being rejected.

An airline pilot has a problem with compulsive affairs in an industry in which this problem is all too common. He comes, however, from a very devout and restrictive religious tradition and is tormented with shame and guilt. He is the father of three and a deacon in his church. But he also has had sex with more than five hundred women in about fifteen years. In therapy, he realizes that he has anger toward the church and anger toward his wife. His breakthrough came when he had a fight with his wife and immediately felt an extreme desire to be sexual outside the marriage. His therapist helped him see that his inability to adequately respond to his wife triggered the sexual acting out. He could get revenge without her knowing it and restore internal "equality" for himself. The pilot learned how dysfunctional his inability to get angry with his wife was, how his feelings about the church and its sexual teachings supercharged his acting out, and how his compulsive behavior was fueled in part by his sexualized rage.

A lovely college-educated African-American woman worked as a stripper. She had a history of extensive sexual and physical abuse by men in her family. She described to her therapist the sexual gratification she felt when men took out their wallets to get money to put on the stage or in her garter. In her view, she had humiliated them and saw them as despicable. She felt superior, powerful, and sexual. Her therapist pointed out how this situation merely recycled the abuse experiences in her family. She became powerful and rageful when sexual. Nor was this dynamic restricted to her dancing. She had a history of being sexual with teachers, a college professor, and her doctor. Sex was the great equalizer with the many men with whom she had been sexual. Unfortunately, it also left her with suicidal feelings, a deep emptiness, a sexual addiction, and a pernicious drug habit.

A white accountant who had always lived by the rules discovered his wife had had a series of affairs with African-American men. He felt very betrayed and angry, but also obsessed about and aroused by what she had done. He reported that the hottest sex they had ever had was when he was gathering details of her exploits. He then discovered cybersex and went to the sites that featured African-American men with white women. He went downhill fast. He was averaging thirty hours a week doing cybersex and neglecting his job. He started to collect pornography of African-American and white couples and became a regular customer for prostitutes. His asking his wife for details became badgering and harassing. When he was asked by his therapist if he had stalked his wife, he said that he would never do that. The therapist rephrased the question and asked if he had followed his wife. "Absolutely," he responded. Actually, he had her under surveillance all the time. The therapist helped the patient understand the role of unresolved anger in his now-sexually compulsive pattern. In therapy, his wife also admitted that even her selection of African-American men was about her anger.

The wife of a high-profile man went to a therapist because of her extreme unhappiness and depression. She had been sexually acting out in many ways for more than a decade. She reported she had even had oral sex with a male stripper in public. Her husband did not know about this or her other activities. But that he *could* learn of it was erotic for her. This woman's therapist observed that it may have been erotic, but it was also angry. Such a public display was designed to humiliate and embarrass her successful partner. It was as if she was toying with his humiliation while not actually carrying it out. In addition, she could then obsess about it. Her therapist explained that the "perverse" part of perversion is often vengeful or defiant anger.

In each of these cases, anger and eroticism became intertwined or fused. The mechanisms for this process are easy to understand, but to begin, we have to look at arousal templates more closely.

As we grow up, we incorporate our life experiences and our sexual experiences with what we are told or learn about sex into a sexual belief system, or template. What we learn about relationships and family also becomes part of our template. This template builds on preferences already determined by our genetic code. Whether we like tall or short, blonds or redheads—all our preferences are determined by a mix of physiology and culturally based learning. As we move through adolescence and into adulthood, this template becomes our guide to what we feel to be erotic. Much of this template remains at an unconscious level.

Almost anything can become part of the arousal template. A rural child growing up where there was no running water might have snuck up behind an outhouse to peer in and watch female family members urinate. Curiosity and arousal could then become connected with urination. As an adult, this person might view urination as a cue for arousal. Pornography of women urinating or spy-cams in rest rooms or prostitutes willing to give "golden showers" could all become extensions of that original scenario or story. Similarly, some men become fascinated as adolescents with girls who smoke. As adults, they seek restaurants or parks near high schools where they can watch girls smoke, or they might drive by areas where girls smoke. They might also take a short-cut by logging on to the Net and seek out the many websites dedicated to girls (who are not necessarily nude) smoking.

As objects, situations, or scenarios become eroticized, so do feelings that accompany them. Many psychology experiments have consistently shown that people were viewed as more attractive when the subjects perceived fear or risk either to themselves or that person. Fear and risk is a well-documented neurochemical escalator of the sexual experience, as is pain. Many female victims of violent childhood sexual abuse report that as adults, they are unable to be orgasmic unless their male partner is hurting them. I have had many traumatized female clients tell me that they could not even masturbate unless they put astringent or abrasive materials in their vaginas. They could not even stimulate themselves without the pain.

Consider the very successful scientist who told of a violent childhood. He can remember his father battering his mother so badly, he could hear her body hit the wall in the next room. He would masturbate to comfort himself in his anxiety. He also had a problem wetting the bed and defecating in his nightclothes until he was six. As an adult, he found fear erotic—any kind of fear. He would compulsively seek high-risk sex. Even his own feces and urine were highly arousing. To use the clinical term, "coprophilia," hardly captures the full picture of what happened to this man. Behind what many would call perverse behavior is a severely traumatized child.

In the same fashion, anger becomes eroticized. First, anger occurs in situations of high risk and fear. Anger adds intensity to the sexual experience and becomes a neurochemical escalator, just as fear does. Second, anger often lies at the core scenarios, stories, and beliefs embedded in the arousal template. Therefore, current sexual behavior can draw enormous energy from past wounds and experience. Finally, anger becomes the sexual stimulus for some people. In order to make sense of how anger can have such an effect, we have to break the situations down into component types or profiles.

Power and the Restoration of Self

In this profile, sex is used to restore power in some way. In the case above in which the husband could not deal with conflict with his spouse, he restored his sense of self by acting out in a way in which she had no control. He believed that he deserved sex because he was so misunderstood and that his wife deserved what he did because her behavior was so bad. How can this be retaliation if she never finds out what he's doing? The possibility that she might find out makes the behavior's value for her husband almost as great as if he had done it in front of her. (It is also important to note that their relationship also involved an intimacy disorder because their inability to create intimacy is part of their problem.) The husband's misguided attempt to deal with his frustrations resulted in the sexually compulsive behavior of a sex addict. Addiction is often the "solution" to an intimacy deficit.

Attempting to achieve relationship parity in this way is one of the most common profiles of eroticized rage. Coincidentally, it is also one of the most common causes of affairs. Consider the story of Tammy. While she was growing up, Tammy was often embarrassed by her father's frequent sexually inappropriate behaviors in public. Her father acted similarly at home, walking around in the nude, for example. He had many affairs and sexually abused Tammy's three sisters. Therein began Tammy's problem. Like many siblings of abused children, Tammy often asked herself why her father had not approached her for sex. He did, however, like to look at her body and often commented about her sexual development. Tammy would deliberately take showers in her father's bathroom so he would have the opportunity to observe her, even though she had a bathroom of her own to use.

Tammy grew into a statuesque, beautiful woman. When she was seventeen, she was caught shoplifting clothes. The shopkeeper pulled her into a back room and told her she could keep the clothes if she would show him her breasts. She did and he pleasured himself. She left with the clothes and a unique feeling. She felt he had betrayed his vulnerability. Sex had reversed the situation in that she was no longer a desperate teenager about to be turned into the police by an authority figure. That power figure had instead become pathetic and disgusting in her eyes. Moreover, exhibiting her body was very sexually arousing and satisfying to her. And she had the clothes.

This scenario repeated over and over again in various ways in the coming years. As a high-powered advertising executive, Tammy kept accounts on several occasions where she was asked to have sex by a client. She would have relationships, usually with older men who were powerful and unattractive. She still felt that she was in control because of their sexual desperation. For a time she was engaged to a man who was much older and weighed three hundred pounds. She enjoyed sex with him. The best sex for her, however, came after they broke up when he would leave her money. Watching a man take money out of his wallet was very erotic for her, and she knew she had "won" at that point.

Tammy also liked to drive down the freeway with her dress hiked up to expose her genitals and her blouse open to expose her breasts. She would pull up next to trucks and feel great pleasure when truckers would pull their air-horn cords in approval. When Tammy got into recovery for alcoholism, she was extremely sexually active with men she met in A.A. meetings. The list goes on. Suffice it to say that Tammy's life was out of control and eventually, she became suicidal.

In treatment, Tammy admitted that she had several standing arrangements with the owners of prestigious clothing stores on fashionable Rodeo Drive in Hollywood. She could pick out the clothes she wanted if she would strip for these merchants. They would pleasure themselves and she would walk away feeling superior. This behavior, as you can see, was simply a repetition of what had happened to her when she was a teenager. Her therapist helped Tammy understand that it also replicated her taking showers in her father's bathroom to get him to notice her. Tammy admitted that the clothing store where she loved to do this was around the corner from her father's upscale apartment. Something about his proximity made her sexual acting out even more compelling. It was then that she confessed to actually having sex with a man in her father's bed on the night of one of his weddings.

Tammy's story illustrates a common phenomenon among trauma survivors in that her behavior replicates the way she was abused as a child. Trauma specialists have described this as "repetition compulsion" or "addiction to the trauma." This sexually compulsive behavior provides a "rush" based on an arousal template she evolved while trying to make sense of her own relationship with her father. Note further, however, that Tammy was also trying to "complete" herself. It's also important to recognize the cyclic nature of her feelings during her sexual acting out. Tammy was desperate for her father's approval however she could get it. Though she was angry about his treatment of her and despised how he behaved, getting his attention and then feeling that she was a better person than he was by exposing him for what he was created the internal dynamic and payoff that drove her dysfunctional behavior. When Tammy finally understood all of this, she was able to arrest her compulsive cycles. She also realized that while on the surface she looked like a victim who was being used by men, at a deeper part she was actually the predator driven by her anger and hatred of men.

Sexualized anger can be used in an attempt to restore a sense of self, and when this happens, it commonly involves some form of abuse and power. In studies of women and sex addiction, this power dynamic and an attempt to "prop up" the self are frequently present. Sex-offender literature regularly describes parallel behaviors in offenders who attempt to compensate for poor self-image by replicating childhood abuse and a rage for women that comes out sexually. Sexualized anger becomes a vehicle for addicts to feel better about themselves by creating a new relationship parity using sex.

Humiliation, Vengeance, and Retaliation

You may have noticed that the examples we have used thus far in this discussion involve some form of humiliation or revenge. The attempt to restore the self via sexualized rage can extend to diminishing another person. This might be a sexual partner—the merchants to whom Tammy felt superior, for example, or a stripper feeling disgust for the men who tip her. This might also be a marital partner, such as in the woman who performed public oral sex. Further, it might be, again in Tammy's case, humiliating a parent in person or indirectly, such as despoiling his marital bed on his wedding night. Posting a nude picture of one's ex-wife for all to see without her permission has both a sexual and a vengeful component. Usually when sexualized rage becomes vengeful, the root issues are deep and profound. Consider this next example.

When Louise was sixteen, she became pregnant and gave up her son for adoption. Unknown to her, her son, Sam, was raised in a physically abusive home. He became a drug addict and went through several cycles of rehabilitation. When he was thirty-three years old, he conducted a successful search for his birth mother. Louise was thrilled to be able to have contact with her son. She was in a second marriage of sixteen years and had raised two children. She had settled into a middle-class, orderly life and had a somewhat matronly appearance. She still had many unresolved feelings, however, about having given up her son for adoption.

Louise went to visit her son while he was in an extended-care facility. In her hotel room, she massaged his shoulders which he said were hurting. The massage ended up with mother and son having sex. When Sam left the extended-care facility, he asked Louise if he could come to live with Louise and her husband until he found a job and got on his feet. Louise agreed, and within a month, their home had turned into chaos. Part of the cause stemmed from Louise and Sam continuing to have sex—which came to a stop when Louise's husband found them in bed together. Sam was asked to leave and Louise became suicidal and began using amphetamines. Her routine, uneventful, middle-class existence had evaporated.

During treatment, Louise was stunned to realize how she had violated her own value system and hurt her husband, whom she dearly loved. Using the details of her sexual experience with her son—that it was more angry than passionate and that she was naked while he remained mostly dressed, for example—Louise's therapist and group helped her realize that it was intended to degrade and humiliate her. Sam's anger at being abandoned was compounded by his physical abuse in the home in which he was raised. Sex became a vehicle for his rage. Louise said she actually understood this at the time, which added to her amazement at her continuing to have sex with him. Her therapist then introduced her to the concept of traumatic bonding, explaining how Sam's presence induced fear and drew power from the guilt and sadness of an old wound. This new understanding allowed Louise to begin to see which parts of this sad situation she was responsible for and those for which she was not.

What happened to Sam and Louise actually happens to many people. Anger and pain related to old betrayals and abuse can be carried into adulthood sexually. Sam blamed his mother for what happened to him, when in fact Louise had taken a responsible action in trying to give him a better life. Sam's perception was, obviously, different and he acted out sexually in an attempt to humiliate his mother. Yet having sex with one's mother only brings up another dimension of sexualized rage: perversion.

Perversion

One of the great researchers on perversion, Robert Stoller, tells the story of his initial investigation into the pornography industry. Every pornography producer he interviewed said that if pornography were legal and had widespread acceptance (or even tolerance), they would never have bothered to become involved. These producers essentially said that the thrill in making sexually explicit movies came from finding pleasure in disapproval. By putting sex in "its face," they were striking back at our culture for its control and rigidity. This rebelliousness or defiance of convention also grows out of anger.

Individual sexual behavior is sometimes simply perverse. For the wife of a public official to publicly perform oral sex on male strippers is perverse. To barter sex for clothes at a store just around the corner from the residence of a controlling father is perverse. To have sex with your mother is more than just an act of defiance. To have many affairs behind the back of the woman with whom you live in a restrictive and judgmental religious community is clearly to break the rules. This perversity also sends a message about convention, control, and relationships. Notice, however, that such perversity is often a private joke. By acting out sexually, one is toying with the possibility that the person with whom you are angry might discover your actions. In this sense, it has elements of a gambling obsession. All of this behavior also clearly adds to the risk and intensity of the act. Perversion works best if it outrages others. Perverse behaviors outrage only when they are very "unusual," yet there is irony here because we know that such behaviors are, in fact, quite common.

Obsession

Anger can also fuel sexual obsession. This occurs especially in cases of betrayal and jealousy. In the case we examined earlier in which a man's wife had had affairs with African-American men, he tortured himself with his preoccupation about her behavior. This obsession was intensely sexual and overtly hostile. That it evolved into stalking behavior is not at all unusual, either. When obsessive anger is present, conventional societal rules are suspended. The stalkers, for example, justify their behavior because they keep "building their case" against the person who they believe betrayed them. Sex addiction coaddicts can also justify stalking. They can become sexually obsessed with the sex addict's behaviors and will then go to the extreme of breaking their spouse's privacy by, for example, hiring a private detective to spy on the spouse, go through personal papers and diaries, and review bills and credit card statements.

There is even a website dedicated to helping people with this type of surveillance. A woman had discovered that her husband was using their computer for cybersex. When she learned that he was having affairs via e-mail and downloading pornography, she was outraged. She found a surveillance website that was designed to track men who cheat on the web. From it, she learned how to use her work computer to disguise her identity and then initiated a torrid chatroom affair with her husband. She also installed a surveillance system on their home computer that automatically tallied and e-mailed to her work computer a description of everything he did on his computer. She was aware of all his online behavior while he had no idea that this was happening. She also discovered and regularly visited a website whose participants (approximately three thousand people per week) talked about what their husbands were currently up to. Anger, perversity, getting even, finding revenge, and obsessiveness—all the components of eroticized rage were there. And she completed the charade by continuing to have sex with her husband as though nothing had changed.

Addicts and co-addicts are surprised to learn that anger is a component of their sexual behavior. They overlook the obvious for several reasons. First, they are aware of the sex, but not of the anger. People caught up in compulsive cycles or repetitive patterns are especially prone to this trap. No feelings—anger, fear, sadness, or pain—survive their obsession. Second, these people have created a complex web of thought distortions and rationalizations that preclude feeling any responsibility whatsoever for their actions. When an activity is not viewed as your fault, any feelings of guilt or remorse or shame are hidden.

Addicts need the help of their group, their sponsor, and a therapist to discover the dynamics of their family or the legacy of abuse in their life. Typically, addicts do not initially welcome these realizations, but over time they can see them as the breakthrough events they truly are.

Anatomy of Arousal

To gain a greater understanding of your own behavior patterns, you must begin by making them explicit. The following exercises will help you do so. First, embedded in most arousal templates is an ideal fantasy that needs to be understood. The following exercises will also help you discover this. In addition, you will be asked to examine those ideal fantasies and determine where the fantasies come from. This is difficult work and is best done in consultation with your support network.

Remember that fantasies are a way of "envisioning" the future. Recovering people recognize that specific fantasies are key components of the obsessive preoccupation that leads to relapse. Examining these fantasies to discover how they started and to acknowledge their probable outcomes helps diminish their power. Begin by describing the fantasy and specify what makes it ideal. Let us use the example of Art, a man who came to treatment because he was caught in his best friend's home masturbating with the underclothes of his friend's wife. Here is his fantasy:

Fantasy: *Sneaking into a woman's home and watching pornography on her TV. Going into her bedroom, finding undergarments, and masturbating.*

When asked what would make the fantasy ideal he said:

The home would be of someone whom I knew and was attracted to. I would bring my own videos, but the ultimate would be if I could find pornographic videos used or viewed by this person. It would be incredible if these tapes contained home videos of this person. The very best would happen when I next saw the person and I could tell she had undergarments on that I had touched. The whole idea is to be very sexual around this person without her knowing I'd been using her stuff. I am the perfect sex burglar.

When asked whether such a fantasy was possible to achieve, Art wrote:

It is possible and I have done it. But it has never been perfect. The chances of finding other people's home videos are pretty remote. Never happened for me. The truth is that it takes a tremendous amount of work for little payoff, even if you set aside the legal risks.

When asked about the risks and the most likely result, Art wrote:

Exactly what happened. I got caught and now all my friends know. In part, it has cost me my marriage and all the friendships I had. The possibility of doing this without a problem is zero. Plus, I still have the legal problems.

Every sexual fantasy has embedded in it a story or scenario. It is critical to understand where that story comes from and what it has done to your life. The hardest part for some is just to see the story. Once the story is clear, you must next ask where this came from? Family? Childhood abuse? Accidental discovery? And why do you think it is so compelling? When Art was asked these questions, he wrote:

[About the story]

Basically, it is about sneaking in and being sexual with that person without her knowing.

[About where it came from]

When I was a kid, I was left alone at a friend's house where I discovered his father's pornography and watched it. I was so aroused that I went through his mom's dresser, found her panties and bras, and masturbated. Later on, I found it very stimulating to notice something she had on that I had looked at. My ideal fantasy virtually replicates the whole event that occurred when I was thirteen.

[About impact on life]

The biggest loss is not my family and friends, although that is huge. This fantasy changed everything. I did not relate to women except as homeowners. To be sexual, sex had to be stolen.

The following pages include fantasy worksheets that will ask you to describe a fantasy, the ideal, the probability of it happening, the risks involved in doing so, the history, and the impact.

Before you begin, it would be a good idea for you to return to chapter 6 and examine the worksheets you did there on relapse scenarios (page 169). Start by reviewing the fantasy driving each relapse scenario you diagrammed in that chapter. If other fantasies are part of your addictive obsession, complete worksheets on them as well. Use your therapy and support group to discuss the results of this work. Remember, this can be triggering material. Do not work on this alone, and pay attention to the painful feelings this work brings out in you.

Fantasy Worksheet 1

This worksheet will help you analyze fantasies that would be part of relapse for you. Complete a worksheet for each fantasy that plays a part in your addiction. Start with fantasies that were part of the relapse scenarios you outlined in chapter 6. Incorporate any others that are appropriate. Use extra paper if necessary. Use this material with your group and therapist.

Describe the fantasy.

_____

_____

_____

_____

_____

_____

What would make the fantasy ideal—in other words, the best it could possibly be?

_____

_____

_____

_____

_____

_____

Is the fantasy actually possible?

_____

_____

_____

_____

_____

What are the risks involved with carrying out this fantasy? What most likely would be the result of doing it?

_____

_____

_____

_____

_____

Is there a story or scenario in the fantasy? If so, how is it like other parts of your life?

_____

_____

_____

_____

_____

Where did the story come from? (Start with your earliest memory of the fantasy if you cannot pinpoint how it started.)

_____

_____

_____

_____

_____

How has this fantasy affected your life?

_____

_____

_____

_____

Fantasy Worksheet 2

Describe the fantasy.

_____

_____

_____

_____

_____

What would make the fantasy ideal—in other words, the best it could possibly be?

_____

_____

_____

_____

_____

_____

Is the fantasy actually possible?

_____

_____

_____

_____

_____

_____

What are the risks involved with carrying out this fantasy? What most likely would be the result of doing it?

_____

_____

_____

_____

_____

Is there a story or scenario in the fantasy? If so, how is it like other parts of your life?

_____

_____

_____

_____

_____

Where did the story come from? (Start with your earliest memory of the fantasy if you cannot pin-point how it started.)

_____

_____

_____

_____

_____

How has this fantasy affected your life?

_____

_____

_____

_____

_____

Fantasy Worksheet 3

Describe the fantasy.

_____

_____

_____

_____

_____

What would make the fantasy ideal—in other words, the best it could possibly be?

_____

_____

_____

_____

_____

_____

Is the fantasy actually possible?

_____

_____

_____

_____

_____

What are the risks involved with carrying out this fantasy? What most likely would be the result of doing it?

_____

_____

_____

_____

_____

Is there a story or scenario in the fantasy? If so, how is it like other parts of your life?

_____

_____

_____

_____

Where did the story come from? (Start with your earliest memory of the fantasy if you cannot pinpoint how it started.)

_____

_____

_____

_____

How has this fantasy affected your life?

_____

_____

_____

_____

Fantasy Worksheet 4

Describe the fantasy.

_____

_____

_____

_____

_____

What would make the fantasy ideal—in other words, the best it could possibly be?

_____

_____

_____

_____

_____

_____

Is the fantasy actually possible?

_____

_____

_____

_____

_____

_____

What are the risks involved with carrying out this fantasy? What most likely would be the result of doing it?

_____

_____

Is there a story or scenario in the fantasy? If so, how is it like other parts of your life?

_____

Where did the story come from? (Start with your earliest memory of the fantasy if you cannot pin-point how it started.)

_____

How has this fantasy affected your life?

_____

Fantasy Worksheet 5

Describe the fantasy.

_____

_____

_____

_____

_____

What would make the fantasy ideal—in other words, the best it could possibly be?

_____

_____

_____

_____

_____

_____

Is the fantasy actually possible?

_____

_____

_____

_____

_____

_____

What are the risks involved with carrying out this fantasy? What most likely would be the result of doing it?

_____

_____

_____

_____

_____

Is there a story or scenario in the fantasy? If so, how is it like other parts of your life?

_____

_____

_____

_____

_____

Where did the story come from? (Start with your earliest memory of the fantasy if you cannot pin-point how it started.)

_____

_____

_____

_____

How has this fantasy affected your life?

_____

_____

_____

_____

_____

Arousal Template

Your next task is to detail the components of your arousal patterns. The components listed below usually appear in an arousal template:

Feelings that have become eroticized in some way—eroticized rage, fear, shame, or pain

Locations you are in—such as hotel rooms, shopping centers, parks, certain parts of town, specific cities or countries, beaches

Sensations—sounds (modem starting), smells (certain perfumes), visual cues (type of dress)

Objects—automobiles, computer keyboards, sex toys, school uniforms, lingerie

Processes—smoking, urination, violence, degradation, humiliation

Body types/body parts—builds, shapes, muscles, wrinkles, stretch marks

Partner characteristics—age, marital status, personality (do you, for example, prefer a vulnerable, hurting woman; an unreachable, elegant woman; unavailable men)

Culture—Catholic schoolgirls, Asian women, African-American men, Hispanic gay men

Courtship stages and beliefs—parts of courtship that become obsessive; dysfunctional courtship beliefs (women tease; men only want sex)

Beyond fantasies, there are usually categories of specific triggers for arousal. In the following pages, you will be able to explore each category. Complete each one and then pay attention to how you feel and what you think as you realistically assess what arouses you.

Eroticized Feelings

List specific feelings (anger, fear, sadness, shame, loneliness) that have become eroticized for you. Remember that when you were acting out, you may not have noticed what you were feeling. Identifying these feelings now, however, is very important for your recovery. Feelings become an important source of information about your sexual behavior. Identify the feelings you had and how they played a role in your compulsive behavior.

Feeling: _____

Role in your behavior: _____

_____

_____

_____

Feeling: _____

Role in your behavior: _____

_____

_____

_____

Feeling: _____

Role in your behavior: _____

_____

_____

_____

Feeling: _____

Role in your behavior: _____

_____

_____

_____

Situations and Places

When you were acting out, certain situations and places became eroticized. By now, just to be in them becomes a source of arousal and part of your addiction cycle. Examples might include hotel rooms, shopping centers, parks, beaches, certain parts of town, and even specific cities or countries. In the spaces provided below, make a list of the situations or places that arouse to you.

1. _____

2. _____

3. _____

4. _____

5. _____

6. _____

7. _____

8. _____

9. _____

10. _____

Review your list and decide in which situation you would most likely relapse. Place a 1 in front of that item. Place a 2 in the next most probable situation for relapse to occur. Continue until you have ranked all the items. Then, record the reason *why* you think that situation is so powerful for you.

Sensations

Specific sensations can stimulate preoccupation and may even be incorporated into your reactions. Examples include:

Sounds—modem starting, specific songs

Smells—perfumes, body odors, incense, massage oil, food

Visual cues—types of dress, computer screen, windows

Touch—the feel of lingerie; crowded spaces like shopping centers, subways, airplanes, lap dances in a strip bar; dancing

Taste—food, lipstick, gum, breath mints

Record below the sense reactions that you now recognize as a part of your arousal patterns.

_____

_____

_____

_____

_____

_____

Objects

Objects can become sexualized as well. Automobiles are used for cruising for prostitutes, exhibitionism, voyeurism, and anonymous sex. Sometimes they are used as a place in which to have sex. Computer keyboards take on a sexual quality when they are what you touch as you access pornography, chatrooms, and sex-related e-mail. Objects such as school uniforms, lingerie, whips, and sex toys are often a critical part of a fantasy life. Almost every creature on the planet, it seems, including snakes and insects, has been sexualized by someone. Specific types of clothing or even a specific article of clothing (examples would be shoes, socks, high heels, and pantyhose) can become highly sexualized. In the space below, specify what objects have become sexualized for you.

_____

_____

_____

_____

_____

_____

Processes

Sometimes arousal becomes fixated on actions or processes. Watching young girls smoke or women urinate can be erotic for some people. Violence, humiliation, and degradation can also be erotic acts. Stealing and burglary can be eroticized. Car washing, cheerleading, and even gardening, though seemingly benign activities, can become part of compulsive ritualization for some people. What processes have become obsessional for you?

_____

_____

_____

_____

_____

Body Types, Parts, and Characteristics

Arousal often is conditioned on a specific body build or physical characteristic. Shape, muscle, and hair color can determine the quality of arousal. Individual features such as wrinkles, moles, and stretch marks can also become part of desire. Fetishes can be organized around specific body parts such as armpits or feet. Being overweight, pregnant, or extremely thin turns some people on. Sometimes the loss of a limb or being disabled in some way becomes a source of arousal. Indicate below what physical attributes are part of your arousal patterns.

_____

_____

_____

_____

_____

Partner Characteristics

Age, marital status, and personality factor into the arousal quotient. What a person does for a living can be critical. People fantasize about a wide range of professions including teaching, body building and the priesthood. Specific attributes such as being wealthy or impoverished, successful or inexperienced, virginal or promiscuous can be arousing. Usually people have a specific type or types that attract them emotionally. Examples include vulnerable, hurting women; elegant, unreachable women; the unavailable, mysterious man; or the "bad boy" who is misunderstood. In your past, what have been the ideal types of persons who were arousing to you? There may be more than one. Why do you think those people were so attractive? Specify each ideal type below and summarize why they were so attractive to you.

Ideal Type:

_____

_____

_____

_____

Origin of Type:

_____

_____

_____

_____

Ideal Type:

_____

_____

_____

_____

_____

Origin of Type:

_____

_____

_____

_____

_____

Culture

Cultures and subcultures—Catholic schoolgirls, Asian women, African-American men, and Hispanic gays, for instance—can become eroticized. Does culture, race, religion, or ethnicity play a part in your sexual arousal? If so, record in what ways they do in the space below.

_____

_____

_____

_____

_____

Courtship Stages and Beliefs

In chapter 3, we asked you to reflect on the stages of courtship. We pointed out that sexually compulsive behavior was often fixated on a specific act of courtship. For example, exhibitionism is really a distortion of the flirtation and demonstration aspects of courtship. Review your work in that chapter and write a summary statement detailing which of your courtship stages have become distorted.

Courtship summary statement:

_____

_____

_____

_____

_____

What aspects of courtship are underdeveloped?

_____

_____

_____

_____

_____

Sometimes dysfunctional courtship beliefs exist in an arousal template. They take the form of sexual prejudices that affect our sexual decisions. Examples include:

• Women are capricious and cannot be relied upon.

• Women tease.

• All women want is money and gifts. Sex has to be bought.

• Men only want sex.

• No man can be trusted.

• "No" really means "yes" (a man or woman is really asking for sex even though he or she says no to it).

What beliefs do you have that you can now identify as being untrue but to which you still react emotionally?

Belief One: _____

Belief Two: _____

Belief Three: _____

Belief Four: _____

Belief Five: _____

Drawing Your Template

The arousal template is highly individualized. After doing this work, can you see how many different aspects there are to your acting-out behavior? What is important now is to understand your template. This template is a way to describe how each of us makes decisions. If a specific stimulus occurs, what will your next choice most likely be? If there are two options, how do you decide which one to take? Consider the man who drives by a strip club and finds himself stimulated. (See figure 7.5) He has a number of choices. He can turn around and go in. He can drive back and forth until he is so stimulated he goes in. He can cruise past other clubs. He can go straight to a massage parlor. He can go home and approach his partner. He can go home, get on the Internet, and go straight to a website where he can have a woman strip for him. If he goes to the web site, there is a certain type of woman he is looking for. If he ends up in the strip club, there is a certain type of woman or behavior he is looking for. If he approaches his partner, what makes that erotic? Here is another example: a woman who sees an old lover who is dangerous to her has several choices. She can walk away from him. She can contact him and then walk away. Or they can agree to meet. No matter the scenario, the important step is to make the choice points explicit.

In business, athletics, and science, we call this structure an expert system. Many people who excel at some activity have a difficult time explaining how they do actions that seem almost miraculous in their insight or understanding or accomplishment. A very accomplished surgeon may have difficulty teaching his skill to other physicians. By carefully thinking through and describing each step, however, the physician can see the steps and others can see how the task is done. The physical actions of world-class athletes and performers seem so easy and effortless. These people, however, have actually created a highly evolved "system" of decision-making that has become unconscious. By making their decision-making process explicit, they can improve their performance. Destructiveness also has its templates. Every addiction—whether drugs, alcohol, gambling, or compulsive spending—has a decision template that continually intensifies its power. You are an expert in your sex addiction, but shame, pleasure, and risk prevent you from understanding yourself and limit your ability to get help from others. Now that you have completed all this work, the task before you is to look at how you make your decisions.

To do so, take a large piece of paper, such as a piece of newsprint, and carefully diagram how your sexual choices have been made. Notice how you make your choices. What makes one action superior to another? What creates a point of no return? Figure 7.5 shows an example of how the man in our strip club example makes his decisions.

Figure 7.5

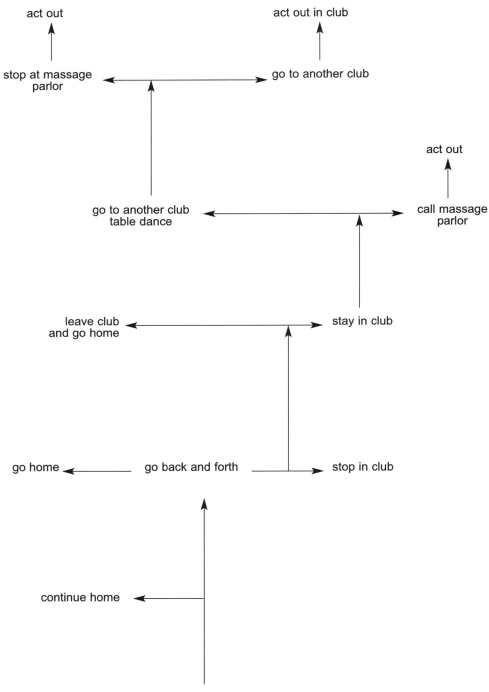

act out

act out in club

stop at massage parlor ←—————————————→ go to another club

act out

go to another club table dance ←—————————————→ call massage parlor

leave club and go home ←—————————————→ stay in club

go home ←————— go back and forth —————→ stop in club

continue home ←—————

START BY DRIVING BY STRIP CLUB

There are several very good reasons for you to work through this task and reveal your decision tree to yourself. First, understanding how you make these decisions will enable you to change your decisions. Sex addicts usually experience their bodies as being driven by forces beyond their control. By recognizing and becoming aware of your choice points, you can create the psychological distance you need to see that you have choices—that your behavior is not inevitable. If you recognize the neuropathways involved, you will understand that addictive arousal is about wiring and templates. It is not the "cosmic person" or sexual reality. Second, carrying out this task will lay the foundation for the long-term reclamation of your sexuality. Your arousal templates have been vandalized, courtship has been distorted, and addiction cycles have taken over. The great irony for many recovering people is to realize that despite incredible amounts of sexual activity, they have really not experienced their sexuality. Rather, they have only experienced the distortions of others. Recovery literally means recovering what has been lost or taken. By stepping back from yourself and looking at how the "system" works, you can decide what you want to keep, what is missing, and what you need to develop.

Following these suggestions will help you enormously as you work through this task:

Stay focused on the pain. Working on your arousal patterns may become stimulating in itself. Keeping in mind just how hard life as an addict has been will help you avoid being distracted by your old patterns.

Do not do this work in isolation. This activity should be shared with others to maximize your insight. You will also feel grief and pain over losses, and you will need support from your therapist, sponsor, and group mates to help you through this difficult experience.

Be thorough. These activities will make a huge difference in your success, but for that to happen, you have to give them the time and energy to make them work for you.

Be honest with yourself. Some of what you discover may be very hard to write down. Being explicit is part of breaking through your feelings of shame and your need for secrecy. Remember second-order change. Remember that changing behaviors will bring some other changes. Changing your internal belief system will make a significant change in your life.

Behind the Arousal Template

Harry Potter in *The Sorcerer's Stone* discovers the Mirror of Erised. As he gazes in the mirror he sees his parents looking back at him with love and approval. Harry's parents died protecting him from the evil wizard Voldemart – or he whose name we dare not mention. To be able to gaze at his parents was his most ardent wish. He found leaving the mirror difficult. He keeps revisiting the mirror and brings his friend Ron to show him how he could see his parents. When Ron gazed in the mirror he saw himself successful and out of the shadow of his brothers – his very most ardent wish.

The Dean of Hogwarts, Albus Dumbeldore, learns that the boys have found the mirror and intervenes. He explains that the mirror reflects your deepest desire (Erised is the reverse of desire). He further tells Ron and Harry that people have literally been captured by the mirror and unable to leave. The mirror of Esired illustrates how living in the fantasy falls far short of living in the reality. As the story unfolds, Ron is fundamentally better off creating his achievements. Further, in Harry's case, there is no way to make up for the wound of the loss of his parents. To use the words of Carl Jung, this is Harry's legitimate suffering. Loss adds to Harry's understanding of the world and strengthens his determination to do well.

Providing the illusion of what we have always wanted appears in our cultural stories in many ways. The "holodeck" of the Star Trek series was a place to enjoy history and fantasy. Those who sought their heart's desire there could end up with Holo-addiction in which a person ended up preferring fantasy to real life. When Faust traded his soul for his desires on earth, Mephistopheles knew just what to promise. When Faust asked Mephistopheles who he was, the response was "I am spirit who denies."

Our fantasies – especially our sexual ones – reflect our own most ardent wishes. In this way the fantasies become in sexologist Michael Bader's words, the "window to the soul." Consider the story of James, who grew up in an alcoholic family and with a physically abusive father. As a boy he was very talented but was also much neglected and learned to rely solely on himself. He became very successful as a real estate investor and prided himself on the fact that in his business all his "deals" created independence. Further, he never had to rely on one person, institution, or market. Yet inside he was desperate for people to notice his exceptional talent. His most ardent wish was to make up the deficit he experienced in his family. He wanted to be noticed and acknowledged. In therapy, his therapist pointed out the obvious. His business was set up in a way so that he would not feel others' rejection. At the same time, being so solitary meant that few could see his genius. He often was bombastic and righteous which served to have few people want to know him.

Sexually, the problem James had was a series of arrests for exhibitionism. He realized he had to do something and entered therapy. One day he made a comment to his therapists on how he was disgusted by women who strip for men in strip clubs. His therapist asked him to reflect on the obvious. When James pressed his therapist on what he meant, the therapist explained that those women James despised were also doing what he did. It was as if a jolt of lightening went through James. He realized he hated what he did but loved what he did. This became the gateway to James' deepest pain. His sexual obsession about exposing himself to women was an extension of the profound search throughout his life for acknowledgement. Thus James began the inner search of connecting his arousal to his deepest, most ardent wishes. Therein lies the core of therapy and recovery. It is a task that takes time and effort to make explicit and why a good therapist is so important to making these significant changes.

Like the mirror of Erised, we can lose ourselves in the fantasy and not understand the core issues of the self that must be addressed. Gazing at the fantasy is like pouring water into a bottomless glass. It never fills. In this way our addiction is an ally to the self, protecting some truth we wish not to face. Almost always addiction's presence means some unbearable truth resides within. The addiction evolved so the addict would not have to face that critical reality. This is why addictions frequently have different forms and combinations. If we resolve one addiction, others surface to keep that truth obscured. Addiction is in many ways an important ally desperate to save the addict from experiencing profound inner wounds. Thus cravings are communications that the self is in distress. No amount of abstinence will be achieved until the wounds are addressed. Nor will any amount of abstinence take away the fundamental obsession until there is resolution and understanding of the hurt.

If addictive behavior contains unacknowledged anger, fear or shame, addicts experience their genitals but not their woundedness. If they have guilt or strengths that are unbearable, the addiction protects the truth about those aspects of self. Thus seeking degradation or humiliation may really be about behavior we have done to others (guilt) or true abilities and aspects of self with which there is discomfort. As with James, if acknowledgement is desperately sought, it will surely emerge sexually in some form.

James' therapist asked him to list his sexual and non-sexual fantasies. His non-sexual fantasies included telling someone off and making a scene, usually in front of a group. With the help of his group and therapist, he was able to see the commonalities between the fantasies. In both, he fantasized about an angry behavior forcing others to notice him. The underlying issue for James was the profound neglect of his childhood that he needed to acknowledge and grieve.

More than any other vehicle for sexual obsession, cybersex is like the Mirror of Erised. Almost any "ardent desire" can be found. Accessing the unresolved is the portal through which many addicts start to live in obsession versus in reality. Finding what you have always been searching for becomes a way to dissociate from who you really are and what you must do. Internet sex can become more than information or confirmation that you are not alone. Gazing on your heart's desire means that somewhere else sex is better, although the truth is you can never get to that somewhere else. You join Faust, Harry Potter, and those trapped in the Holodeck. Addiction is sustained when illusion becomes reality. The very fantasy can, however, serve as a vehicle to understanding issues core to your soul.

Mirror of Desire

Imagine you have a mirror in which you could see that which you want the most. Make a list of what you would see in that mirror. Be honest with yourself. One way to approach it is to ask for what would you give up everything. This is the proverbial list of those things for which you would trade your soul. All of us have them. They are important to acknowledge as part of your healing. Make sure that half of your list is sexual. Start with listing your most ardent non-sexual desires. What scenes would appear in your mirror? Please list them below:

1._____

2._____

3._____

4._____

5._____

6._____

7._____

8._____

9._____

10._____

Now make a list of your ideal sexual fantasies. These are the fantasies that are the most power-ful in your life. Gazing in the mirror, what sexual fantasies would appear? List them below:

1._____

2._____

3._____

4._____

5._____

6._____

7._____

8._____

9._____

10._____

Reflect on themes that emerge. Talk with your therapist, sponsor, and recovery support people. What parallels exist between the lists?

Now record what they have in common.

_____

_____

_____

_____

Looking at the commonalities, where do you think your most "ardent desires" come from. They may have come from early wounds or experiences in your life. Or they could be a difficult truth about you which has been too painful to face. Harry Potter gazed in the mirror which gave him relief from grieving about his parent's deaths. Addiction "protects" like gazing in the mirror. Part of woundedness for addicts is behaviors which are used to cope, such as James' artful skills at isolation. Behind damaged coping, and addictive refocusing are core experiences. List the sources of your "ardent desires."

Sources of Deep Desire

No.1_____

_____

No.2_____

_____

No.3_____

_____

No.4_____

_____

No.5_____

_____

What have been the costs in not acknowledging these wounds. Include both addictive and non addictive costs:

_____

_____

_____

_____

_____

Reflect on what steps you could take to heal those experiences that have supported dysfunction and addiction in your life:

_____

_____

_____

_____

Recommended Readings

Milkman, Harvey, and Stanley, Sunderwirth. *Craving for Ecstasy: The Chemistry and Consciousness of Escape*. New York: Free Press, 1987.

Carnes, Patrick J. *Sexual Anorexia: Overcoming Self Hatred*. pp. 217-365. Center City, MN.: Hazelden, 1997.

Carnes, Patrick J., David Delmonico and Elizabeth Griffin. *In the Shadow of the Net*. Chap. 4, "What Turns You On." Center City, MN: Hazelden. 2001.

Additional Reading

Bader, Michael. *Arousal: The Secret Logic of Sexual Fantasies.* New York: St. Martin's Press. 2002.

Crenshaw, Theresa L., M.D. *The Alchemy of Love & Lust*. New York: Putnam Berkeley Group, 1996.

Covington, Stephanie, and Liana Beckett. *Leaving the Enchanted Forest: The Path from Relationship Addiction to Intimacy*. San Francisco: Harper & Rowe, 1988.

Fisher, Helen. *Journal of Sex Education and Therapy*. Vol. 25, (no. 1) pp. 96-104.

Fisher, Helen. *Anatomy of Love: The Natural History of Monogamy, Adultery, and Divorce.* 1992.

Fisher, Helen. *Why We Love?* New York: Henry Holt & Co., 2004.

Klausner, Mary Ann, and Bobbie Hasselbring. *Aching for Love: The Sexual Drama of the Adult Child*. San Francisco: Harper & Rowe,1990.

Maltz, Wendy. *The Sexual Healing Journey*. New York: Harper Collins, 1991.

Mellody, Pia. *Facing Love Addiction*. San Francisco: Harper & Rowe, 1992.

Money, John W. *Love Maps*. Amherst, New York: Prometheus Books, 1990

Schaeffer, Brenda. *Is It Love or Is It Addiction?* Center City, MN.: Hazelden, 1987.

CHAPTER EIGHT: Where Is Your Support?
Creating Your Support Systems

If sex is very troublesome, we throw ourselves the harder into helping others. We think of
their needs and work for them. This takes us out of ourselves.
It quiets the imperious urge, when to yield would mean heartache.
—ALCOHOLICS ANONYMOUS, The Big Book

THROUGHOUT THIS BOOK we have identified the importance of being in a Twelve Step program. To summarize:

- Abuse victims and children raised in dysfunctional families find it difficult to engage in therapy unless they are with an ongoing group of people who have had similar experiences.•
Participation in a Twelve Step group helps addicts make up developmental deficits—that
is, skills they did not get from their families—in such areas as intimacy, trust, and accountability.

- The Twelve Steps teach an existential position that can help addicts better manage grief,
loss, and anxiety.

- Starting with the First Step, the Twelve Steps initiate a profound change process. We have
described this shift as a second-order change in which the core beliefs of the system are
now altered (rather than a first-order change in which the addicts attempts to control
behavior by "trying harder").

- At its most basic level, the recovery process requires connection and consultation with
others. Addicts who are isolated make poor choices. To succeed in recovery, they need
the help of therapists and of other recovering people. Starting with the initial debriefing
with a sponsor and continuing through relapse planning and arousal template work, we
have emphasized the importance of having recovering people involved in your work.

Therapy makes a fundamental difference in how successful recovery is. In fact, some addicts have been able to stay relapse-free with only therapeutic support for a brief time. Research shows that long-term recovery will consistently hold for those who immerse themselves into a Twelve Step culture. Going to therapy is not enough. Attending Twelve Step groups is not enough. You have to start participating in the life of your Twelve Step community. How do you do that? This chapter will assist you in integrating Twelve Step recovery into your life.

Learning about the Twelve Step Process

To begin, it will help you to know more about the original Twelve Step group. We strongly suggest that you read the Big Book of Alcoholics Anonymous. The recommended reading list at the end of the chapter cites a "study" version of the Big Book, which also contains a copy of the original typed manuscript. You will find this an extraordinary story of great courage and hope. Table 8.1 lists the original Twelve Steps of AA. By reading and reflecting on the original Twelve Step story, you will become familiar with phrases that have become the hallmarks of recovery, including "a day at a time," "an easier, softer way," and "cunning and baffling." You will be surprised when you find phrases that speak directly to you as a sex addict, such as those passages about the "voices who cry for sex and more sex." Moreover, you will become familiar with famous passages such as the "promises of AA" that have inspired generations of recovering people (see pages 83 and 84 of the Big Book).

Table 8.1

STEP ONE We admitted we were powerless over alcohol—that our lives had become unmanageable.

STEP TWO Came to believe that a Power greater than ourselves could restore us to sanity.

STEP THREE Made a decision to turn our will and our lives over to the care of God *as we understood Him.*

STEP FOUR Made a searching and fearless moral inventory of ourselves.

STEP FIVE Admitted to God, to ourselves, and to another human being the exact nature of our wrongs.

STEP SIX Were entirely ready to have God remove all these defects of character.

STEP SEVEN Humbly asked Him to remove our shortcomings.

STEP EIGHT Made a list of all persons we had harmed, and became willing to make amends to them all.

STEP NINE Made direct amends to such people wherever possible, except when to do so would injure them or others.

STEP TEN Continued to take personal inventory and when we were wrong promptly admitted it.

STEP ELEVEN Sought through prayer and meditation to improve our conscious contact with God *as we understood Him*, praying only for knowledge of His will for us and the power to carry that out.

STEP TWELVE Having had a spiritual awakening as the result of these steps, we tried to carry this message to alcoholics, and to practice these principles in all our affairs.

Books describing the development of AA will also be useful to you. You will start to realize how truly revolutionary the Twelve Step process was and what it took for it to grow. Two books listed in the recommended reading are Nan Robertson's *Getting Better: Inside Alcoholics Anonymous* and Francis Hartigan's *Bill W.* One of the most intriguing discoveries you will make is that Bill Wilson, the famous co-founder of AA, struggled with sexual issues himself. His struggles in this area of his life appear to parallel the lives of many people who have become sober from alcoholism only to have their sexual behavior go out of control. Nan Robertson describes it this way:

> *Bill Wilson was a compulsive womanizer. His flirtations and his adulterous behavior filled him with guilt, according to old-timers close to him, but he continued to stray off the reservation. His last and most serious love affair, with a woman at AA headquarters in New York, began when he was in his sixties. She was important to him until the end of his life.*

No wonder his words speak to sex addicts today.

Sadly, Bill W. did not have the benefit of using the Steps for his other addictions, nor did countless sex addicts who came after him. This sad situation changed, however, in the summer of 1977. In three different parts of the country, groups were established using Twelve Step principles for sex addiction. In Boston, the groups came to be called Sex and Love Addicts Anonymous (SLAA). In Simi Valley, California, the groups were called Sexaholics Anonymous (SA). And in Minneapolis, Minnesota, Sex Addicts Anonymous (SAA) started. Since that time, two other fellowships of significance also emerged: Sexual Compulsives Anonymous (SCA), which was initiated by gay men, and Sexual Recovery Anonymous (SRA), which has been strong in the northeastern part of the country. They all have the Twelve Steps in common and draw heavily on the heritage of AA. Here are some of the differences:

- **SLAA** (Sex and Love Addicts Anonymous) is perhaps the most inclusive (and the largest) of all the fellowships simply because it also acknowledges compulsive romance and relationships. It also has led the way in looking at sexual anorexia as part of this illness.

- **SAA** (Sex Addicts Anonymous) also is quite inclusive and is making progress on sexual anorexia as well. Like SLAA, it asks participants to realistically view their bottom line behaviors and to take responsibility for them.

- **SA** (Sexaholics Anonymous) has the strictest standards for sobriety, emphasizing the importance of commitment, heterosexuality, and spirituality. Homosexual activity is currently not accepted within the parameters of recovery in this fellowship.

- **SCA** (Sexual Compulsives Anonymous) was started by gay men but now includes a strong contingent of heterosexual women who found the meetings especially safe for them. Of all the fellowships, it does the best job of helping individuals develop their "sex plan."

- **SRA** (Sexual Recovery Anonymous) is a program that started in New York and has aggressively developed outreach in the northeastern part of the country. It is very inclusive, though still regional in its scope.

Such diversity has encouraged great creativity and growth in our understanding of how to recover from sex addiction. This diversity, however, has probably limited the development of a strong centralized support network like those in Alcoholics Anonymous or Overeaters Anonymous. Many addicts report the benefit of having attended groups from a number of different fellowships and of learning different perspectives within the Twelve Step umbrella. Ongoing dialogue continues among these fellowships about collaboration and resource sharing. In some cities, there are intergroups that serve all the S-fellowships—and this shows how the differences between them are starting to blur. Table 8-2 summarizes this fellowship information and the additional reading section specifies key publications from various fellowships.

Table 8.2

COSA (Partners)
9337-B Katy Freeway
Suite 142
Houston, TX 77024
612-537-6904

NCSAC (National Council on Sexual
Addiction and Compulsivity)
1090 Northchase Parkway
Suite 200 South
Marietta, GA 30067
770-989-9754
www.ncsac.org

RCA (Recovering Couples Anonymous)
PO Box 11029
Oakland, CA 94611
510-336-3300
www.recovering-couples.org

SA (Sexaholics Anonymous)
PO Box 111910
Nashville, TN 37222-1910
615-331-6230
www.sa.org

SAA (Sex Addicts Anonymous)
PO Box 70949
Houston, TX 77270
713-869-4902
www.saa-recovery.org

S-Anon (Partners)
PO Box 111242
Nashville, TN 37222
615-833-3152
www.sanon.org

SCA (Sexual Compulsive Anonymous)
PO Box 1585
Old Chelsea Station
New York, NY 10011
www.sca-recovery.org

SLAA (Sex and Love Addicts Anonymous)
The Augustine Fellowship
PO Box 338
Norwood, MA 02062-0338
781-255-8825
www.slaafws.org

SRA (Sexual Recovery Anonymous)
PO Box 73
Planetarium Station
New York, NY 10024
212-340-4650
www.sexualrecovery.org

www.onlinesexaddict.com
Online Sexual Addiction Homepage

www.sexaddict.com
Sex Addiction Recovery Resources

www.sexhelp.com
Dr. Carnes's Online Resources

The best action you can take, however, is to find a really good meeting—just as it is in AA. There may be thirty to fifty meetings in your city, but finding one within a good time slot that has good sobriety with people you like may be hard and take some time. That is, however, what makes the difference. More important than which fellowship you belong to is the quality of the meeting that you attend. Here are some signs to help you recognize a good meeting:

- Strong regular attendance.
- Members take responsibility for leadership positions.
- Each week, someone in the group takes responsibility for presenting either a Step or a topic.
- The Step presentations or topic presentations are prepared and thoughtful.
- There is a well-understood and supported process for welcoming newcomers.
- The group has strong ties with a codependency support group such as S-Anon, Co-SA, or Co-SLAA.
- There is a group life outside of the meeting in the form of regular meals together, workshops, or retreats.
- Periodically—at least every quarter—the group stops to do a "group conscience," which means the members hold an extended discussion about how the group is doing.
- Leadership and "jobs" in the group rotate regularly.
- There is a steady influx of new persons.
- There is steady attendance of veterans who have successful sobriety.

A good meeting is the heart of recovery. If you find one you really like, it is worth restructuring your schedule so you can attend regularly. It takes a while to know whether a given meeting is "right" for you. Many people suggest that you go to at least six meetings before you draw any conclusions. Every meeting can have an "off" night or two, but usually the character of the meeting will emerge over six weeks. Spend time outside the meeting over a meal or in some fellowship function getting to know some of the members. It would be unusual not to misjudge a meeting in some way early in the process. In part it is because of the nature of meetings, but also it can be our own issues.

Early Barriers to Meetings

Addicts resist going to meetings because recovery principles are so different from the way addictions work. Meetings rely on their members to be open, consultative, vulnerable, accountable, and consistent. Addiction thrives best in secrecy, isolation, willfulness, and chaos. No wonder addicts find reasons not to go. The following are typical reasons people offer for not attending, as well as some observations about each:

I might meet someone I know.

You probably will, but that will help reduce feelings of shame for both of you. Reflect on the fact that while you were acting out, you ran the risk of meeting someone you would know and it did not stop you. Under which circumstances would you rather meet others you know? The real reason you do not want to go has to do with feelings of pride. You've tried to create an image of yourself that is different from who you really are. If someone recognizes you at a meeting, that person will know the truth about you. But this is exactly why you should attend. You will find that the pretense is unnecessary; people will respect you for who you really are, faults included.

I might meet someone I know professionally.

Physicians, therapists, attorneys, judges, politicians, CEOs, and business leaders worry about meeting clients, patients, or employees. This has been, of course, an issue in Twelve Step programs for years, one that people, particularly those in small towns, have successfully overcome. Several points should be remembered. First, this is a problem for everyone, and so this is where judicious use of boundaries apply. Being in the same program does not mean that you tell everything to people whom you know outside the program. Second, most cities have groups called "boundary groups" that are designed for people who would have a serious problem being in an open meeting. It would probably not be a good idea for a therapist to share struggles in the same group as his or her patients. Finally, it is very important to observe the "traditions" of the various fellowships and leave non-program issues at the door. It is not appropriate to talk to a CEO of a company about job possibilities at a meeting. Anonymity must be observed for the benefit of everyone.

I cannot find a meeting that does not conflict with my schedule.

If so, then start a new one. Get some help from existing meetings and your local intergroup, or call the national office of the fellowship of your choice. Tell local clergy and mental health professionals where and when you wish to start a meeting. Most meetings begin either because of a lack of meetings or the availability of meetings at a convenient time. This task becomes harder, however, if you have never been in a meeting before. The fellowships have lots of experience in helping people start from scratch. So ask for help.

I do not fit well with the people in the meeting I went to.

The most common discovery mentioned by people who've joined Twelve Step programs is that they seriously misperceived the people in their group when they started. This happens most often because of the newcomer's shame, distrust, and uncertainty. Over time, they realize what tremendous resources the group members have become in their lives. You do have to get to know them, and the key to this task is spending time with them outside of a meeting. Frequently, groups meet before or after a meeting. In other cases, groups set up time during the week in which everyone gets together for a meal. **Go to some of those events before you make up your mind about a group.** *This is one of the most important things you can do for your recovery besides finding a sponsor.*

Everyone is slipping in the group I go to.

If a pattern of slipping occurs in your group, then it is time for a meeting called a "group conscience." During that time, group members talk about how the group is doing and whethe it is meeting the needs of its members. Members can share with one another how important mutual sobriety is. If people are struggling, they need to get more help until they are able to stay sober. Usually the group starts targeting topics that will help people with their sobriety. Sponsorship, regular check-ins by phone, and getting therapeutic support can also make a difference. Ironically, groups will often take the people who are struggling the most and give them more responsibility in the group, such as taking on the weekly "trusted servant" leadership role. Many people finally achieve sobriety when they are in a leadership position. Remember, some people may need a higher level of intervention such as an outpatient or residential program to give their recovery momentum. For them, simply being a leader may not be enough and they will need to be encouraged to get more help. Remember also the old aphorism "You are only as healthy as your group." Even as a newcomer, you have a responsibility to help the group be as healthy as possible. Not going to the meeting provides neither you nor the group with a solution. Sometimes, it is newcomers who provide the positive energy needed to make a group healthier. To say to yourself "because everyone is slipping there is no hope" is addictive thinking. Clearly, the real issue is to determine what you can do to make the group better.

I do not go to meetings because I have been slipping and it is hard to admit to my struggle.

All the above applies to you. Admit you are struggling. Start calling and meeting other people. Volunteer for leadership roles and fellowship tasks. Sign up to give talks and meetings. Start going to meals and get-togethers. Get more help if you need it. Above all, be honest with yourself about how you got outside of your recovery zone. The very worst things you can do are to avoid meetings and to tell no one. Do them and the boulder we pictured in chapter 6 starts to roll. You simply must reimmerse yourself in the recovery culture.

Going to meetings is the bedrock of recovery. But attendance is not really the issue; involvement is. Do you have a sponsor who is coaching you? Even temporary sponsors make a huge difference. Do you participate in the life of the group? Have you presented a Step or a meeting? Have you supported the group by doing service work? Do you sponsor people? It is really "throwing ourselves into helping others" that makes the difference.

Consider the story of James. He was a very successful and entrepreneurial man with a rather poor sexual track record. Therein was the problem. There were very few things he had set out to do that he had not achieved, but he simply failed repeatedly in his attempts to stop his risky sexual behavior. James was seeing a therapist and he had found a Twelve Step group to attend. When he acted out, James did not tell his therapist. He hated going to his Twelve Step meeting and acted like all was well when he was there. Admitting failure at something was still beyond what he could do. When his Twelve Step meeting finished, with most everyone adjourning to a nearby Chinese restaurant, James would head straight home. James always felt wistful about missing the restaurant time because his meeting colleagues all laughed so hard and seemed to enjoy each other's company so much. He felt left out, and there were very few places in his life where he was not at the center of the action. As an excuse, James told himself that they did not have the stress he did nor had most of them achieved what he had. And then with time, James would allow the press of his schedule to interfere with his Twelve Step meetings. He would frequently cancel and reschedule therapy. As his recovery work became more erratic, James's acting out became even more frequent.

James's life unraveled when one of his affairs—with a woman who worked in one of his companies—became public. He had counted on her to never reveal their love affair—a trust she kept until her husband discovered their love letters and her diary. He promptly called James's wife and then told his own wife that if she did not sue James for sexual harassment, the marriage was over. The incident became public knowledge in James's various companies. Other women came forward. A vengeful activist in the accounting department checked travel receipts. A number of hotel records showed local numbers called to escort services and outcall massage agencies. The company being sued called an emergency meeting. A key stockholder on the board was a woman with whom James flirted all the time. In fact, her support was vital to his power base in that company, and it was their emotional affair that he believed kept her in his camp. This woman became furious to learn about the other women with whom James had been involved. Even worse, James had confided in her about matters about which the rest of the board did not know and which would upset them. In short, this was a mess.

James went to see his therapist, Don, and reported what was going on. Some of this, of course, was news to the therapist—which he pointed out. Don asked James about his Twelve Step support, specifically who knew the whole story. James could point to no one. Don explained the concept of "shopping" your story. The addict will tell pieces of his or her story to different people and consider himself to have "shared" the story. In James's case, no one person knew about the extent of his acting out or of his current relapses. Don told James that if they were to continue in therapy, everything had to come out—and he also insisted that James contact members of his group.

James called a group member named Jack that night. Jack said that he would invite some guys to meet together for breakfast the next morning. Three men met with James at a local pancake house. Coming up to the breakfast table, James felt teary realizing that these people whom he did not know well had changed their schedules to help him after all he had done. Their welcome was warm and kind—though not without a touch of gallows humor. Laughing felt good to James, however. As he told his story in hushed tones, James fell again into tears first and then deep sobs. Here was the guy who would not let anyone know what was happening crying in the middle of a pancake house. Being with men who cared about what happened to him broke down James's walls.

His group mates were very practical. They started with what needed to happen today. It was very clarifying for James to realize that all he had to do was to get through today. Then they asked if he would talk to the group about his dishonesty with them. James agreed to do that the next night at the meeting. They stayed in touch with him until then. At the meeting, James admitted that he had been coming and saying things were fine when, in fact, they were not. Now he was facing the loss of career, marriage, and financial well-being. When he finished his story, there was a long silence. And then people spoke slowly, thoughtfully. Some pointed out that they had done the same because it was the nature of the illness to hide shame. Others were relieved and glad that he was really finally joining the group. And still others offered their support and help. That night they all sat in the Chinese restaurant and helped James think through his next steps. They had suggestions for the board, for therapy, and for dealing with an angry spouse. James came to two realizations sitting in that restaurant: his life had changed significantly because of these people and he had seriously misjudged them. They were competent and resourceful. And they were working hard to keep him from making his life even worse.

James was asked by his board to go to a residential facility for treatment. When he went to see Don about it, his therapist said that he had come to the same conclusion. James had not been getting enough help, given how badly his illness had progressed. Don had also been talking with Judy, James's wife. In Don's opinion, to go into a program was his best shot at recovery and saving his marriage. So James went. There, James was overwhelmed to discover just how much he did not know about himself. When he returned from treatment, he reported this to the group amidst cheers and laughter. He was elected to be the group's "trusted servant" for a three-month term. It was then that James really discovered the heart of the Twelve Step program. He became very close to his sponsor (Jack took on the task), although he heard from almost everybody while he was in treatment. It had meant a lot to him to get supportive cards and calls. He now was sponsoring others and remembering them when times were difficult. He had discovered the secret. Service to others is how things get better. Back in the beginning of AA, Bill W. was told by Carl Jung that "passing it on" was how they would get better. The correspondence between Bill W. and Dr. Jung are now regarded as documents of great significance because of the recipe for success they contained. Addicts helping other addicts—"throwing ourselves into helping others," as Bill W. eventually described it—is a key to the Twelve Step program's success.

James's story is not unique. Many people who went through the motions of recovery were finally forced to surrender to the recovery process. Full disclosure to trusted people is one of those moments of surrender. Participating fully in a culture of Twelve Step support is another. In the following pages, you will find a series of exercises related to the "important" people in your life. The goal of the exercises is to ensure that you make a full disclosure to those in your life who need to know and whom you trust. Complete them and then record your reflections.

Important People Inventory

The following inventory asks you to list people who are important to you. You will categorize them in two ways. First, you will list people according to how much they know about you. Start with those who know everything. Then list those who know most of the story. Follow this with a list of those who know about your addiction, but not much of the story. Finish with another list of people whose relationship you value but who know nothing of your addiction or recovery. After completing the four lists, go back and rate each person on a scale of 1 to 5 as to how close you feel to that person. A score of 1 means not close at all and a score of 5 represents a very close and trusting relationship. Then, follow the directions provided at the conclusion of the exercise.

1. Important people who know the whole story (those who know everything past and present).

Name	Closeness Rating
a.	1 2 3 4 5
b.	1 2 3 4 5
c.	1 2 3 4 5
d.	1 2 3 4 5
e.	1 2 3 4 5
f.	1 2 3 4 5
g.	1 2 3 4 5
h.	1 2 3 4 5
i.	1 2 3 4 5
j.	1 2 3 4 5

2. Important people who know most of your story (those who know most everything past and current).

Name	Closeness Rating
a.	1 2 3 4 5
b.	1 2 3 4 5
c.	1 2 3 4 5
d.	1 2 3 4 5
e.	1 2 3 4 5
f.	1 2 3 4 5
g.	1 2 3 4 5
h.	1 2 3 4 5
i.	1 2 3 4 5
j.	1 2 3 4 5

3. Important people who know about your addiction but have only few details (those who know of the illness, but do not know about the story, or recovery, or current progress).

Name	Closeness Rating
a.	1 2 3 4 5
b.	1 2 3 4 5
c.	1 2 3 4 5
d.	1 2 3 4 5
e.	1 2 3 4 5
f.	1 2 3 4 5
g.	1 2 3 4 5
h.	1 2 3 4 5
i.	1 2 3 4 5
j.	1 2 3 4 5

4. Important people who know nothing of your addiction or recovery (those whose relationship you value but with whom you have shared nothing about your story or recovery).

Name	Closeness Rating
a.	1 2 3 4 5
b.	1 2 3 4 5
c.	1 2 3 4 5
d.	1 2 3 4 5
e.	1 2 3 4 5
f.	1 2 3 4 5
g.	1 2 3 4 5
h.	1 2 3 4 5
i.	1 2 3 4 5
j.	1 2 3 4 5

Reflection Questions

The following questions are designed to help you reflect on your *Important People Inventory.*

1. How do you feel about the number of people who truly know all of your past story and your current status?

_____

_____

_____

_____

2. What discrepancies did you notice? Are there people you trust who do not know? People who know but with whom you do not feel close?

_____

_____

_____

_____

3. Look at your inventory from a Twelve Step perspective. Who are the people in recovery on your list? Are there sponsors and sponsees? If not, why?

_____

_____

_____

_____

4. Who in your family is on that list? In your extended family? Do you wish to change that?

_____

_____

_____

_____

5. Where is your therapist on this list? Do you need to talk to your therapist about your relationship? About further disclosure? About this list?

_____

_____

_____

_____

6. This list often reveals unfinished business that needs to be addressed or relationship work that needs to be done. List any action steps you now need to take.

a. action step:_____

b. action step:_____

c. action step:_____

d. action step:_____

e. action step:_____

Use this work when you reflect in your journal or talk to your groups. Show your work to your sponsor, therapist, or people in your consulting circle.

Couples Recovery

When doing the research for *Don't Call It Love,* I learned some important facts about successful recovery. If a person was in a committed relationship, the likelihood of successful recovery went up if the partner was involved in therapy early in recovery. The quality of recovery improved dramatically if the partners also committed to recovery for themselves. This means that they actually went to a Twelve Step program for co-sex addiction such as S-Anon or Co-SA. In this way, they learned how they participated in this illness. They also were able to apply Twelve Step principles to their codependency. And finally, the overall quality of recovery was highest for those people who attended a Twelve Step program for couples.

Recovering Couples Anonymous (RCA) uses the metaphor of a three-legged stool. There is "my recovery," "your (spouse or partner) recovery," and "our recovery together"—the three legs of couples recovery. The idea of "coupleship in recovery" was new in the 1980s but long overdue. Therapists had known for a long time that to treat people individually for issues that also involved the couple's relationship often made things worse. In Twelve Step programs, there was no place for couples to systematically use the Steps as a couple. Sadly, I believe Twelve Step programs actually undermined relationships at times. Groups like RCA became a format for looking at relationship deficits and for using Twelve Step principles for change. (See Table 8.2 for fellowship listings.) The result is a consistent, cohesive shift both in partners individually and in their relationship. Readers who are single and think this does not apply to them should still take note. When you do get into a relationship, you will find the waters will be a lot smoother if you and your partner participate in a Twelve Step couples community. The principles of recovery when shared with a partner can make dramatic differences in the quality of intimacy. RCA describes it this way:

> If we are honest about our commitment and painstaking about working the Twelve Steps together, we will quickly be amazed at how soon our love returns. We are going to know a new freedom and a new happiness. We will learn how to play and have fun together. As we experience mutual forgiveness, we will not regret the past nor wish to shut the door on it. Trust in each other will return. We will comprehend the word serenity, and we will know peace.
>
> No matter how close to brokenness we have come, we will see how our experiences can benefit others. That feeling of uselessness, shame and self-pity will disappear. We will lose interest in selfish things and gain interest in our partners, families and others. Self-seeking will slip away. Our whole attitude and outlook on life will change. Fear of people and of economic insecurity will leave us. We will intuitively know how to handle situations that used to baffle us. We will be better parents, workers, helpers and friends. We will suddenly realize that God is doing for us what we could not do for ourselves.

James and Judy went to their first RCA meeting at the insistence of Don, their therapist. James was reluctant because he did not want to have other people's spouses hear about his behavior. Judy also was reticent. First of all, she did not want to go to any group and, in fact, had not yet attended a group for codependence. She was an atheist and did not want religion "shoved down her throat." Further, she was so mad at James that she was not sure the relationship would survive anyway. The only reason she went was because Don had asked her if she could live with leaving without really looking at possible sources of healing. She knew that she could not, but she nevertheless had one foot out the door.

Both James and Judy were surprised. They quickly recognized that their struggles were no different from what other couples were going through. They found themselves laughing heartily with the group about the ironies they faced. Judy broke into sobs as she told of how embarrassed and distraught she felt. She virtually melted when two women took her aside during a break and invited her to join them at a Co-SA meeting. It was like meeting a welcoming extended family. James and Judy left feeling exposed and raw, but they knew they would return.

A year later, James and Judy gave a meeting on the second Step and the meaning of spirituality in their coupleship. Judy moved the group to tears as she recounted how she started with a deep distrust of God. She was a sexual abuse victim who thought that no loving God would allow something like that to happen. She told of how the care of others transformed her understanding of care for herself. Because of their care, her understanding of a Higher Power in her life with her husband evolved out of her agony. She reflected on the promises and how they had come true for her, including her new understanding of "serenity."

To Be of Service

To be of service means more than just helping in your group. Service may mean helping in your local intergroup, or serving on a national committee, or going to a national conference. Service may also mean helping with some of the national support organizations. Join the National Council for Sex Addiction and Compulsion which, like the National Council on Gambling or the National Council on Alcoholism and Drug Dependency, works to reduce the stigma attached to sex addiction and to make resources available to recovering people. Also consider the National Council on Couple and Family Recovery, which is dedicated to supporting couples in recovery. There are many meaningful avenues for you to help.

By now, it should be clear that working the program does not mean merely attending meetings. Nor is it just about sponsorship and doing Step work—although no change or growth will happen without those components. The real key is becoming an active proponent for the lives of those in recovery. Helping the organizations that support recovery is as important as helping after a meeting. Remember: helping others "takes us out of ourselves."

Recommended Reading:

Alcoholics Anonymous. Study Ed., Croton Falls, New York: 1994.

Recovering Couples Anonymous. 3d Ed.

Carnes, Patrick, Debra Laaser, and Mark Laaser. *Open Hearts: Renewing Relationships with Recovery, Romance, and Reality.* Wickenburg, Ariz.: Gentle Path Press, 1999.

Additional Reading

Robertson, Nan. *Getting Better: Inside Alcoholics Anonymous*

Hartigan, Francis. *Bill W.: A Biography of Alcoholics Anonymous Cofounder Bill Wilson.*

The following literature is available from the offices listed in Table 8.2:

SAA Literature

From Shame to Grace
The Bubble
Group Guide
Three Circles
First Step
Abstinence and Boundaries
Getting Started
Abstinence

SCA Literature and Suggested Reading

Hope and Recovery
Twelve Steps and Twelve Traditions
Out of the Shadows (by Patrick Carnes)
Contrary to Love (by Patrick Carnes)
Women Who Love Too Much (by Robin Norwood)
Answers in the Heart (meditations)

SLAA Literature

Introduction to Sex and Love Addicts Anonymous
Questions Beginners Ask
Suggestions for Newcomers
12 Recommended Guidelines
Sex and Love Addiction—40 Questions
Sponsorship
Addiction and Recovery
Anorexia (Sexual, Social, Emotional)
Gateway to Freedom, Hope, and Joy

SA Literature

Member Stories
Recovery Continues
Discovering the Principles
Practical Guidelines for Group Recovery
SA Manual audiocassettes

CHAPTER NINE: What Makes for Long Term Success?
Deepening Recovery for Profound Life Change

"Do or not do. There is no 'try.'"
—YODA TO LUKE SKYWALKER in, THE EMPIRE STRIKES BACK

GEORGE LUCAS' STAR WARS TRILOGY was based on the research of Joseph Campbell, the famous expert on heroes and heroines. This story was created in part as a metaphor about meeting the challenges of twenty-first century life. At one point in the epic, young Luke Skywalker arrives on the planet Degobah in search of a master teacher of Jedi Knights named Yoda. Yoda, however, turns out to be very different from how Luke imagined he would be. He is green, short, big eared, and always placing his verbs in the wrong place when he speaks. Though clearly very funny, Yoda's humor nonetheless is always just beyond Luke's understanding. Yoda resembles what Native Americans call the "trickster"—the fun medicine man who teaches through paradox and practical jokes. Further, he always presses Luke to think beyond his worldview categories and to question his assumptions. Luke soon learns that beneath Yoda's frumpish exterior and seemingly dim-witted manner is a very learned, wise, powerful, and compassionate elder.

Above all, Luke learns from Yoda that being a Jedi Knight involves profound commitment. At one point, Yoda encourages Luke to attempt to raise his X-wing star fighter, which had sunk in a swamp. Luke makes progress but ultimately loses heart, thus allowing the ship to sink back into the goo. Luke tells Yoda that he "tried" to do as he was asked, but he concluded that raising the star fighter was impossible. Yoda responded by saying, "And that is why you fail!" Yoda then turns and raises the ship clear of the swamp and places it on dry land. Next, he turns to Luke and says, "Do or not do. There is no try"—and then he walks away.

I have often been struck by the profound truth in that scene. In therapy, I have seen many addicts who failed because they did not believe it was possible for them to recover. They could acknowledge the possibility of others' success, but in their heart of hearts they believed they were too "defective" to succeed. But they always seemed to want credit for "trying."

These individuals failed because they never made the "decision" to change. In fact, one of the most often asked questions among people in early recovery is this: "Does it get better?" This very question was, in part, the impetus behind the research for *Don't Call It Love*. We wanted to learn more about the people who had gotten better to see what actions and thoughts contributed to their success. We found much more than we had ever anticipated. We found many measures of quality of life and health. We found that recovery made dramatic life changes for the better in their lives. We also found that the people who had the greatest success took the same steps in a relatively predictable fashion. Sobriety was but one part of their life changes. They all had made a deeper commitment to making their lives better. Out of our research an overall pattern emerged. Here is the general profile of those who succeeded in recovery:

1. **They had a primary therapist.** Whether they went to residential programs, intensive workshops, or took part in specialized therapy with others, each was involved with a therapist whom they stayed with over a three-to-five year period. Working through a relationship with a therapist appears to be essential to recovery. Even more important, they each allowed themselves to have an "examined" life in which one person (the therapist) knew them extraordinarily well and had skills to help them through the challenges they encountered as they moved through recovery.

2. **They were in a therapy group.** Whether some of these hours were in a residential or outpatient setting seemed to make little difference. Those who did well spent time in a group setting with a therapist (who might or might not be their primary therapist). The optimum amount of time in such a group was approximately 175 hours, typically spent over a period of eighteen months to two years.

3. **They went regularly to Twelve Step meetings.** Further, they became deeply involved in the program, including participation in service, sponsorship, and Step work. Working through all the Steps does make a critical difference; those who did not continue Step work either struggled in their sober life or lost their sobriety altogether.

4. **If other addictions were present, they were addressed as well.** Addicts went to other Twelve Step meetings as appropriate for them. They came to understand how their addictions interacted (negatively!) with one another and how they all related to the deeper problems in their lives.

5. **They worked to find clarity and resolution in their family-of-origin and childhood issues.** They used the Steps and therapy to understand the deeper character issues they faced, and they did everything they could to find serenity with them.

6. **Their families were involved early in therapy.** Clearly, early family involvement and support plays a significant role in recovery. We found a clear difference between people who simply were involved on their own in treatment and those whose partners and family members also committed to therapy and recovery for themselves. Oftentimes, the addict's recovery was the impetus for recovery and healing in other family members, too—though in some cases, years passed before this happened.

7. **If they were in a primary relationship, the couple went to a Twelve Step couples' group such as Recovering Couples Anonymous.** Those who attended such a meeting clearly did the best of all. Having a partner in recovery is significant, but for the best result, the couple needs to participate in a Twelve Step–based couples' support network.

8. **They developed a spiritual life.** What their spiritual life consisted of was as important as practicing it on a regular, even daily, basis. Those whose spiritual life flourished were also usually active participants in a spiritual community.

9. **They actively worked to maintain regular exercise and good nutrition.** Those whose recovery blossomed exercised regularly, if not daily, and were also conscientious about making good food choices as part of their self-care.

As a general profile, this information was helpful. But after *Don't Call It Love* was completed, we felt that it was important to more clearly determine the steps taken by people who were successful in recovery. We were able to break recovery down into thirty specific tasks on which we then carried out extensive research. This workbook, and this workbook series, are based on these tasks. You might think of them like a food recipe: if you follow the recipe, you will have a predictable result. You can, of course, add extra ingredients and enhance the recipe. But that's not necessary. In general, if you want good recovery results, follow this well-proven recipe. The thirty recovery tasks are listed in table 9.1.

Each task is finished by completing activities we call "performables." We have tried to define the performables as concretely as possible. By using the experience of others, we have created a road map to recovery. In other words, while you still may not know what challenges await you around the turns on your recovery road, you now know what has helped others succeed in recovery. Follow their lead and you will increase your chances of recovery enormously.

Table 9.1

RECOVERY TASK	PERFORMABLES	LIFE COMPETENCY
1. Break through denial.	• Creates a problem list • Records a secret list • Completes list of excuses • Completes Consequences Inventory • Learns 14 ways to distort reality • Inventories 14 distortion strategies in personal life • Accountability—Victim Empathy Exercise • Makes full disclosure to therapist	• Understands the characteristics of denial and self-delusion • Identifies presence of self-delusion in life • Knows personal preferred patterns of thought distortion • Accepts confrontation
2. Understand the nature of addictive illness.	• Completes assigned readings on sex addiction • Learns different ways to define sex addiction • Understands addictive system • Understands deprivation system • Maps out personal addictive system • Understands criteria for addictive illness • Applies criteria to personal behavior • Learns key factors in the genesis of sex addiction	• Knows information on addictive illness • Applies information to personal life
Sexual Addiction Component	• Understands sexual modularity • Understands sexual hierarchy • Knows ten types of behavior • Reviews ten types for personal patterns • Understands stages of courtship • Reviews personal courtship patterns • Matches courtship patterns with acting out patterns • Understands context of change, grief, commitment	• Understands sexually compulsive patterns • Understands courtship patterns and intimacy issues
3. Surrenders process.	• Understands existential position on change—essence of recovery • Understands principles of anxiety reduction • Completes sexual addiction history • Completes powerless inventory • Completes unmanageability inventory • Completes financial costs inventory • Identifies ten worst moments • Understands guidelines of step completion • Gives First Step	• Acceptance of addiction in life • Knows personal limitations • Discerns difference between controllable and non-controllable events
4. Limit damage from behavior.	• Understands 1st and 2nd order change • Understands concept of paradigm shift • Records provisional beliefs • Completes damage control plan • Completes a disclosure plan • Completes a Second and Third Step	• Integrates self-limitation into personal paradigm • Responds to crisis plan fully • Uses boundaries at a minimum level • Has internal skills for anxiety reduction • Develops resolve for change and commitment

RECOVERY TASK	PERFORMABLES	LIFE COMPETENCY

5. Establish sobriety.	• Understands sobriety as boundary problem
	• Understands sobriety challenge
	• Completes recovery essentials exercise
	• Completes sobriety challenges worksheet
	• Writes sobriety statement including
	  –abstinence list
	  –boundaries list
	  –sexual health plan
	• Understands relapse process
	• Completes Relapse Prevention sequence including
	  –scenario worksheets
	  –fire drill planning
	  –letter to self
	  –emergency first aid kit
	  –relapse contract
	  –celibacy contract
	• Establishes a date
		• Uses clearly stated boundaries of sobriety
		• Manages life without dysfunctional sexual behavior

6. Ensure physical integrity.	• Learns physical aspects of addiction
	• Learn about sexually transmitted diseases
	• Completes physical
	• Completes psychiatric assessment
	• Learns neuropathways of addiction
	• Learns sexual neuropathways
	• Learns sexual addiction matrix
	• Completes matrix exercise
	• Understands arousal template
	• Maps personal arousal template including
	  –fantasy worksheets
	  –arousal template worksheets
	  –drawing decision tree
		• Understands physical aspects of addiction
		• Identifies neuropathway interaction
		• Identifies dysfunctional arousal patterns

7. Participate in a culture of support.	• Participates in a Twelve Step program • Knows different fellowships • Develops relationship with sponsor • Participates in program life • Presents Steps in program • Does service in program • Knows signs of a healthy group • Has celebration date • Completes important people inventory • Maintains a healthy support system	• Knows differences in fellowships • Maintains relationships with members of recovering community • Knowledge of Twelve Step work • Knows signs of healthy support group • Uses steps "therapeutically" • Understands control/anxiety paradigm of Twelve Step life

Table 9.1 continued

RECOVERY TASK	PERFORMABLES	LIFE COMPETENCY
8. Reduce shame.	Complete Steps Four and Five.	Recognize and manage toxic shame.
9. Grieve losses.	Define clear grieving strategies and use them.	Recognize grief and have skills for grieving.
10. Understand multiple addictions and sobriety.	Complete an Addiction Interaction Disorder screen. Complete a Multiple Addiction Relapse Prevention Plan.	Remain relapse free from all concurrent addictions.
11. Acknowledge cycles of abuse.	Complete Survivors Week. Complete Abuse Inventory.	Identify abuse and exploitation.
12. Bring closure and resolution to addictive shame.	Complete Steps Eight and Nine.	Keep current on shame, resentment, and relationship issues.
13. Restore financial viability.	Live within financial means (spend less than earned). Work a recovery financial plan.	Maintain financial viability.
14. Restore meaningful work.	Establish a meaningful career path.	Have meaningful work.
15. Create lifestyle balance.	Use a Personal Craziness Index for eight weeks.	Live in balance/harmony.
16. Build supportive personal relationships.	Find and use a sponsor. Attend a therapy group for 175 hours. Be a sponsor to others.	Initiate and sustain enduring life relationships.
17. Establish healthy exercise and nutrition patterns.	Have a weekly aerobic exercise pattern. Remain in appropriate weight range for age and height.	Stay physically fit.
18. Restructure relationship with self.	Complete eighteen months of individual therapy. Clarify boundaries, goals, and needs.	Have a workable, compassionate relationship with self in order to be self-determining and autonomous.
19. Resolve original conflicts-wounds.	Do therapy specific to family-of-origin or trauma issues.	Identify and manage recurring dysfunctional patterns.
20. Restore healthy sexuality.	Write a sex plan and keep it updated.	Have sexual health.
21. Involve family members in therapy.	Family members attend Family Week. Family members attend therapy sessions.	Capacity to ask for help from immediate family.
22. Alter dysfunctional family relationships.	Full disclosure to primary partner and immediate family as appropriate.	Remain true to self in the presence of dysfunction.
23. Commit to recovery for each family member.	Family members enter a recovery program for themselves.	Take responsibility for self.

RECOVERY TASK	PERFORMABLES	LIFE COMPETENCY
24. Resolve issues with children.	Share secrets and make amends to children when appropriate.	Resolve conflict in dependent relationships.
25. Resolve issues with extended family.	Share secrets and make amends to extended family when appropriate.	Resolve conflict in interdependent relationships.
26. Work through differentiation.	Write a Fair Fight contract.	Sustain intimacy without loss of self.
27. Recommit/commit to primary relationship.	Commit to a primary relationship, or recommit to a primary relationship.	Capacity to maintain a committed relationship.
28. Commit to coupleship.	Attend Twelve Step meeting for couples regularly.	Participate in a community of couples.
29. Succeed in primary intimacy.	Have a primary relationship that is satisfying.	Be vulnerable and intimate.
30. Develop a spiritual life.	Find and use a spiritual director or mentor. Join a spiritual community.	Be spiritually conscious.

Table 9.2

THE FIRST SEVEN TASKS—PERFORMABLES CHECKLIST

Listed below are each of the seven tasks you have accomplished. Under each is an additional list of performables—the specific activities you completed that make up each task. Review your work. Check off each performable if you wish. Notice how good it feels to "finish" what you set out to do.

1. **Break through denial.**
   - ☐ Make a problem list.
   - ☐ Make a secret list.
   - ☐ Make a list of excuses and rationales.
   - ☐ Complete a Consequences Inventory.
   - ☐ Make a list of people hurt.
   - ☐ Find a therapist.
   - ☐ Find a sponsor.
   - ☐ Make full disclosure to therapist and sponsor.

2. **Understand the nature of the illness.**
   - ☐ Read at least one book on sex addiction.
   - ☐ Map out your own addiction cycle and addiction system.
   - ☐ Make a list of unmanageable moments.
   - ☐ Learn about sexual anorexia and binge-purge cycles.
   - ☐ Learn about "collateral indicators."
   - ☐ Conduct self-assessment for sex addiction and sexual anorexia.
   - ☐ Complete sexual history and sexual Problem Inventory.
   - ☐ Complete a Courtship Inventory.

3. **Surrender to the process.**
   - ☐ Complete Sex Addiction History.
   - ☐ Complete Powerlessness Inventory.
   - ☐ Complete Unmanageability Inventory.
   - ☐ Complete Financial Costs Worksheet.
   - ☐ Itemize Ten Worst Moments.
   - ☐ Share your First Step.

4. **Limit damage from behavior.**
   - ☐ Complete a Damage Control Plan.
   - ☐ Complete a Disclosure Plan.

5. **Establish sobriety.**
   - ☐ Complete Sobriety Challenges Worksheet.
   - ☐ Identify your relapse scenarios.

- ☐ Develop Fire Drill Plan.
- ☐ Write Abstinence List, Boundaries List, and Sexual Health Plan.
- ☐ Use a Personal Craziness Index for twelve weeks.
- ☐ Write a letter to yourself.
- ☐ Create an Emergency First Aid Kit.
- ☐ Sign a relapse contract.

6. Ensure physical integrity.

- ☐ Complete a physical exam.
- ☐ Complete your Sex Addiction Matrix.
- ☐ Complete your Sexual Health Matrix.
- ☐ Complete Arousal Template Assessment including:
  - ☐ Fantasy worksheet
  - ☐ Eroticized feelings
  - ☐ Situations and places
  - ☐ Sensations
  - ☐ Objects
  - ☐ Body types, parts, characteristics
  - ☐ Partner's characteristics
  - ☐ Culture
  - ☐ Courtship stages and beliefs
- ☐ Draw your own Arousal Template.

7. Participate in a culture of support.

- ☐ Find a "home" meeting and attend regularly.
- ☐ Have regular contact with sponsor(s).
- ☐ Give meeting presentations.
- ☐ Perform program "service" in some capacity.
- ☐ Join activities outside of meetings.
- ☐ Present First Step and additional Steps as you complete them.
- ☐ Know differences among sex addiction fellowships.
- ☐ Observe daily rituals, such as readings, meditations, and writing a journal, that promote recovery.
- ☐ Attend Twelve Step meetings for other addictions as appropriate.

At this point, you have in effect completed the first seven of the thirty tasks. There are several areas of concern that you ought to think about at this point. First, you need to share what you have done with those who have been part of this process—therapists, sponsors, group mates, and friends. Allow them to congratulate you, and think of some ways that you can thank them for their help. Also, figure out a way to celebrate what you've accomplished. If you are in a Twelve Step program, there may already be a celebration as part of the process. If you are doing this work individually, it is still important to take time to notice what you have accomplished. You deserve much credit for getting this far! At the conclusion of this chapter we have provided a page on which you can have people write wishes and comments .

Your next challenge is a workbook called *The Recovery Zone*, which takes you from task eight to task nineteen. The remaining tasks are all about family and intimacy and they, too, have their own workbook. Also check into www.recoveryzone.com and become part of the Recovery Zone community. More information about the sequential workbooks in the series and recoveryzone.com can be found immediately following this chapter.

I am grateful that you have taken the risk to live in the solution. All of us share the same challenge our storytellers have discerned as our lot as humans. The stories of Luke Skywalker and Frodo Baggins are not just for entertainment. They are about you and me and making the commitment to change. It matters a great deal that you have.

Comments and Reflections . . .

The user of this workbook has now completed the tasks of beginning recovery from sex addiction. This person is asking those who have helped in the process to write reflections, comments, and wishes as this person moves on to the next challenge. Please take a moment to add your thoughts in celebration of this hard work.

_____

_____

_____

_____

_____

_____

_____

_____

_____

_____

_____

_____

_____

_____

_____

_____

_____

_____

_____

_____

Contact List for More Information

Two recovery-supporting websites are available; access them at www.sexhelp.com and www.recoveryzone.com.

For general or purchasing information about *The Recovery Zone Workbook*, please go to www.sexhelp.com or www.gentlepath.com or call 1-800-708-1796.

For information on both inpatient and outpatient treatment services, contact us at 1-800-708-1796.

For more information about Dr. Patrick Carnes and his speaking engagements, access his website at www.sexhelp.com or call him at 1-800-708-1796.

For information on training for counselors and other helping professionals, call the International Institute for Trauma and Addiction Professionals at 1-866-575-6853 or access them via the Internet at www.iitap.com.

Appendix

The Twelve Steps of Alcoholics Anonymous[1]

1. We admitted we were powerless over alcohol—that our lives had become unmanageable.

2. Came to believe that a Power greater than ourselves could restore us to sanity.

3. Made a decision to turn our will and our lives over to the care of God *as we understood Him*.

4. Made a searching and fearless moral inventory of ourselves.

5. Admitted to God, to ourselves, and to another human being the exact nature of our wrongs.

6. Were entirely ready to have God remove all these defects of character.

7. Humbly asked Him to remove our shortcomings.

8. Made a list of all persons we had harmed, and became willing to make amends to them all.

9. Made direct amends to such people wherever possible, except when to do so would injure them or others.

10. Continued to take personal inventory and when we were wrong promptly admitted it.

11. Sought through prayer and meditation to improve our conscious contact with God *as we understood Him*, praying only for knowledge of His will for us and the power to carry that out.

12. Having had a spiritual awakening as the result of these steps, we tried to carry this message to alcoholics, and to practice these principles in all our affairs.

The Twelve Steps of Alcoholics Anonymous Adapted for Sexual Addicts[2]

1. We admitted we were powerless over our sexual addiction—that our lives had become unmanageable.

2. Came to believe a Power greater than ourselves could restore us to sanity.

3. Made a decision to turn our will and our lives over to the care of God, *as we understood Him*.

4. Made a searching and fearless moral inventory of ourselves.

5. Admitted to God, to ourselves, and to another human being the exact nature of our wrongs.

6. Were entirely ready to have God remove all these defects of character.

7. Humbly asked Him to remove our shortcomings.

8. Made a list of all persons we had harmed, and became willing to make amends to them all.

9. Made direct amends to such people wherever possible, except when to do so would injure them or others.

10. Continued to take personal inventory and when we were wrong promptly admitted it.

11. Sought through prayer and meditation to improve our conscious contact with God *as we understood Him*, praying only for knowledge of His will for us and the power to carry that out.

12. Having had a spiritual awakening as the result of these steps, we tried to carry this message to others and to practice these principles in all our affairs.

1. The Twelve Steps of AA are taken from *Alcoholics Anonymous,* 3d ed., published by AA World Services, Inc., New York, N.Y., 59-60. Reprinted with permission of AA World Services, Inc. (See editor's note on copyright page.)
2. Adapted from the Twelve Steps of Alcoholics Anonymous. Reprinted with permission of AA World Services, Inc., New York, N.Y.

Resource Guide

The following is a list of recovery fellowships that may be helpful to you in your particular situation.

Adult Children of Alcoholics
310-534-1815
www.adultchildren.org

Alateen (ages 12–17)
800-356-9996
www.al-anon-alateen.org

Al-Anon
800-344-2666
www.al-anon-alateen.org

Alcoholics Anonymous
212-870-3400
www.aa.org

Co-Dependents Anonymous
602-277-7991
www.codependents.org

Co-Dependents of Sex Addicts (COSA)
612-537-6904
www.cosa-recovery.org

Cocaine Anonymous
800-347-8998
www.ca.org

CoAnon
www.co-anon.org

Debtors Anonymous
781-453-2743
www.debtorsanonymous.org

Emotions Anonymous
651-647-9712
www.emotionsanonymous.org

Families Anonymous
310-815-8010
www.familiesanonymous.org

Gamblers Anonymous
213-386-8789
www.gamblersanonymous.org

Marijuana Anonymous
212-459-4423
www.marijuana-anonymous.org

Narcotics Anonymous
818-773-9999
www.na.org

National Council for Couple and Family Recovery
314-997-9808

Society for the Advancement of Sexual Health
770-541-9912
www.sash.net

Nicotine Anonymous
www.nicotine-anonymous.org

Overeaters Anonymous
www.oa.org

Recovering Couples Anonymous
314-997-9808
www.recovering-couples.org

Runaway and Suicide Hotline
800-RUN-AWAY
www.1800runaway.org

S-Anon
615-833-3152
www.sanon.org

Sex and Love Addicts Anonymous
210-828-7900
www.slaafws.org

Sex Addicts Anonymous
713-869-4902
www.sexaa.org

Sexual Addiction Resources/ Dr. Patrick Carnes
www.sexhelp.com

Sexual Compulsives Anonymous
310-859-5585
www.sca-recovery.org

Sexaholics Anonymous
866-424-8777
www.sa.org

Survivors of Incest Anonymous
410-282-3400
www.siawso.org

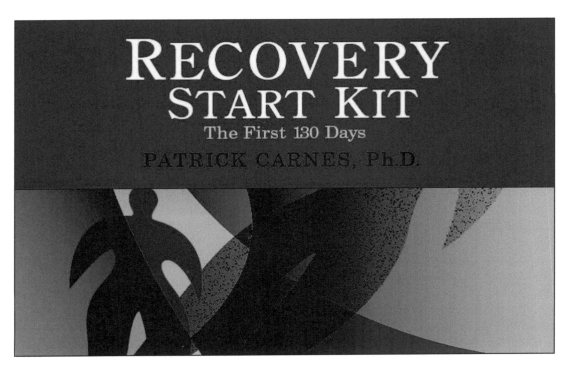

This comprehensive recovery tool includes:

- ◆ One kit for 130 days
- ◆ Three workbooks
- ◆ Four CDs
- ◆ One DVD
- ◆ A "90-Day Pocket Planner" to help the individual seeking long-term recovery.

Gentle Path Press
P.O. Box 3172
Carefree, AZ 85377
Phone: (800) 708-1796
Fax: (480) 488-9125
Www.gentlepath.com

* Use with a Certified Sex Addiction Therapist is highly recommended

Books of Related Interest Written by Dr. Patrick Carnes

The Betrayal Bond: Breaking Free of Exploitive Relationships (Deerfield Beach, Fla.: Health Communications, 1998).
In a savage, psychic twist, victims of abuse and violence often bond with their perpetrators to the stunning point that they will die rather than escape. Carnes's breakthrough book focuses on how betrayal intensifies trauma and illuminates the keys to escaping destructive relationships.

Sexual Anorexia: Overcoming Sexual Self-Hatred (with Joseph M. Moriarity) (Center City, Minn.: Hazelden, 1997).
The devastating mix of fear, pain, and betrayal can lead to obsessive sexual aversion. Tracing the dysfunction's roots in childhood sexual trauma, neglect, and abuse, Carnes explores dimensions of sexual health, targeting key issues that let recovery proceed.

Out of the Shadows: Understanding Sexual Addiction, 3d ed. (Center City, Minn.: Hazelden, 2001).
The groundbreaking book that first identified and defined sexual addiction. A must for anyone looking to understand the illness, it's an expert and in-depth look at the origins of sexual addiction and the addiction cycle.

Contrary to Love: Helping the Sexual Addict (Center City, Minn.: Hazelden, 1989).
This sequel *to Out of the Shadows* traces the origins and consequences of the addict's faulty core beliefs. Building upon his earlier work, Carnes describes the stages of the illness and lays the groundwork for potential recovery.

Don't Call It Love: Recovering from Sexual Addiction (Phoenix, Ariz.: Gentle Path Press, 1991).
This landmark study of one thousand recovering sex addicts and their families explores how people become sex addicts and the role of culture, family, neurochemistry, and child abuse in creating addiction.

A Gentle Path through the Twelve Steps: The Classic Guide for All People in the Process of Recovery (Center City, Minn.: Hazelden, 1994).
A guidebook for people in recovery that helps them understand their own story and begin planning a new life of recovery. With more than 325,000 copies sold, it holds invaluable insights for beginners and old-timers alike in any Twelve Step program.

DVD'S AND CD'S BY GENTLE PATH PRESS

For more information or to order videotapes from Gentle Path Press, call 800-708-1796.

Trauma Bonds: When Humans Bond with Those Who Hurt Them
Often victims cling to destructive relationships with baffling desperation. In this riveting videotape, Dr. Patrick Carnes analyzes how trauma bonding develops and outlines strategies for breaking free from its compulsive torment.
Addiction Interaction Disorder: Understanding Multiple Addictions

Few addicts—about 17 percent—have only one addiction. More commonly, assorted compulsions combine in a complex systemic problem called addiction interaction disorder. This videotape outlines how to screen for the disorder (a major factor in relapse) and explores the role of addiction as a "solution" to trauma.

Contrary to Love: Helping the Sexual Addict
This is a twelve-part PBS video in which noted addiction psychologist Dr. Patrick Carnes discusses the spectrum of compulsive-addictive behavior and its treatment. The titles of the twelve parts are

"Our Addictive Society"
"Cultural Denial of Addiction"
"Am I an Addict?"
"Interview with Three"
"The Addictive Family"
"Interview with Melody Beattie"
"Child Abuse"
"The Twelve-Step Recovery Process"
"Healthy Sexuality and Spirituality"
"Finding a Balance in Recovery"
"Coping in a World of Shame"
"The Ten Risks of Recovery"

AUDIO CDS BY GENTLE PATH PRESS

For more information or to order audio CDs from Gentle Path Press, call 800-708-1796.

Facing the Shadow Workshop
Multiple Addictions Workshop
Addiction Interaction Disorder: Understanding Multiple Addictions
Toward a New Freedom: Discovering Healthy Sexuality
Eroticized Rage: Courtship, Compulsion and Cybersex
Spiritual Skill Set: Part 1 - Discernment
Spiritual Skill Set: Part 2 - Resilience

For Further Reading

The following list contains books referenced in this book, as well as further readings that you may find helpful.

Co-Sex Addiction Recovery

Beattie, Melody. *Codependent No More: How to Stop Controlling Others and Start Caring for Yourself.* New York: Walker, 1989.

Calof, David L., and Robin Simons. *The Couple Who Became Each Other and Other Tales of Healing of a Master Hypnotherapist.* New York: Bantam Books, 1996.

Carnes, Patrick J. *The Betrayal Bond: Breaking Free of Exploitive Relationships.* Deerfield Beach, Fla.: Health Communications, 1998.

Fossum, Merle A., and Marilyn J. Mason. *Facing Shame: Families in Recovery.* New York: Norton, 1989.

Friel, John, and Linda Friel. *Adult Children: The Secrets of Dysfunctional Families.* Deerfield Beach, Fla.: Health Communications, 1988.

Schaeffer, Brenda. *Is It Love or Is It Addiction?* 2d ed. Center City, Minn: Hazelden, 1997.

Schneider, Jennifer. *Back from Betrayal: Recovering from His Affairs.* New York: Ballantine Books, 1990.

Schneider, Jennifer P., and Burt Schneider. *Sex, Lies, and Forgiveness: Couples Speaking Out on Healing from Sex Addiction.* Center City, Minn.: Hazelden, 1991.

Family

Bradshaw, John. *Bradshaw on the Family: A Revolutionary Way of Self-Discovery.* Pompano Beach, Fla.: Health Communications, 1988.

Bradshaw, John. *Family Secrets, What You Don't Know Can Hurt You.* New York: Bantam Books, 1996.

Evans, Patricia. *The Verbally Abusive Relationship: How to Recognize It and How to Respond.* Holbrook, Mass.: Adams Media Corporation, 1996.

Love, Patricia. *Emotional Incest Syndrome: What to Do When a Parent's Love Rules Your Life.* New York: Bantam Books, 1991.

Mellody, Pia, with Andrea Well Miller and J. Keith Miller. *Facing Codependence.* San Francisco: Harper San Francisco, 1989.

Key Recovery Works

Beattie, Melody. *Journey to the Heart: Daily Meditations on the Path to Freeing Your Soul.* San Francisco: Harper San Francisco, 1996.

Bradshaw, John. *Healing the Shame That Binds You.* Deerfield Beach, Fla.: Health Communications, 1988.

Breton, Denise, and Christopher Largent. *The Paradigm Conspiracy: Why Our Social Systems Violate Our Human Potential—and How We Can Change Them.*

Center City, Minn.: Hazelden, 1996.

Bryan, Mark, and Julia Cameron. *The Money Drunk: Ninety Days to Financial Sobriety.* New York: Ballantine Books, 1993.

Cameron, Julia. *The Artist's Way: A Spiritual Path to Higher Creativity.* New York: Putnam, 1995.

Covey, Stephen R. *First Things First: Everyday.* New York: Simon & Schuster, 1999.

Covey, Stephen. *The Seven Habits of Highly Effective People: Powerful Lessons in Personal Change.* New York: Simon & Schuster, 1989.

Hope and Recovery: The Twelve Step Guide for Healing from Compulsive Sexual Behavior. Center City, Minn.: Hazelden, 1994.

Milkman, Harvey B., and Stanley Sunderwirth. *Craving for Ecstasy: The Chemistry and Consciousness of Escape.* New York: Free Press, 1987.

Millman, Dan. *Way of the Peaceful Warrior: A Book That Changes Lives.* Tiburon, Calif.: Kramer, 1984.

Mundis, Jerrold. *How to Get Out of Debt, Stay Out of Debt & Live Prosperously.* New York: Bantam Books, 1990.

Nouwen, Henri J. *Reaching Out: The Three Movements of the Spiritual Life.* Garden City, N.Y.: Doubleday, 1986.

Peck, M. Scott. *People of the Lie: The Hope for Healing Human Evil.* New York: Simon & Schuster, 1985.

Peck, M. Scott. *The Road Less Traveled.* New York: Simon & Schuster, 1978.

Sex Addiction

Adams, Kenneth M. *Silently Seduced: When Parents Make Their Children Partners.* Deerfield Beach, Fla.: Health Communications, 1991.

Answers in the Heart. Center City, Minn.: Hazelden, 1994.

Earle, Ralph H., and Gregory Crowe. *Lonely All the Time: Recognizing, Understanding, and Overcoming Sex Addiction, for Addicts and Co-Dependents.* n.p.: Bradt, 1998.

Ellison, Marvin M. *Erotic Justice: A Liberating Ethic of Sexuality.* Louisville, Ky.: Westminster John Knox Press, 1996.

Hastings, Anne S. *From Generation to Generation: Learning about Adults Who Are Sexual with Children.* Tiburon, Calif.: Printed Voice, 1994.

Kasl, Charlotte. *Women, Sex, and Addiction.* Harper & Row, 1989.

Nouwen, Henri J. *The Return of the Prodigal Son: A Story of Homecoming.* New York: Doubleday, 1994.

Sexual Health

Bechtal, Stephen. *The Practical Encyclopedia of Sex and Health.* Emmaus, Pa.: Rodale Press, 1993.

Berzon, Betty, ed. *Positively Gay.* Berkeley, Calif.: CelestialArts, 1995.

Covington, Stephanie. *Awakening Your Sexuality: A Guide for Recovering Women.*

Center City, Minn.: Hazelden, 1991.

Diamond, Jed. *Male Menopause: Sex and Survival in the Second Half of Life.* Naperville, Ill.: Sourcebooks, 1997.

Eisler, Riane. *The Chalice and the Blade: Our History, Our Future.* San Francisco: Harper & Row, 1987.

Hastings, Anne S. *Discovering Sexuality That Will Satisfy You Both: When Couples Want Differing Amounts and Different Kinds of Sex.* Tiburon, Calif.: Printed Voice, 1993.

Klausner, Mary A., and Bobbie Hasselbring. *Aching for Love: The Sexual Drama of the Adult Child.* San Francisco: Harper San Francisco, 1990.

Maltz, Wendy. *The Sexual Healing Journey: A Guide for Survivors of Sexual Abuse.* New York: HarperCollins, 1991.

Maltz, Wendy. ed. *Passionate Hearts: The Poetry of Sexual Love.* Novato, Calif.: New World Library, 1997.

Renshaw, Domeena. *Seven Weeks to Better Sex.* New York: Random House, 1995.

Sex and Religion

Elinor, Burkett, and Frank Bruni. *A Gospel of Shame: Children, Sexual Abuse, and the Catholic Church.* New York: Viking Penguin, 1993.

Laaser, Mark. *Faithful and True: Sexual Integrity in a Fallen World.* Grand Rapids, Mich.: Zondervan, 1996.

Laaser, Mark, ed. *Restoring the Soul of a Church: Reconciling Congregations Wounded by Clergy Sexual Misconduct.* Collegeville, Minn.: Liturgical Press, 1995.

Rossetti, Stephen J. *A Tragic Grace: The Catholic Church and Child Sexual Abuse.* Collegeville, Minn.: Liturgical Press, 1996.

Sipe, A. W. Richard. *Sex, Priests, and Power: Anatomy of a Crisis.* New York: Brunner/Mazel, 1995.

Trauma Resolution

Bass, Ellen, and Laura Davis. *The Courage to Heal: A Guide for Women Survivors of Child Sexual Abuse.* New York: HarperCollins, 1994.

Courtois, Christine A. *Healing the Incest Wound: Adult Survivors in Therapy.* New York: Norton, 1996.

Crowder, Adrienne. *Opening the Door: A Treatment Model for Therapy with Male Survivors of Sexual Abuse.* Philadelphia: Brunner/Mazel, 1995.

Davis, Laura. *Allies in Healing: When the Person You Love Was Sexually Abused as a Child.* New York: HarperCollins, 1991.

Dolan, Yvonne. *Resolving Sexual Abuse: Solution-Focused Therapy and Ericksonian Hypnosis for Adult Survivors.* New York: Norton, 1991.

Fossum, Merle A., and Marilyn J. Mason. *Facing Shame: Families in Recovery.* New York: Norton, 1986.

Hunter, Mic. *Abused Boys: The Neglected Victims of Sexual Abuse.* New York: Fawcett, 1991.

Maltz, Wendy, and Beverly Holman. *Incest and Sexuality: A Guide to Understanding and Healing.* Lexington, Ky.: Lexington Books, 1987.

Miller, Alice. *For Your Own Good: Hidden Cruelty in Child-Rearing and the Roots of Violence.* New York: Farrar, Straus, Giroux, 1990.

White, William L. *The Incestuous Workplace: Stress and Distress in the Organizational Family.* Center City, Minn.: Hazelden, 1997.